ENGENDERED

What Was God Thinking?

PATSY CAMENETI

Tulsa, OK

ENGENDERED

Gender Roles & Relationships
What Was God Thinking?
Copyright © 2018 Patsy Cameneti
ISBN 978-1-68031-216-4
Published by Harrison House Publishers
Tulsa, OK 74145
www.harrisonhouse.com

en·gen·dered
/ĕn-jĕn′dərd/

Engendered is the past tense of *engender,* meaning *to bring about, to give rise to,* or in its earliest form, *to propagate or to beget.* Simply put, *to engender* means *to make it happen.*

Right from the beginning, God had a plan for mankind. He engendered the course of human families not simply by suggestion or even direction but by His operation in the creation of humans—male and female.

From the same root word, *genus,* we get *gender.* In its simplest definition, *gender* means *a type, a class of things that share certain traits.* Only in recent times has the term *gender* been used to describe attributes pertaining to sexuality.

On the issue of marriage—male and female—Jesus referred people not to the law or what Moses had said. He referred them to creation— The Genesis—where God engendered gender. God generated or brought about two genders based on how He created mankind— male and female created He them.

The fall of Adam's race fractured and confused God's plan for male and female.

In the pages to follow, we explore just what happened to God's original purpose and design. We come to terms with how it was fractured in the fall and how Jesus redeemed humankind, not simply from the curse of the law but back to what He had *engendered* from the beginning.

Acknowledgements

This book would have never come to be without these wonderful people:

The students of Rhema Bible College, where I've had the privilege of teaching the subject of Christian marriage and family. You have inspired me to study, pray, and learn.

Madonna Clark, you gave me material to start on with the many hours of lessons you cheerfully transcribed.

Jenny Eddison, I'm deeply grateful for all the many things you have done to help get this message from my heart into a book.

Bill and Carol Cooper; Trina Hankins; friends in France, John and Laura Madan and Marie-Héléne Moulin; Michelle Vandusen; and my prayer group of many years, Edith Szilveszter, Diana Ryan, and Jenny Eddison. Your encouragement and prayers for me helped me begin and finish this book.

John McAllan, Mitch Robinson, and Chelsea Perry thank you for reading and giving feedback.

Tony, you helped protect my time, even if it meant the way you saw me was primarily on the other side of my computer.

Dedicated to...

The Creator...I am so grateful to Him for giving me a constant desire to know Him. Everything about Him amazes me.

My wonderful husband, Tony...You loved me first, consistently and faithfully, very much like Christ loves the Church. I love being your wife.

My parents...The characteristics that I adore and cherish in God have been consistently visible and tangible in you. You helped me know God, and I am eternally grateful.

To my beautiful daughters, Liliana and Annalisa...You have given me the opportunity to be a mother and to know a type of love I never could have imagined. You are God's most precious gifts to me.

To my sisters and brothers...Loving the family of God unconditionally began for me with experiencing family love with you. I love us. Forever.

CONTENTS

CHAPTER 1

In the Beginning

In the beginning God created the heavens and the earth.

Genesis 1: 1

I absolutely believe this. However, I'm fully aware there are many who do not and for a variety of reasons. There are brilliant apologists who address these reasons intelligently, historically, and scientifically. I recommend their study[1] and presentation on vital subjects, such as the existence of God, God as Creator of heaven and earth, and the veracity of the Scriptures. These resources are helpful to people searching for answers in these areas.

However, this book has been written for people searching for more specific answers about man and woman, gender roles and relationships, and marriage and family. It's been written with the following people in mind:

- Those who are convinced or, at least, open to believe God exists and is the Creator of all things, including humans.

- Those who believe the Bible reveals God's thoughts, will, and ways.

- Those who want clarity of God's creative intention when it came to making man and woman and the roles they fill.

- Those who are willing for God and the Bible to address with final authority the subject of male and female gender identity, marriage, and family.

- Those who are curious to know more of what the Bible says about God's creative intention for man and woman, marriage, and family.

After all, if you believe Genesis 1:1, you will have no problem believing the rest of God's Word and what it says about man and woman, marriage, and family.

For many years, I've had the privilege of teaching the subject of marriage and family, a topic I believe is very close to the heart of God. The Bible schools where I taught were in different countries with different traditions and cultures regarding the subject, so I prayerfully asked the Lord to help me represent His thoughts and ways and not just the culture I was most familiar with or my personal experience. The answer to this prayer is ongoing, but up to now the Holy Spirit has kindly, yet purposefully, led me to take away the trappings of culture and look away from negative—even positive—personal experience. He's encouraged me to look completely at God's idea of man and woman. What was God thinking when He made man? What was God thinking when He made woman? And what do His intentions have to do with the roles they play? What did the Creator want marriage to look like? What did He want family to look like?

In any culture, there may be good traditions while others run cross-grain with God's intention, but I encourage you to strip away all viewpoints and look at the raw truth of the Bible. This is our goal: To look at the sexes and their roles from God's standpoint and what that has to do with their roles as male and female and within marriage and family.

As we look at what the Bible says, we will be impacted most if we honestly desire to know what it says and then prayerfully accept it. A lot of times when we approach something as core as our gender, or family, and marriage, we bring with us, even subconsciously, our own experiences or what we've witnessed in other people.

Yet, when the validity of the apostle Paul's ministry was being questioned and compared, he said, "Of course we would not dare classify ourselves or compare ourselves with those who rate themselves so highly. How stupid they are! *They make up their own standards to measure themselves by, and they judge themselves by their own standards!*"

2 Corinthians 10:12 (GNT)

Even though this verse is addressing a different subject, what does apply is that people who measure themselves by standards that they themselves make up are not wise. The Good News Translation says they are stupid!

THE MODEL FOR BOTH MALE AND FEMALE IS NOTHING LESS THAN GOD HIMSELF.

We must let God and His Word be the standard of measure! Why? It's true. Unbiased. And it works for all cultures, all ages, and for all time.

To do this, we must determine to look away from our own experience, our parents, our aunts and uncles, and even look away from our own situation as the standard. Society is not a safe standard either. It keeps changing (2 Corinthians 10:12). Instead, we must look to God as the standard! God created the sexes (male and female). What was *He* thinking? He hasn't changed.

Confusion about what it means to be a godly man or woman, husband or wife, father or mother, and confusion about gender and sexuality is cleared up when we look to our Creator. We are *His* idea in the first place.

My purpose in this book is not to argue my opinion or anyone else's for that matter. Instead, my purpose is to carefully examine what the Bible reveals of God's thoughts and intentions in creating male and female in His image.

Of course, words used to communicate are vital. Words may mean one thing to one person while the same words may mean something entirely different to another person. When certain words are used, they serve as buttons that trigger, consciously or subconsciously, everything from a short, simple definition someone picked up and derived from conversations with others all the way to an avalanche of emotions based on personal experience.

In this book, *gender²* and *sex³* are such words, and it's important that you know what I mean when I use them when referring to male and female. The following definitions apply:

Sex⁴ is the biological difference between male and female determined by chromosomes: XX in the case of a female and XY in the case of a male.

Gender⁵ is the range of characteristics that pertain to being either masculine or feminine. It's the state of being—psychologically, socially, or culturally—that defines what it means to be male or female. Gender is demonstrated in behavior, attitudes, and attributes.

Let us prayerfully and humbly look at this glorious subject of man and woman and their roles. We'll see that the model for both male and female is nothing less than God Himself.

PRAYER

Father God, I believe that You are the Creator of heaven and earth and everything in them. Open my heart to understand what Your intention was when You created man and woman in Your image. Open my eyes to see myself and others the way You do. I desire to represent You truly and bring glory to You in the way I express my sex and each role of my gender.

In Jesus' wonderful name. Amen

Notes

1 Recommended reading:

Creation

William Lane Craig & Paul Copan, *Creation out of Nothing: A Biblical, Philosophical, and Scientific Exploration*, Baker Publishing Group, Grand Rapids, MI, 2004.

Hugh Ross, *The Creator and the Cosmos: How the Latest Scientific Discoveries of the Century Reveal God*, Fourth Edition, RTB Press, 2018.

William A. Dembski & Sean McDowell, *Understanding Intelligent Design: Everything You Need to Know in Plain Language*, Harvest House Publishers, Eugene, OR, United States, 2008.

Veracity of the New Testament

John Wenham, *Christ and the Bible*, Baker Publishing Group, MI, 1994.

Craig L. Blomberg, *The Reliability of the New Testament*, B&H Academic, Nashville, TN, 2016.

F.F. Bruce, *The Canon of Scripture*, InterVarsity Press, 1988.

2 *Gender* – Either of the two sexes (male and female), especially when considered with reference to social and cultural differences rather than biological ones.
Oxford Dictionary. https://en.oxforddictionaries.com/definition/gender

3 *Sex* – Either of the two main categories (male and female) into which humans and most other living things are divided based on their reproductive functions.
https://en.oxforddictionaries.com/definition/sex

4 It's widely known that people who inherit sex chromosome X from the mother and Y from the father are genetically male, while people who inherit X from both parents are genetically female. Thus, the sex of an offspring is determined entirely by which of the male's sperm (one carrying X or Y) fertilizes the egg (which always carries X). This fact was not realized until the twentieth century, however. Before that, women were often held accountable for not producing a male heir, and in some cases, were even murdered for it (e.g., Anne Boleyn, second wife of King Henry VIII).
In actuality, it's merely the presence of a Y chromosome that makes a person male, and its absence that makes a person female.

Through accidents of chromosomal sorting (meiosis) during sperm and egg production, some people inherit an XXY combination, but are still male (with Klinefelter syndrome). Others inherit only one X, and are thus denoted XO; they are genetically female (with Turner Syndrome). Such people are often, but not always, sterile. (The YO condition is fatal, because the X carries many genes that are indispensable for survival.) The biological law that XX results in a female and XY results in a male is true not only in humans, but in all mammals.
http://www.biologyreference.com/Re-Se/Sex-Determination.html

When a person has neither XX (female) or XY (Male) chromosomes, he or she is considered to have a disorder in sex development. For example, a karyotype of X0 exhibits

Turner's Syndrome and XXY exhibits Klinefelter's Syndrome. There are other conditions triggered by hormonal fluctuations and genetic markers, especially in the development of the fetus. All such conditions are considered anomalies.
http://www.who.int/genomics/gender/en/index1.html

5 Sexologist John Money introduced the terminological distinction between biological sex and gender as a role in 1955. Before his work, it was uncommon to use the word *gender* to refer to anything but grammatical categories. However, Money's meaning of the word did not become widespread until the 1970s, when feminist theory embraced the concept of a distinction between biological sex and the social construct of gender. Today the distinction is strictly followed in some contexts, especially the social sciences and documents written by the World Health Organization.
https://en.wikipedia.org/wiki/Gender

CHAPTER 2

Precisely the Way He Wanted It

In the beginning God created the heavens and the earth.
The earth was without form, and void; and darkness was
on the face of the deep.
And the Spirit of God was hovering over the face of the waters. Then
God said, "Let there be light"; and there was light.

Genesis 1:1-3

In these first three verses of the Bible, we see the trinity of God. In verse 1, we see God the Father. In verse 2, we see the Spirit of God who moved upon the face of the waters. In verse 3, we see the second person of the Godhead. The word *said* identifies God's Word. Before Jesus Christ was made flesh and dwelled among us, He was in the beginning with God as the Word.

1 In the beginning the Word already existed; the Word was with God, and the Word was God. 2 From the very beginning the Word was with God. 3 Through him God made all things; not one thing in all creation was made without him. 4 The Word was

the source of life, and this life brought light to people. 5 The light shines in the darkness, and the darkness has never put it out.

John 1:1-5 (GNT)

Creation began in Genesis 1:3 when the light the Father willed to be created was commanded to be and was brought into existence by the Holy Spirit. Each day of creation unfolded the same way.

By faith we understand that the entire universe was formed at God's command, that what we now see did not come from anything that can be seen.

Hebrews 11:3 (NLT)

THE PATTERN GOD USED TO MAKE MAN WAS HIMSELF.

God didn't use what already existed on earth as a pattern. He created things that had never existed before by His Word. When it came to making man, God did not use a pattern of anything He had made previously on any other day of creation. *The pattern God used to make man was Himself.*

26 God said, "Let us make human beings *in our image to be like us.* They will reign over the fish of the sea, the birds of the sky, the livestock, all the wild animals on the earth and the small animals that scurry along the ground." 27 So God created human beings *in His own image. In the image of God* He created them, male and female He created them. 28 Then God blessed them and said, "Be fruitful and multiply, fill the earth and govern it. Reign over the fish of the sea the birds in the sky and all the animals that scurry along the ground."

Genesis 1:26-28 (NLT)

The Tabernacle

In addition to all that was created in Genesis 1, the two dwelling places God commissioned to be built in the Old Testament illustrate the fact that God did not use earthly patterns. We also see that God is very specific about what He wants and how He wants it.

Acts 7:44 says, "Our ancestors carried the Tabernacle with them through the wilderness. It was constructed according to the plan God had shown Moses" (NLT). It wasn't constructed according to any design that Moses had seen in Egypt. Although Moses was familiar with the leading architecture of the day, he did not use Egyptian architecture to build the tabernacle. It was a new plan. It came from heaven—not from Egypt.

In Scripture, Egypt is a nation, but it's also used as a type or symbol of the world. When God wants to build something, He doesn't get His plan from the world. It originates in Himself, so the plan for the tabernacle began in heaven. In fact, when Moses was preparing to build the tabernacle, God gave him this warning in Exodus 25:40, "Be sure that you make everything according to the *pattern* I have shown you…." In Egypt? No! "…*on the mountain*" (NLT).

God had Moses come away from every other influence and even took him away from the people he was leading. The tabernacle was not some kind of concoction that emerged from a group discussion or a special committee assigned to come up with what it should look like. No, God took Moses away from every other influence, up onto the mountain of God, and there, God gave him the pattern of the original that came from heaven itself.

The words *be sure* in Exodus 25:40 are not a casual instruction. God didn't tell Moses, "It would be nice!" Or, "I would kind of like it!" No. God said, "Be sure!" In fact, God said, "Be sure that you make everything—not most everything—according to the *pattern* I have shown you here on the mountain."

Notice again in Exodus 26:30 God says, "Set up this Tabernacle according to the *pattern* you were shown on the mountain" (NLT). God wasn't trying something on a whim or as an experiment. No. He had a pattern in Himself, and He showed it to Moses.

> **The altar must be hollow, made from planks. Build it just as you were shown *on the mountain*.**
>
> **Exodus 27:8 (NLT)**

The entire lampstand, from its base to its decorative blossoms, was made of beaten gold. It was built according to the *exact design* the Lord had shown Moses.

Numbers 8:4 (NLT)

They serve in a system of worship that is only a *copy*, a shadow of the real one in heaven....

Hebrews 8:5a (NLT)

The words *they serve* refer to the system of worship that the priests and Levites carried out, which was only a copy or a shadow of the real one in heaven.

...For when Moses was getting ready to build the Tabernacle, God gave him this warning: "Be sure that you make everything according to the *pattern* I have shown you here on the mountain."

Hebrews 8:5b (NLT)

The Temple

The next building that God had built was the temple, and God was just as precise about it.

11 Then David gave his son Solomon the plans for the vestibule, its houses, its treasuries, its upper chambers, its inner chambers, and the place of the mercy seat; 12 and *the plans for all that he had by the Spirit,* of the courts of the house of the Lord, of all the chambers all around, of the treasuries of the house of God, and of the treasuries for the dedicated things.

1 Chronicles 28:11-12

Like the tabernacle, Solomon's temple was built exactly according to the specs and design that came from God. As a result, both were filled with the glory of God upon their completion.

Just know this: God never fills man's plans with His glory. Man may even dedicate his plan to God. Still, He won't fill it with His glory. The only thing that God fills with His glory is what comes from Him. If man does the work, God won't take the credit (Psalm 127:1a).

For my birthday one year, an intern of ours who is an exceptional artist presented me with a beautiful picture she had painted. However, I noticed when she gave it to me that it was unsigned. So, I asked her to please sign it. Her signature said it was indeed her work and finished. A true artist won't sign a painting if somebody else does the work on his or her painting. The artist may say, "Well, I contributed," but he or she won't sign it unless it's original and complete.

God signed the tabernacle and the temple with His glory. Do you want the glory of God on your life as well? It comes on a life that represents and reflects Him. God's glory is His signature.

Adam

Like other Bible genealogies, the one found in Luke 3 names each man and his father. Let's look at the final verse of this genealogy in Luke 3:38, "…the son of Enosh, the son of Seth the son of Adam the son of God." That's just profound! Adam didn't come from anybody else. God made him. And what pattern did He use?

To answer that question, let's look once again at the creation of man in Genesis. God said, "Let Us make man in *Our image,* according to *Our likeness*" (Genesis 1:26). God said it again two more times in verse 28, "So God created man *in His own image. In the image of God* He created him; male and female He created them" (Genesis 1:28). God is not redundant; He's purposeful. For Him to repeat this phrase so many times is a big deal.

One primary reason we know that man didn't evolve from any other type of life created earlier is that God very plainly said four times in these verses the pattern He used to make man was Himself. The pattern was not from something He made from some plant or animal He made some other time in His creation. No, the verses make it abundantly clear. God Himself is the pattern in the creation of man. That's pretty cool!

Just how significant is it to be made in the image and likeness of God, and what does it mean? To help us wrap our heads around the concept, let's look at some words and definitions that describe *image* and *likeness.*

Webster's Dictionary defines *image* as *a physical likeness; a representation as is produced by reflection from a mirror; form, appearance, resemblance counterpart, copy, embodiment, illusion or imaged, imaging, counterpart, embodiment; to reflect the likeness of; to mirror, to resemble; a tangible or visible representation;*[1] *an optical counterpart or appearance of an object, as is produced by reflection from a mirror.*[2]

Strong's Concordance uses these words for *likeness:*[3] *similitude, figure, form, like, pattern, model, shape.* In using these words, we can see that man was created as a model, figure, form, shape, profile, and a similitude of God. Adam was made to represent, resemble, reflect, and image God like a mirror. God was the pattern for man.

Man and woman were perfect visible images of the invisible God. Like a mirror is *not* a person but images or reflects a person, Adam and Eve were made to image and reflect God. You couldn't see God, but you could see man. In other words, if you could see man, there wouldn't be any confusion about what God was like. Man was God's likeness.

Notes

1 Image – Webster's Definition includes: exact likeness; semblance; A tangible or visible representation; incarnation. Example: A person strikingly like another person as in "she is the image of her mother." God created man in his own image, (Genesis 1:27 RSV). https://www.merriam-webster.com/dictionary/image

2 Dictionary.com uses these words: (1) a physical likeness or representation of a person, animal, or thing, photographed, painted, sculptured, or otherwise made visible. (2) an optical counterpart or appearance of an object, as is produced by reflection from a mirror, refraction by a lens, or the passage of luminous rays through a small aperture and their reception on a surface. (3) a mental representation; idea; conception.

3 Likeness – Strong's Concordance 1823 – Original Word: תּוּמֻד
http://biblehub.com/hebrew/1823.htm

CHAPTER 3

What God Looks Like

…what you learned about Christ.

Ephesians 4:20 (NLT)

It's a beautiful and interesting thing to study the doctrines of the Bible. We can study an entire lifetime and never exhaust the teachings of the Bible. Yet, my question is this: What do you personally know of God? What do you know of His personality and His characteristics? What have you experienced of Him? Without using "churchy" clichés, what have you personally learned not only about Christ but about the Father and Holy Spirit as well?

Surely all of us want to know God more because nothing compares to the delight of every discovery. Bible studies through colleges, great books, and sermons can help you learn about God's personality, but life actually gives you the opportunity to experience different aspects of God. That's why I don't mind getting older. Bring on the years! Each season of life gives me more opportunities to know God more deeply and richly.

This in itself takes the sting out of any season of life. With God, bad seasons in life don't have to be remembered for the bad. Even the most awful tragedy or complicated problem in any season gives you an opportunity to lean into God, get His perspective, and come to know and experience Him more. In this way, every season is known by what you've come to know and discover about God rather than by something sinister or disastrous.

EACH SEASON OF LIFE GIVES ME MORE OPPORTUNITIES TO KNOW GOD MORE DEEPLY AND RICHLY.

Below is a list compiled by Bible school students from many countries and backgrounds that describes the characteristics they have personally learned of the Father, Son, and Holy Spirit. Something that stood out to me every time I had a different group of students compile a list of God's characteristics is that no matter where a person is born or what language they speak, when they come to know God, the same wonderful characteristics are identified world over!

Obviously, these characteristics are not exclusive to just one person of the Godhead, but the characteristics are shared by the Father, Son, and Holy Spirit. However, the purpose of these lists is to identify specific characteristics of each that someone would come to know through personal interaction.

In the list below, circle the characteristics you personally know of the Father, Son, and Holy Spirit. Feel free to add characteristics of your own. We'll be referring to this list as *List A* repeatedly in the chapters to come. For easy reference, you'll find List A on page 278 as well.

LIST A:
Characteristics of God

Characteristics of the God the Father

accepting	forgiving	kind	strong
accessible	good	long-suffering	smart
affectionate	gracious	loving	trustworthy
consistent	generous	merciful	welcoming
creative	giving	patient	wise
disciplines	honest	provider	
enduring	impartial	protector	
ever-present	just and fair	restoring	

Characteristics of Jesus the Son

assertive	consistent	humble	sacrificial
available	decisive	joyful	selfless,
caring	faithful	loving	serving
committed	forgiving	mature	submissive
communicates	friendly	meek	true
compassionate	gentle	obedient	
conquering	good listener	peaceful	

Characteristics of the Holy Spirit

able	counselor	helper	revealer
activator	defending	honest	supportive
advocate	dependable	instructor	teacher
attentive	edifier	loving	trusted friend
bold	encourager	loyal	truthful
comforting	ever-present help	nurturing	wise
convincing	forewarner	peaceful	
corrects	guide	personal	
communicator		powerful	

These characteristics of God that you know and have experienced to be true are personal and very beautiful, and many of them would have an accompanying story. Each of the characteristics of God are worthy to study and experience. Songs, poems, and whole books have been written about His love, fairness, faithfulness, humility, strength, kindness, and Him being a friend or protector. Can you see how we'll not grow bored with Him even after thousands of years in heaven?

CHAPTER 4

The Fall That Broke the Mirror

In addition to these beautiful traits we've identified in God's personality, He also has numerous divine attributes and characteristics such as the fact that He is eternal with no beginning or end. He is holy, all knowing, and everywhere at the same time.

God Is Invisible

Another divine characteristic we want to consider in particular is that God is invisible. Several verses in the Bible clearly describe God this way.

> For ever since the world was created, people have seen the earth and the sky. Through everything that God made, they can clearly see *his invisible qualities*—his eternal power and divine nature. So they have no excuse for not knowing God.
>
> Romans 1:20 (NLT)

He (Jesus) is the image of the *invisible God,* the firstborn over all creation

Colossians 1:15

[Jesus said] *"God is a Spirit...."*
John 4:24 (KJV)

Now to the king eternal, immortal, *invisible,* to God who alone is wise, be honor and glory forever and ever. Amen.

1 Timothy 1:17

By faith he forsook Egypt, not fearing the wrath of the king; for he endured as seeing *Him who is invisible.*

Hebrews 11:27

Faith enabled Moses to see the invisible God. Yet, He is real even if you haven't touched Him. He is real even if you haven't seen Him in a vision. Even if you've never tangibly encountered Him, it doesn't make God any less real. That's because what the Bible makes such a big thing about is not what you see in a vision but that by *faith* you're able to connect with God who is invisible. Jesus even said, "Blessed are you who believe and haven't seen" (John 20:29). Our faith is not attached to something we've seen; our faith is attached to Someone invisible.

Nature Reveals God

Even though God is invisible, He delights in making Himself known and real to people and uses nature to make His invisible qualities obvious. Even the triune Father, Son, and Holy Spirit are expressed in nature. Romans tells us:

19 ...because what may be known of God is manifest in them, for God has shown *it* to them. 20 For since the creation of the world His invisible *attributes* are clearly seen, being understood by the things that are made, *even* His eternal power and Godhead, so that they are without excuse.

Romans 1:19-20

However, the Bible doesn't say anything was created in God's image until God created man: "So God created man in His own image; in the image of God He created him; male and female He created them" (Genesis 1:27). While we can see godly attributes in nature, it was the human that God specifically created with the purpose and the ability to image Himself.

It is true that the image of God cannot be reduced to a list of characteristics; He's far more extensive. He is God. Every detail certainly could not be contained on a page, in a book, or in a library. However, these beautiful characteristics in List A certainly are included in God's image that was used as a pattern to create man.

When God made man and woman, He made a perfect representation of Himself. As imagers of God, we were made and meant to reflect or mirror Him. Because God is invisible, His intention was for us to be His visible representation.

Man Was Made to Mirror God's Image

By seeing someone's reflected image in a mirror, you can know what that person looks like even though the mirror itself is not the person. In the same way, man isn't God, but like a mirror, man reflects His image and likeness. God is omnipresent; only as a spirit could that be true. Not only that, but as a spirit, we cannot see Him. Man was created to make the likeness of God tangible. It's also important to point out that after using Himself as the pattern or model to make man and woman, He told them to be fruitful and multiply and fill the earth.

Have you ever seen a series of mirrors or "house of mirrors" in an amusement park that multiplies the image of yourself? It's the same concept. God originally meant to have His image reflected and then reflected again in the next generation and again in the next generation and on and on it would go. Because God said to be fruitful and multiply and fill the earth, His earth would literally have been filled with His image.

What would that look like? Practically speaking, the earth would be filled with List A characteristics. That would have been so amazing that it's difficult to comprehend! Sadly, that didn't happen. What did happen?

The Fall

Genesis 2:16-17 says, "And the LORD God commanded the man, saying, "Of every tree of the garden you may freely eat; but of the tree of the knowledge of good and evil you shall not eat, for in the day that you eat of it you shall surely die."

The command God gave to man wasn't a long list of do's and don'ts. Adam and Eve could eat freely of every tree, including the Tree of Life, but they were not to eat of the Tree of the Knowledge of Good and Evil. In other words, God gave them the choice to eat freely of what God said was good to eat, which is life. But rather than trusting God's definition of good and evil, Adam and Eve took it upon themselves to make their own definitions.

Everything would have proceeded according to God's design, and His perfect image would have been multiplied in the earth had it not been for the serpent and his successful temptation to choose against God.

1 The serpent was the shrewdest of all the wild animals the Lord God had made. One day he asked the woman, "Did God really say you must not eat the fruit from any of the trees in the garden?" 2 "Of course we may eat fruit from the trees in the garden," the woman replied. 3 "It's only the fruit from the tree in the middle of the garden that we are not allowed to eat. God said, 'You must not eat it or even touch it; if you do, you will die.'" 4 "You won't die!" the serpent replied to the woman. 5 "God knows that your eyes will be opened as soon as you eat it, and you will be like God, knowing both good and evil." 6 The woman was convinced. She saw that the tree was beautiful and its fruit looked delicious, and she wanted the wisdom it would give her. So she took some of the fruit and ate it. Then she gave some to her husband, who was with her, and he ate it, too.

Genesis 3:1-6 (NLT)

The serpent deceived Eve into thinking they would be like God *if* they ate of the Tree of the Knowledge of Good and Evil. What a lie about their identity *that* was! They already *were* like God. They were *perfect imagers* of Him. From the first words of the serpent or the devil, he has always gained mastery over people by using their senses against them, confusing them about their identity.

Through the serpent's deceptive temptation, man disobeyed that direct command, choosing autonomy from God. Basically, the meaning of *sin* in both Hebrew and Greek means *to disobey* and *to miss the mark* or *the bullseye*. If you are shooting an arrow at a target and the arrow misses the bullseye, it may be completely off the entire target or just a little to the right or the left or even just a sliver off. Yet, regardless, you miss the bullseye. That's exactly what sin is.[1]

What does the bullseye represent? It's God's standard in that particular thing, or in other words, what God's design and will is. If you miss that by a long or narrow margin, it's called sin.

There are countless opinions in the world, about everything: "Well, I think this…." "My opinion is…." "I've always felt that…." "My personal belief is…." Yet, God being perfect, holy, just, and righteous *is* the standard of what is right and true. If we take it upon ourselves to decide right and wrong, we miss the mark. It doesn't matter if everyone in the world agrees with us. If we miss the mark, we miss God, because He is right. We're wrong. And what we did is called sin.

> FROM THE FIRST WORDS OF THE SERPENT OR THE DEVIL, HE HAS ALWAYS GAINED MASTERY OVER PEOPLE BY USING THEIR SENSES AGAINST THEM, CONFUSING THEM ABOUT THEIR IDENTITY.

As a result of sin, Romans 3:23 says all have *fallen* short of the glory of God. When Adam and Eve disobeyed and chose against what God had said and revealed as His way of life, they fell from the glory of God.

God warned Adam and Eve:

15 Then the Lord God took the man and put him in the garden of Eden to tend and keep it. 16 And the Lord God commanded the man, saying, "Of every tree of the garden you may freely eat; 17 but of the tree of the knowledge of good and evil you shall not eat, for *in the day that you eat of it you shall surely die.*

Genesis 2:15-17

Notice the last phrase once again: "…in the day that you eat of it you shall surely die." The Hebrew carries the significance of this phrase with the literal Hebrew meaning: *in dying thou shalt die.*[2] In other words, the first "dying" will cause the second death. What does that mean?

Let's look closely at the first dying. When Adam and Eve partook of the fruit, did they keel over? Of course, if you know the story in Genesis, you know they did not. That's exactly what the serpent said. He said, "You won't surely die." In other words, the devil was saying, "What God said was not true. Did God really say you would die?" Yet, is God's Word true? *Yes!*

So, if Adam and Eve didn't keel over when they ate the fruit, what did God mean when He told them they would die? God meant they would die the first death. Obviously, God was not referring to their bodies, but their spirits. God was talking about the spirit that He breathed into their bodies that He formed from the dust that made them live.

TO BE SPIRITUALLY SEPARATED FROM GOD WHO IS LIFE, LOVE, AND LIGHT, IS TRULY DEATH.

In the Bible, the word *die* doesn't only mean to die physically. That is not the only meaning of *death* as we see it in the Bible, and it is certainly not the first use of the word *die*. But what did happen when they died? True to what God said, their spirits separated from God. In choosing against God's direction, they chose separation or death.

We get the English word *sin* from the Latin word *sine* meaning *without.*[3]

Without God, man is spiritually dead and suffers the products of spiritual death in his or her life—spirit, soul, and body.

To be spiritually separated from God who is life, love, and light is truly death. Immediately, there was an image distortion in man. His spirit is no longer as it was before—as God breathed into man. It is no longer connected to life (John 11:25), light (1 John 1:5), love (1 John 4:8), and God.

So, what happened to the image of God in the fall? In the same way your mobile phone or a glass object would fall from a counter and shatter and break into pieces, so did man. Man—a reflection of God and His mirror image—fell from the glory of God and broke.

This is what we refer to as *the fall*—and clearly, there was no bigger fall known to man.

The Spirit Separated from God

In turning away from God's commandment to respond to the serpent's temptation, man's spirit does not reflect God anymore.

John put it this way:

> *You are of your father the devil, and the desires of your* father you want to do. He was a murderer from the beginning, and does not stand in the truth, because there is no truth in him. When he speaks a lie, he speaks from his own resources, for he is a liar and the father of it.
>
> John 8:44

Jesus' description of the devil in this verse is quite powerful. But what is really scary is His statement, "You are of your father the devil, and the desires of your father you want to do." Jesus was speaking spiritually, and He said, "The works of your father you will do." Basically, He was saying, "Like father like son." Yet, the devil was never to be our spiritual father. It was never intended to be that way, but it became that way as a result of Adam's choice.

We live in a generation where tolerance of everything is important. Sadly, it's often more important than truth. Truth is often not spoken if it's confrontational or contrary. This verse, and a lot of other things Jesus said, run cross-grain to our culture of tolerance. Jesus would be censored and forbidden to speak publicly today. His words infuriated people of His day as well.

The point Jesus was making in John 8:44 is that being dead spiritually and having the devil as your spiritual father will affect the way people act. Even more to the point here, being dead spiritually won't just remain a spiritual problem. It will display itself for all the world to see. We'll see why.

As a result of spiritual separation from God, the image originally intended to perfectly reflect the unseen God has been fractured in varying degrees in every human, from a slight distortion graduating up to hideous and grotesque distortions. This is awful. It's sad. It's so far from God's original and *very good* plan for man.

The Fractured Soul

Man's nature[4] is composed of three parts: spirit, soul, and body, and all three parts were impacted by his fall and separation from God. Think of man's spirit like a factory. Proverbs 4:23 says that out of our heart come all the issues of life. If there is death in his spirit, it's not just latent. The spirit produces death, which works up into the soul—works up into the mind, works up into the will, and works up into the emotions to break and darken them.

The soul, then, becomes an expresser of whatever is happening in the spirit, as well as what is negatively happening around about externally. As a result, the soul can be a terrible distortion of what was originally designed to image God. The distorted soul becomes not God's intention at all.

Think again about the example of mirrors in an amusement park fun house that do weird things to your appearance. It's kind of funny to see yourself all distorted—stretched, slanted, warped, and twisted. But there's a point in real life where distortion is not at all fun. That point is when the distortion of who you're intended and designed to be becomes more real than the original design. It is tragic what sin has done to the image of God in mankind and what the fall has done to fracture the image.

The Fractured Body

What about the body? The body was also designed to image the Lord. God doesn't have a physical body, but the human body He fashioned expresses His spiritual form. The Bible in various scriptures speaks of God's hands, arms, face, and back. Ezekiel saw a being who from the waist up was fire and from the waist down was fire. So, God evidently has form from the waist up and waist down.

Yet, even as wonderfully as God created the human body to image His own being, man's body also was tragically affected by the fall. To whatever degree man's body was affected by spiritual death and psychological dysfunction, his body bears the brunt and is indirectly oppressed by the devil. Acts 10:38 tell us "how God anointed Jesus of Nazareth with the Holy Spirit and with power, who went about doing good and healing all who were *oppressed by the devil.*"

DISEASE IS THE FOUL OFFSPRING OF ITS FATHER SATAN AND ITS MOTHER SIN.

Sickness is an oppression either directly or indirectly from the devil. Not every sickness is brought to a person's body and enforced by a demon. Yet, even if sickness is indirect, it's a result of the fall. Sickness was not a part of the original design for man's body.

In this book, we will look all the way back to the original design. What was God thinking when He designed the body? Certainly, He did not design for it to be sick. God loves your body, and it is very precious to Him (1 Corinthians 6:13).

Sin is what opened the door to malfunctions in the body. Sickness assaults God's original design for the body, and Jesus doesn't like it! He fought against it by healing people everywhere He went.

John Alexander Dowie, who is known for his powerful ministry to the sick in the late 1800s said disease is the foul offspring of its father Satan and its mother Sin.[5] What a powerful statement. Certainly, God didn't create anything broken, diseased, or sick.

Notes

1 Strong's Concordance – Hebrew – *chata: to miss, go wrong, sin* – Original Word: חָטָא
Phonetic Spelling: (*khaw-taw'*).
NAS Exhaustive Concordance: Definition – *to miss, go wrong, sin* – http://biblehub.com/hebrew/2398.htm
Strong's Concordance – Greek – *hamartia: a sin, failure* – Original Word: ἁμαρτία, ας, ἡ – phonetic spelling: (*ham-ar-tee'-ah*)
Definition: *missing the mark; hence:* (a) *guilt, sin,* (b) *a fault, failure (in an ethical sense), sinful deed.*
266 *hamartía* (a feminine noun derived from 1 /A "not" and 3313 /méros, "a part, share of") – properly, *no-share* ("no part of"); *loss* (forfeiture) because not hitting *the target*; *sin* (*missing* the mark).
266 /*hamartía* (*sin, forfeiture because missing the mark*) is the brand of sin that emphasizes its *self*-originated (*self*-empowered) nature – i.e. it is not originated or empowered by God (i.e. *not* of *faith*, His inworked persuasion, cf. Ro 14:23). http://biblehub.com/greek/266.htm

2 The phrase *you shall surely die* can be literally translated from the Hebrew biblical text as *dying you shall die*. In the Hebrew phrase we find the imperfect form of the Hebrew verb (*you shall die*) with the infinitive absolute form of the same verb *(dying)*. This presence of the infinitive absolute intensifies the meaning of the imperfect verb (hence the usual translation of *you shall surely die*). This grammatical construction is quite common in the Old Testament, not just with this verb but others also, and does indicate (or intensify) the certainty of the action. Clearly in the context of Genesis 3, Adam and Eve died spiritually instantly. They were separated from God and hid themselves. Their relationship with God was broken, so both spiritual death and physical death are the consequences of Adam's fall. https://answersingenesis.org/death-before-sin/genesis-2-17-you-shall-surely-die/

3 http://latindictionary.wikidot.com/preposition:sine
S*in:* from the Latin word *sine*, meaning *lacking or without*. Literally, *sin* is anything *without God*.
https://www.online-latin-dictionary.com/latin-english-dictionary.php?parola=sine

4 Man is a threefold being: (1) Spirit - the part of man which deals with the spiritual realm; (2) Soul - the part of man which deals with the mental realm: his reasoning and intellectual powers; (3) Body - the part of man which deals with the physical realm. Paul made a distinction between them in 1 Thessalonians 5:23, "…I pray God your whole *spirit* and *soul* and *body* be preserved blameless unto the coming of our Lord Jesus Christ. http://www.cfaith.com/index.php/blog/22-articles/christian-living/20520-the-three-part-nature-of-man

5 John Alexander Dowie spoke of the foul effects of sin after seeing its ravages on people's bodies: "It seemed sometimes as if I could almost hear the triumphant mockery of fiends ringing in my ear whilst I spoke to the bereaved ones the words of Christian hope and consolation. Disease, the foul offspring of its father, Satan, and its mother Sin, was defiling and destroying the earthly temples of God's children and there was no deliverance…No, sir, that is the devil's work, and it is time we called on Him Who came to 'destroy the work of the devil,' to slay that deadly foul destroyer, and to save the child." http://healingandrevival.com/TestimonyDowie.pdf

ENGENDERED

CHAPTER 5

Like Father Like Son

The son of Enosh, the son of Seth, the son of *Adam,*
the son of God.

Luke 3:38

As we study scriptures that describe the very beginning of humanity, we see God and His son Adam. From Adam came Eve, and the two were created as a perfect reflection of the Creator. Yet, when Adam sinned, it all broke down, and the perfect image was fractured. Initially, Adam perfectly reflected God, but after he fell, there was a distortion to that reflection that continued with Adam's son and way beyond.

And Adam lived one hundred and thirty years, and begot a son in
***his own likeness, after his image,* and named him Seth.**

Genesis 5:3

Do you see that? Adam had a son in whose image? In *his own image.* Essentially, Adam broke, and then he had a son in his broken image. How did that affect the spirit then? Adam passed death and the sin nature on to us all.

Nevertheless death reigned from Adam to Moses, even over those who had not sinned according to the likeness of the transgression of Adam, who is a type of Him who was to come.

Romans 5:14

SIN HAS A FRACTURING EFFECT ON A HUMAN'S SOUL AS WELL.

Adam had a direct command from God, and he broke it. The scripture says we haven't transgressed exactly like Adam did because he had personal contact and a direct command from the Creator. Death nonetheless was passed on because we have all sinned. In sinning, we've all fallen. And in falling, we all broke. There is not one human who hasn't suffered fracture.

...For if by the one man's offense many died....

Romans 5:15

That one man's offense caused everyone to die. That spiritual death affected us all, and the fractures were passed on and on.

For if by the one man's offense death reigned through the one....

Romans 5:17

Because of one man's transgression it says that death reigned. Everybody was affected by Adam's fall because what he passed on was a fractured image.[1]

What about the spirit of babies?

Furthermore, we have had fathers of our flesh which corrected us, and we gave them reverence: shall we not much rather be in subjection unto the *Father of spirits*, and live?

Hebrews 12:9 (KJV)

Notice, God is called the *Father of spirits* in this verse. In other words, the spirit of every baby who is conceived comes from God, not their parents (Ecclesiastes 12:7). However, a baby's spirit is not born again as a person's is when he or she believes in the heart that God raised Jesus from the dead and confesses Jesus is Lord. Yet, because a baby's spirit comes from God, it is alive to God and perfect in essence. But watch what happens!

> For all have sinned and fall short of the glory of God.
>
> Romans 3:23

Even though every human spirit comes from God, it's only a matter of time until that person sins. When they do, his or her spirit dies or is separated from God, and sin has its fracturing effect. Those effects are passed to another generation.

Sin has a fracturing effect on a human's soul as well. Those fractures in the soul are often passed on to the next generation. In fact, particular fractures can even run in a family. Let's look closer at the effects of these fractures from one generation to another.

Notes

1 The Bible says that "life is in the Blood" (Leviticus 17:11). Sin was passed down through the blood from father to child. A child inherits his or her blood type from both their parents. Jesus, therefore, inherited His blood type from His Father. During pregnancy, a baby's blood and mother's blood never mix. They are kept separated by the placenta. Jesus did not inherit sin nature. His blood was perfect and full of the life of God

CHAPTER 6

Thoroughly Fractured

Some disorders that are influenced by family genetics are schizophrenia, alcoholism, obesity, and depression. Drugs have been designed to help deal with these disorders although they cannot cure them. Temper, abuse, and unfaithfulness are other examples of characteristics of a fractured soul that may not have come genetically but often still appear from generation to generation. Through medicine, self-helps, counseling, and therapy, these fractures can be patched—taped up to hold things together somewhat.

Yet, outside of a new birth into Christ and a transformation in thinking, these ways of holding the fractures together, coping with them, or disguising them with some good emotional makeup are all that can be offered. There's even instruction on how to highlight our good parts in order to distract us from the broken parts. "Yes, I'm a mess here, but look at me in this other area. I'm great!"

Then there is a level of fracture that is too difficult to disguise. People with these extreme fractures have a difficult time functioning in society and often live together in special facilities or prisons to keep themselves and other people safe.

We're all pretty used to normal level fractures, however. We walk around confidently, all the while a little askew, a little messed up. Then we comfort one another and maybe even joke about it: "We have the same mess ups. Let's be friends!" We have clubs built around fractures. We go on special vacations with people who have the same fractures we do. Movies and film plots thrive off dysfunctional people.

I'm thankful for anything that soothes and helps people suffering from fractures in their lives, and I'm certainly thankful for every social help. We often pray that God infuses social workers with life, light, and help because they are amongst hurting people every day doing what they've been trained to do. Too often the Church has been quite removed from the people who really need help while social agencies are actually out among them. God certainly uses people who work in these fields to help in every way they possibly can.

By all these means, a person can try to glue the fracture and hold things together, but under pressure it will pop out again or break out in another area. In reality, these methods of help are broken Adam trying to help broken Adam.

The Broken Soul Breaks the Body

The body also took a hit as a result of the fall. It didn't show up immediately because people still lived for nearly a millennium for 10 generations. Noah was 950 years old when he died. But in time, the body progressively broke down and gradually reduced the life span. Isn't a fracture a sorry thing to pass down to your kids?!

> **Whoever sheds man's blood, by man his blood shall be shed; for in the *image of God He made man.***
>
> **Genesis 9:6**

In the story of Noah, many years after the creation of Adam, it says that man was made in the image of God, as opposed to being made in the image of a tree, or in the image of an ape, or in the image of a star, or in the image of a fish. No. Man was made originally in the image of God, and there is a sacredness about that. There is something sacred about the human body because it was patterned from the image of God.

Notice what James says:

> **With it we bless our Lord and Father, and with it we curse men, who have been made** *in the likeness of God.*
>
> **James 3:9 (AMP)**

In the most general sense, it's not right to bless God and then turn around and curse men. That includes even mean people, because the pattern for every human, good or bad, was originally God. You just don't curse people. Period.

Although God originally formed Adam's body out of the dust and Eve's body from part of Adam's, the body you have came from your mom and dad's genes[1] and chromosomes;[2] it was knit together in your mother's womb.

The body expresses the spirit that is separated from God as we saw in the previous chapter. Your body also is the expresser of the soul, your thoughts, will, and emotions. Because the body expresses the fallen spirit and the darkened soul, it is consequently weakened by disease, sickness, and degeneration.[3]

The origin and cause of the eruption of sickness in the human body is often either spiritual or psychological. When things go amok in the soul through stresses and fears, it affects the human body by releasing toxins that make way for sickness or disease.

Notes

1 *Gene* – Microscopic, yet powerful, a gene is segment of DNA, the molecule that stores the code for building living bodies. A gene is a single unit of genetic information, stored on twisting strands in every cell of every living being. In sexual reproduction, the parents' genes mix together to make the child. Although people would like to think that genes code for discrete traits, like friendliness or mathematical genius, that's not the case. Genes control the color of your eyes and the shape of your toes, not your personality. https://www.vocabulary.com/dictionary/genes

2 *Chromosome* – A chromosome is a strand of DNA encoded with genes. In most cells, humans have 22 pairs of these chromosomes plus the two sex chromosomes (XX in females and XY in males) for a total of 46. https://www.vocabulary.com/dictionary/chromosome

3 Scientists are discovering a strong link between behavior and physical well-being. For instance: • Expressing affection lowers cholesterol. • A 30-minute argument will cause a surge in cytokines, the immune molecules that trigger inflammation. High levels of cytokines are linked to arthritis, diabetes, heart disease, and cancer. • Exposure to chronic stress has been found to raise risk of cardiovascular disease and diabetes. • Angry outbursts may last only a few minutes, but they can cause surges in blood pressure and heart rate, raising the risk of heart attack by 19 per cent, concludes a study at University College, London. • Falling in love raises levels of nerve growth factor for about a year, according to researchers at the University of Pavia in Italy. • "Low mood is linked to low levels of serotonin and dopamine, the feel-good neurotransmitters in the brain," says London GP Dr Jane Flemming. • "Serotonin plays a role in regulating pain perception and could be the reason why 45 per cent of patients with depression also suffer aches and pains." • Cardiologists at the University of Maryland Medical Center found that laughing can reduce the risk of a heart attack by curbing unwanted stress.
https://www.psychologies.co.uk/self/the-link-between-emotions-and-health.html

CHAPTER 7

Stereotypical Male and Female—Post Fall

The devastation the fall had upon the spirit, soul, and body is apparent. But what about the characteristics of God that were to be tangibly imaged and experienced through male and female? If we examine the sexes and the characteristics of their gender roles, will we find damage done there as well?

In chapter 3, we looked at a list compiled by students from various countries outlining the characteristics of God the Father, Son, and Holy Spirit (List A). It's always been interesting to me that no matter where people come from, what race, sex and gender, age, language and social standing they have, the same wonderful characteristics are listed.

Let's also look at a couple of other lists compiled by the same groups of people. These characteristics, like the list of God's characteristics, are the same no matter how diverse the background of students. However, unlike the characteristics of God in List A, the next two lists feature man and woman. List B identifies negative stereotypical characteristics of the male in his roles as a man, father, and husband. List C records negative stereotypical characteristics of the female in her roles as a woman, wife, and mother.

LIST B:
Negative Male Characteristics

abusive
absent
angry
arrogant
cold
controlling
cruel
detached
dictatorial
disrespectful
domineering
egotistic

hard heart
harsh
inconsiderate
indecisive
insensitive
irresponsible
insecure
intimidating
jealous
judgmental
lazy
lover of themselves

manipulative
non- communicative
possessive
selfish
stubborn
temperamental
unaffectionate
unaware
unfaithful
unteachable
violent

LIST C:
Negative Female Characteristics

annoying
bossy
catty
clingy
competitive
cold
conniving
condemning
controlling
demanding
depressed

domineering
emotional
fault-finding
fragile
gossipy
gullible
hysterical
indecisive
insecure
irrational
jealous

judgmental
nagging
manipulative
materialistic
mean
needy
passive
prideful
scheming
self-absorbed
self-conscious

spiteful
stingy
stubborn
talkative
unstable
vain
vindictive
weak

Have you ever before seen a compilation of such uncomplimentary descriptions? The making of these lists was actually fun, and we laughed a lot. In real life, however, a person with any of these traits is not a laughing matter. It would be ugly, indeed.

The characteristics in List B make monsters out of men, and the stereotypes in List C make even the most gorgeous of women hideous. Of course, the entire list does not apply to every man and every woman. Nonetheless, this is a general list of stereotypes by which men and women around the world in all walks of life are known and recognized. It's important to remember that this is not the way we were intended to be, but these fractures have become the stereotypes each gender is known to have.

Let these descriptions soak into your consciousness, and then compare them with the characteristics of God that male and female were created to image and reflect found in List A below:

LIST A:
Characteristics of God

Characteristics of God the Father

accepting	forgiving	kind	strong
accessible	good	long-suffering	smart
affectionate	gracious	loving	trustworthy
consistent	generous	merciful	welcoming
creative	giving	patient	wise
disciplines	honest	provider	
enduring	impartial	protector	
ever-present	just and fair	restoring	

Characteristics of Jesus the Son

assertive	consistent	humble	sacrificial
available	decisive	joyful	selfless,
caring	faithful	loving	serving
committed	forgiving	mature	submissive
communicates	friendly	meek	true
compassionate	gentle	obedient	
conquering	good listener	peaceful	

Characteristics of the Holy Spirit

able	counselor	helper	revealer
activator	defending	honest	supportive
advocate	dependable	instructor	teacher
attentive	edifier	loving	trusted friend
bold	encourager	loyal	truthful
comforting	ever-present help	nurturing	wise
convincing	forewarner	peaceful	
corrects	guide	personal	
communicator		powerful	

Look again at the stark contrast that Lists B and C present and how they misrepresent God's nature. Remember, it was in God's image male and female were created, and His characteristics were to have been on display through them. Adam and Eve would have visibly reflected the characteristics of the invisible God and were created to do just that.

Yet it's also abundantly clear that to observe a fallen and fractured male or female, you might misunderstand God completely. Humans—God's imagers on the earth—have become so marred that He is misunderstood and often unrecognizable.

For this reason, the fall was a tragedy for God as well as a terrible outcome for humans. How could God be "seen" and correctly understood in the earth? Would the man and woman He created ever be able to naturally represent His characteristics again and make Him visible?

CHAPTER 8

He Made Them Male and Female

At the climax of creation as the crowning achievement of all He had designed, God created the human being—male and female—to image and represent Himself. The pattern for the male and female genders came out of God Himself—completely original, perfect, and pure.

Do you remember from Chapter 2 that Moses was not to take his pattern for the construction of the tabernacle from anything around him or from his memory of architecture in Egypt? God took him to a mountain, apart from any other influence, and gave him the pattern for the tabernacle. In the same way, the pattern for the male and female genders originated with God but was far more sacred and unprecedented.

When Jesus was questioned on the subject of marriage, He didn't go back to the law for His standard. He went back further yet—to creation. In the same way, for clarity regarding sex and gender, we need to follow Jesus' example and go back to creation.

Separating the Sexes

26 Then God said, "Let Us make man in Our image, according to Our likeness; let them have dominion over the fish of the sea, over the birds of the air, and over the cattle, over all the earth and over every creeping thing that creeps on the earth." 27 So God created man in His own image; in the image of God He created him; *male and female He created them.*

Genesis 1:26-27

What was the beginning for the male and female sexes? True, they were created on the sixth day, but is there more to be understood about their creation?

As we read above, Genesis 1:27 gives the final outcome of God's creation of male and female. However, Genesis 2 reiterates and adds a few details to the creation story. Then, verse 4 begins to break down the process for creating man and woman.

To gain more insight about this process, let's take a look at the Hebrew language that gives us intriguing clues. There are two Hebrew words translated *man* in the scripture we're studying. The first one *ha'adam*[1] means *the human or humanity. Humanity,* as we know, includes both sexes. The other word, *Ish*, is translated *man* and means *a male.* Another word that is marked in the scripture below is the Hebrew word *ishsha*[2] *or isha* which is translated *woman.*

Now, let's read in Genesis below in light of this. *The human* is italicized and used every place where the Hebrew word *ha'adam* is in the passage below and replaces the word *man:*

1 Thus the heavens and the earth, and all the host of them, were finished. 2 And on the seventh day God ended His work which He had done, and He rested on the seventh day from all His work which He had done. 3 Then God blessed the seventh day and sanctified it, because in it He rested from all his work which God had created and made. 4 This is the history of the heavens and the earth when they were created, in the day that the Lord God made the earth and the heavens, 5 before any plant of the field was in

the earth and before any herb of the field had grown. For the Lord God had not caused it to rain on the earth, and there was no man to till the ground; 6 but a mist went up from the earth and watered the whole face of the ground. 7 And the Lord God formed man [*the human*] of the dust of the ground, and breathed into his nostrils the breath of life; and man [*the human*] became a living being. 8 The Lord God planted a garden eastward in Eden, and there he put the man [*the human*] whom he had formed. 9 And out of the ground the Lord God made every tree grow that is pleasant to the sight and good for food. The tree of life was also in the midst of the garden, and the tree of the knowledge of good and evil. 10 Now a river went out of Eden to water the garden, and from there it parted and became four riverheads. 11 The name of the first is Pishon; it is the one which skirts the whole land of Havilah, where there is gold. 12 And the gold of that land is good. Bdellium and the onyx stone are there. 13 The name of the second river is Gihon; it is the one which goes around the whole land of Cush. 14 The name of the third river is Hiddekel; it is the one which goes toward the east of Assyria. The fourth river is the Euphrates. 15 Then the Lord God took the man [*the human*] and put him in the garden of Eden to tend and keep it. 16 And the Lord God commanded the man [*the human*], saying, 'Of every tree of the garden you may freely eat; 17 but of the tree of the knowledge of good and evil you shall not eat, for in the day that you eat of it you shall surely die.' 18 And the Lord God said, "It is not good that man [*this human*] should be alone; I will make him a helper fit for him." 19 Out of the ground the Lord God had formed every beast of the field and every bird of the air, brought them to Adam [*the human*] to see what he would call them. And whatever Adam [*the human*] called every living creature, that was its name. 20 So Adam [*the human*] gave names to all cattle, to the birds of the air, and to every beast of the field. But for Adam [the *human*] there was not found a helper comparable to him. 21 And the Lord God caused a deep sleep to fall on Adam [*the human*], and he slept; and He took one of his ribs, and closed up the flesh in its place. 22 Then the rib which the Lord God had taken from man [*the human*] He made into a woman [*ish*], and He brought her to the man [*the human*]. 23 And Adam said: "This is now bone of my bones And flesh of my flesh; She shall be called Woman [*ishsha or isha*], Because she was taken out of Man" [the word here is not *ha'adam* but *'ish*].

Genesis 2:1-23

Basically, what stands out from reading the text with these words marked is that the being God initially created was a human that contained both male and female. After this human had named the animals, it was evident that among the animals there was nothing compatible to the human. So, God performed an operation on the human and separated the female from the male—creating two distinct sexes.

SEPARATION WAS A PART OF GOD'S CREATIVE PROCESS.

It may be noted here that the sex chromosomes support this "separation." Male is XY while female is XX. God obviously took the X chromosome from the first human to form an XX counterpart—Eve.

Actually, separating the female from the male was not the first time God separated something while creating. Separation was a part of God's creative process on three other days as well. Let's take note of the separation that happened on the first, second, and fourth days of creation that perhaps are overlooked. While reading these verses, look particularly at the italicized words.

Day 1 – "3 Then God said, 'Let there be light,' and there was light. 4 And God saw that the light was good. *Then he separated the light from the darkness.* 5 God called the light 'day' and the darkness 'night.' And evening passed and morning came, marking the first day" (Genesis 1:3-5 NLT).

Day 2 – "6 Then God said, *'Let there be a space between the waters, to separate the waters of the heavens from the waters of the earth.'* 7 And that is what happened. *God made this space to separate the waters of the earth from the waters of the heavens.* 8 God called the space 'sky.' And evening passed and morning came, marking the second day" (Genesis 1:6-8 NLT).

Day 4 – "14 Then God said, 'Let lights appear in the sky to *separate the day from the night.* Let them be signs to mark the seasons, days, and years. 15 Let these lights in the sky shine down on the earth.' And that is what happened. 16 God made two great lights—the larger one to govern the day, and the smaller one to govern the night. He also made the stars. 17 God set these lights in the sky to light the earth, 18 *to govern the day and night, and to separate the light from the darkness.* And God saw that it was good. 19 And evening passed and morning came, marking the fourth day" (Genesis 1:14-19 NLT).

On day six after God performed an operation on the human He made, separating the female from the male. Then God brought the woman to the man, who says this:

> "At last!" the man exclaimed. "This one is bone from my bone, and flesh from my flesh! She will be called 'woman,' *[ishsha or isha]* because she was taken out of '*man*' [the word here is not *ha'adam* but *'ish].*"
>
> **Genesis 2:23 (NLT)**

Again, quite literally, the woman *had* been bone[3] of his bone and flesh of his flesh until woman was taken out of man. God took one human being and made two distinct sexes. Now notice the next two verses:

> 24 Therefore a *man* shall leave his father and his mother and be joined to his wife, and they shall become one flesh. 25 And they were both naked, the man *[the human]* and his wife, and were not ashamed.
>
> **Genesis 2:24-25**

Sexual intercourse makes them one again. Even though the act of sex can be expressed in a myriad of ways other than exclusively between man and woman in marriage, it still remains that it is only when male and female come together in intercourse that the human race continues naturally—without medical assistance and intervention.

The Genesis Pattern

Think about this from the devil's standpoint. If the devil's goal was to deface and desecrate the image of God that he saw in the human, he would need to begin by spiritually separating man from God. Then the devil went on to fracture what is essentially the epicenter of our human identity: the male and female genders.

At this point, I'm not referring to sexual orientation but only to the way a person identifies with and expresses his or her particular sex. The twisted characteristics of Lists B and C are indicators that the identification and expression were both included in all that was fractured and distorted. They require redemption and reconciliation to God and His original purpose for mankind to image Him accurately as in List A.

Going all the way back to the Creator and His divine pattern for the male and female He designed is the *only* way to have real clarity regarding sex and gender identity without prejudice, bias, and bigotry.

What was in the mind of the Creator when he made humans in the first place?

Genesis 1:27 says, "He made them male and female." That's all. Just male and female.

The sex chromosomes—either XX or XY—are given at conception, and how the baby develops before birth determines the sex identified when the baby is born.

APART FROM A PERSON'S SPIRIT, THERE IS NOTHING MORE CORE TO HIS OR HER IDENTITY THAN HIS OR HER SEX.

Of course, like every other area, the fall made way for fractures in this area to God's original pattern, and there are numerous chromosomal and developmental anomalies that impact the development of the sex organs. These are commonly called *intersex*[4] conditions or disorders in sexual development. They happen either at conception or during the baby's development during gestation and are not at all the same as transgenderism and homosexuality and don't in and of themselves affect sexual orientation.

Even considering these anomalies in sex development, by the time a baby is born the sex of the child is established. The appearance of a person's sex can be surgically altered and hormonally modified to change specific physical development and functions. Even the paths in the brain can be forged and developed to express another gender.[5] Still, that person's sex, determined by their DNA[6] at the time of their conception, is stamped into every cell of their body and remains the same in spite of all modifications.

Male or Female Identity

Apart from a person's spirit, there is nothing more core to his or her identity than his or her sex. At birth, a baby's sex is sometimes even more apparent than the baby's race and is usually the first thing identified—even before eye color and which parents' hands, nose, and ears the babe has. A person's age, health, state of mind, personality, talents, education, environment, social standing, and financial status are marks that characterize them. But all of these can fluctuate and none even come close to the way that a person's sex and gender define their identity.

When a person's thoughts and feelings don't portray their sex, it causes a horrible internal conflict, often heightened at puberty. When the body and soul are at odds with each other, there is gender confusion or dysphoria.[7] It is not surprising that people who suffer the confusion of a body that is one gender, but have feelings and thinking of the other gender, can be so tormented they don't even want to live. Perhaps you or someone you know has experienced this. Misunderstanding and ignorance in this area opens the door to shame and fear, which are perfect ingredients for the devil to torment and bind a person.

WHEN THE BODY AND SOUL ARE AT ODDS WITH EACH OTHER, THERE IS GENDER CONFUSION.

There can be a variety of reasons why a person becomes disoriented regarding the sex he or she was conceived and born as. Many of those reasons are intimate, some even tragic, while for others it is a temporary phase. The purpose of our study is to delve into God's original plan for man and woman *before* the fall—before anything tragic happened. What did the Creator intend for us to look and be like? How can knowing this help?

Personal opinions and experiences may be impacting, but they don't shine light on the subject. Psalm 119:130 says that the entrance of God's Word gives light. The absolute truth that is free from bias and prejudice can *only* be found in the One who is the Truth and in His words. To experience redemption and reconciliation to God's original intent, a person must first know what it is and then accept it as truth. Truth confronts but never condemns or binds. It makes a person free.

Sadly, the sinister plan of the devil against God and His image on the earth—male and female—worked really well. However, God also had a plan for redemption. As clever as the devil's plan was, God's plan to redeem mankind in every way he was damaged was even more brilliant.

Redemption truly means so much more than simply being saved so you go to heaven when you die. Let the scope of redemption include everything that was broken in the fall and everything that required redemption so it can be returned to its original intention. If you can find something in any area of life—spirit, soul, and body—that doesn't image or represent God, there's redemption for it. Total redemption!

Second Corinthians 5:17 says all things become new for the one who is a new creation in Christ. Do you suppose God really means *all* things? And if so, wouldn't that include any challenges regarding gender? Yes! Redemption even includes something as core as any fractured characteristics of our sex and gender as well.

Notes

1 *Adam can mean human and humanity.* The Hebrew word *adam* can mean *human being* and not necessarily a male human being. For instance, in the Hebrew of Genesis 5:2, humankind—both men and women—are referred to as *adam* by God. In Genesis 1:27, it says, "God created humankind (*ha'adam*) in His own image, in the image of God he created him; male and female he created them." In Genesis 2, the first human is fairly consistently referred to as *ha'adam* (הָאָדָם), especially before the "operation." https://margmowczko.com/human-man-woman-genesis-2/

2 Was the first human being male? In Genesis 2 we read the creation account of the first human being. In many English translations of Genesis 2, the first human is simply called "man". This "man" is understood by most people as referring to a male human rather than to a generic human. However, in the Hebrew text, the first "man" is not specifically referred to as a male human (*ish*) until after the "operation" mentioned in Genesis 2:21-22

when a part, or side, is taken out of him.

After the "operation," the now undoubtedly male human sees the female human and says, "This one is bone of my bone and flesh of my flesh! She will be called 'woman' (*ish-shah*) because she was taken out of 'man' (*ish*) (Gen. 2:23). The first woman (*ishshah*) and the first man (*ish*) may have both been a part of, or one side of, the first human being (*ha'adam*). http://margmowczko.com/human-man-woman-genesis-2/

3 Strong's Concordance: *rib, side.* Original Word: צֵלָע –
NAS Exhaustive Concordance: *rib, side.* NASB Translation: *boards (3), chambers (1), hillside* (1), leaves (1), one...another (1), rib (1), ribs (1), side (15), side chamber (1), side chambers (10), sides (5), walls (1).* http://biblehub.com/hebrew/6763.htm

4 *intersex* – What does *intersex* mean? A variety of conditions that lead to atypical development of physical sex characteristics are collectively referred to as intersex conditions. These conditions can involve abnormalities of the external genitals, internal reproductive organs, sex chromosomes or sex-related hormones. *Intersex* was originally a medical term that was later embraced by some intersex persons. Many experts and persons with intersex conditions have recently recommended adopting the term *disorders of sex development* (DSD). They feel that this term is more accurate and less stigmatizing than the term intersex. American Psychological Association. http://www.isna.org/faq/what_is_intersex

4B Katie Baratz – *Growing Up Intersex*
HC: Can you tell us what intersex is not?
KB: *Intersex*, as the name disorders of sex development implies, is a medical condition. Intersex is *not* the same as transgenderism or gender dysphoria and has very little correlation with sexual orientation.
https://www.haverford.edu/college-communications/news/growing-intersex-going-oprah

5 "The surprising truth is that every single thought—whether positive or negative—goes through the same cycle when it forms. Thoughts are basically electrical impulses, chemical reactions, and neurons. They look like a tree with branches. As the thoughts grow and become permanent, more branches grow, and the connections become stronger. As we change our thinking, some branches go away, new ones form, the strength of the connections change, and the memories network with other thoughts. What an incredible capacity of the brain to change and rewire and grow! Spiritually, this is renewing the mind. *Who Switched Off My Brain*, Dr. Caroline Leaf. Distributed by Thomas Nelson Publishers, Copyright ©Dr. Caroline Leaf, Southlake TX, 2009, pp19 -20. Used by permission.

6 People had long philosophized about the observed differences between males and females of a species. If one considers sex a trait, or set of traits, then it followed that sex is inherited. In 1905, closer study of meiosis revealed the chromosomal basis of gender. Scientists noticed an oddball pair among the homologous chromosomes lined up at the cell equator during reduction division. One chromosome (X) was much bigger than the other (Y). In human beings, this mismatched pair of one X and one Y chromosome is

seen exclusively in male cells. A matched pair of X chromosomes is found in female cells. Thus, XX chromosomes determine femaleness, and XY chromosomes determine maleness. Females produce only eggs with X chromosomes; males produce sperm with an X or a Y chromosome. http://www.dnaftb.org/9/

7 *Gender Dysphoria* – Gender dysphoria involves a conflict between a person's physical or assigned gender and the gender with which he/she/they identify. People with gender dysphoria may be very uncomfortable with the gender they were assigned, sometimes described as being uncomfortable with their body (particularly developments during puberty) or being uncomfortable with the expected roles of their assigned gender. People with gender dysphoria may often experience significant distress and/or problems functioning associated with this conflict between the way they feel and think of themselves (referred to as experienced or expressed gender) and their physical or assigned gender. https://www.psychiatry.org/patients-families/gender-dysphoria/what-is-gender-dysphoria

CHAPTER 9

The Creator's Intention for the Man

In a unique way, man was created to reflect or image the Father and the Son. After all, we cannot see the Father; He is a spirit. The Son is in heaven; Jesus was only on earth in His physical body for thirty-three years until His ascension. Yet, we can see man. Through observing a man as a father or as a husband or simply as a man, the Creator meant for the characteristics of the Father and the Son to be displayed and imaged.

By watching a man in the role of a father, it should have been possible to see what loving, just, fair, and patient essentially looks like and what these characteristics sound like. By interacting with a husband, we were to be able to experience kindness, faithfulness, and the presence of One who will never leave or forsake. That's huge! God intended that these characteristics be reflected and modeled, to be made flesh and dwell among us through men, husbands, and fathers.

Though we cannot see God, it was God's intention that by interacting with a man and observing a father or a husband it would be possible to know what God is like. First Corinthians 11:7 says, "For a man indeed ought not to cover his head since he is the image and glory of God...."

That is a very interesting verse of scripture, isn't it? Look at the characteristics again of List A (page 278). If a man looks like that, he is definitely glorious to God. He reflects God! I'm all for women; I *am* a woman. But there is something unique in the way the male sex has the potential of giving glory to God.

Broken Male

Let me ask you a question: What did the devil desire when he—as Lucifer in heaven—was the anointed cherub before God's throne? He wanted God's glory, and through pride, he tried to ascend above the throne of God and take it. As a result, he was cast out of heaven (Luke 10:18; Isaiah 14:12-17).

A MAN, HIS SEX AND GENDER, WAS UNIQUELY DESIGNED TO BRING GLORY TO GOD.

Then God made man in His own image and in His own likeness, and the Bible said He crowned man—male and female—with glory and honor (Psalm 8:5). But in a unique and particular way, the Bible very plainly says that man is the glory of God. A man, his sex and gender, was uniquely designed to bring glory to God.

When the devil saw that man, created to image the characteristics of God, was crowned with God's glory, the devil loathed man. After all, this was the glory he craved but couldn't have. Imagine his horror when the devil realized that through man, the glorious image of God would be duplicated and multiplied to fill the earth. The devil could not tolerate a visible representation of the image of God that was capable of reproducing. He had to do something to stop this from happening, and he surely did.

Through the devil's successful temptation that resulted in Adam sinning against God, the devil struck out at this once-glorious man and reduced him to the laughing stock in sitcoms. Man is poked fun at or, alternatively, becomes hideous due to the fractures and brokenness that have become characteristic, even stereotypical, of the male gender. The entertainment field incorporates weak men or the other extreme of domineering and violent, bigoted, and insensitive men into storylines. These and other fractures become the characteristics of stories people find entertaining.

Even though Lucifer couldn't have God's glory in heaven, through the fall, he's degraded man and robbed the glory due God that was intended to come through the male sex in all of the roles of that gender. It's pretty serious, isn't it? Tragically, every characteristic of God to be seen and experienced through man was in varying degrees distorted, twisted, marred, and disfigured grossly in the fall.

God meant for sons and daughters to look at their dad and see how God the Father looks and come to know God naturally through a relationship with their physical father. Children were to look at their fathers whom they can see and come to know God whom they cannot see. But can you recognize that the evil strategy of the devil was to so degrade man that no one could look at him to know what God is truly like?

For instance, instead of a child naturally understanding the love of God the Father, he or she may think God is cruel or mean or that He doesn't even exist if what was portrayed by the child's father was twisted. A child who looks at the fractured List B father, often ends up with a skewed idea about God the Father. Even the word *father* will come to mean List B characteristics to the child instead of List A characteristics as it should be.

In his book, *The Wild Man's Journey*[1], Richard Rhor gives a powerful example below of how absent, abusive, or simply fractured father figures impact the lives of his children:

> When I was giving a retreat in Peru, a sister who ministers in Lima's Central Prison brought this lesson home to me. She described how, as Mother's Day was approaching during her first year there, the men in the prison kept asking for Mother's Day cards. She kept bringing boxes and boxes of cards for the prisoners to send to mama, but she never seemed to have enough. So as Father's Day approached, she decided to prepare for the onslaught of requests by buying an entire case of Father's Day cards. But that case, she told me, is still sitting in her office. Not one man asked for a Father's Day card. She couldn't even give them away.

She realized this – and as she told me this story with tears in her eyes, I realized it too – that most of the men were in jail because they had no fathers. Not that they were orphans, but they had never been fathered. They had never seen themselves as sons of men who admired them, they had never felt a deep secure identity, and they had never received that primal enthusiasm that comes from growing up in a company of a father. And so, they spent their lives trying to become men in devious and destructive ways. They were insecure men who had to prove that they were macho, and they did this by committing acts of lawlessness and violence.

How a father images God will have immeasurable value or devastating effects on the identity that children have about themselves as well as how they view and interact with God.

By looking at the broken male in the role of a husband, the selfless love and faithfulness of the head of the Church would be completely misunderstood. By looking at the unfaithful husband, a wife won't be able to see the faithfulness of Jesus that a husband was designed to image or reflect.

For every ugly broken characteristic in List B there is an opposite unbroken characteristic in List A that the man was created to image and reflect. Let's contrast 30 characteristics from both lists.

List A	List B
Faithful	Unfaithful
Humble	Proud
Submissive	Arrogant
Selfless	Selfish
Compassionate	Critical
Gentle	Harsh
Caring	Unaffectionate
Serving	Demanding

The Creator's Intention for the Man

Willing	Stubborn
Assertive	Violent
Kind	Angry
Forgiving	Bitter
Good listener	Unaware
Communicates	Closed
Dependable	Irresponsible
Works in obedience to the Father	Lazy
Decisive	Insecure
Available	Detached
Meek	Unteachable
Joyful	Grumpy
Consistent	Temperamental
Friendly	Cold
True/Honest	Deceptive
Powerful	Domineering
Provider	Inconsiderate
Protector	Abandoning
Patient	Impatient
Impartial/Fair	Partial
Correcting / Discipline	Abusive
Wise	Brash

Notes

1 *The Wild Man's Journey: Reflections on Male Spirituality,* pp 85 – 86, Richard Rohr and Joseph Martos, St. Anthony Messenger Press, 1996. Used with permission.

CHAPTER 10

The Creator's Intention for the Woman

L et's look now at what God wanted to be imaged when He made woman. To do that, we don't look at the women we know who are around us. No. Remember, we were made in *God's* image, so we begin at Genesis 1:2 with God.

> **The earth was without form, and void; and darkness was on the face of the deep. And the *Spirit of God was hovering* over the face of the waters.**
>
> **Genesis 1:2**

Notice that it says the Holy Spirit was hovering upon the face of the waters. That's the very first time the Holy Spirit is spoken of in the Bible. That word *hovering* in the Hebrew is *rachaph*, and its primitive root means *brood* [1], *like a mother bird broods over the eggs in her nest and after they hatch, nurtures her chicks. Rachaph* is translated to picture that in Deuteronomy 32:

As an eagle stirs up its nest, *hovers* over its young, spreading out its wings, taking them up, carrying them on its wings.

Deuteronomy 32:11

BOTH GENDERS WERE CREATED TO IMAGE AND EXPRESS THE NATURE AND CHARACTERISTICS OF GOD.

The Holy Spirit certainly does have that kind of characteristic. Again, remember, God is a Spirit, and therefore, is neither male nor female. However, both genders were created to image and express the nature and characteristics of God.

Look again at the beautiful characteristics we've identified of the Holy Spirit in List A. In a unique way, woman was to make those characteristics tangible to reflect the Holy Spirit. As she imaged and reflected God as intended, her children could observe her and come away with a correct understanding of what the Holy Spirit is like. God's intention was for a woman who is visible, to express the personality qualities of the Holy Spirit who is invisible. *She was to model the kind of trusted friend that the Holy Spirit is.* Through observing a woman, you were to be able to see the guide, shepherd, comforter, teacher, forewarner, communicator, activator, inspirer, and edifier the Holy Spirit is. These are beautiful qualities indeed (List A — Holy Spirit. See page 278).

Here's something to consider. Would it be correct to think of women as inferior if woman was made in God's image with the purpose of imaging and reflecting Him? Wouldn't that mean that some part of God is inferior to another part? That's impossible! All of God is good and glorious. Man *and* woman—both—are made in God's image, and both are glorious!

However, as a result of the fall, beautiful qualities have been so broken and compromised that the list of stereotypes describing women, collected from people from various parts of the world, are not glorious at all. Even the majority of Disney stories that capitalize on the negative stereotypes of women being wicked, manipulative, cunning, and jealous have made millions.

Let's take another look at List C that features the negative stereotypes of women:

Negative Female Characteristics

annoying	domineering	judgmental	spiteful
bossy	emotional	nagging	stingy
catty	fault-finding	manipulative	stubborn
clingy	fragile	materialistic	talkative
competitive	gossipy	mean	unstable
cold	gullible	needy	vain
conniving	hysterical	passive	vindictive
condemning	indecisive	prideful	weak
controlling	insecure	scheming	
demanding	irrational	self-absorbed	
depressed	jealous	self-conscious	

These characteristics may make a good story, but they make things miserable in real life.

Created to Influence

The Word of God paints a different picture of woman altogether. Let's look at Genesis 2:

> 18 Then the LORD God said, "It is not good for the man to be alone. I will make a helper who is just right for him." 19 So the LORD God formed from the ground all the wild animals and all the birds of the sky. He brought them to the man to see what he would call them, and the man chose a name for each one. 20 He gave names to all the livestock, all the birds of the sky, and all the wild animals. But still there was no helper just right for him. 21 So the LORD God caused the man to fall into a deep sleep. While the man slept, the LORD God took out one of the man's ribs and closed up the opening. 22 Then the LORD God made a woman from the rib, and he brought her to the man.
>
> Genesis 2:18-22 (NLT)

In Genesis 2:18, for the very first time in all of creation—everything God created from the beginning—He declared, "It's not good." Every other day when God completed His work, He looked it over and said, "It's good." But when it came to observing the human, He said, "It is not good." No, God didn't say man wasn't good; He said it was not good that man be alone even though Adam was perfect and living in a perfect environment.

Why isn't it good for man to be alone? Man alone cannot be the whole expression of God. That's interesting, isn't it? God is triune—He's trinity. He's Father, Son, and Holy Spirit. And as we've already said, some characteristics of God are more expressed and amplified through one gender than the other. It's not that both cannot image all the characteristics of God because, of course, they can. But God chose a combination of male and female to be made in His image.

Man cannot reproduce alone. There are some trees that can't even reproduce alone. Did you know that? I didn't. My son-in-law is a horticulturist, and I was telling him that it would be nice to have a paw-paw tree because I like that fruit. He said, "No, if you want fruit, you can't just have one tree. You have to have at least a pair because they won't reproduce alone." Who knew that? There's a sermon in that! There's just some fruit you'll never bear if you want to be independent and be an all-by-yourself-type of a person.

God wants us to be in company and in a family where our roots get all tangled up with each other. Someone might say, "But I like everything just perfect. I don't want to mix up with anybody else's mistakes." Okay, then be fruitless. Be an amazing, leafy tree with no fruit. But if you're going to be fruitful, you're going to have to mix it up.

The third thing is that the inspirational qualities in women were put there by God to help men to be their best. By examples we see in the Bible, we can understand that God made it so. Women who influenced in the Bible were not only wives but also mothers, sisters, grandmothers, and friends.

It would be wrong to think this influencing capability that God has given to women doesn't kick in until a woman is in her 20s or something. No! It starts very young. It starts as a baby girl. I watched my girls when they were little do it with their father. I thought, *How are they doing that?*

They would just look at Tony, and he would melt, saying, "Whatever you want." It's amazing!

Mind you, due to the fact that this capability was fractured in the fall, women's influence has not always been good. In fact, in many cases, it has been terrible. Nevertheless, good or bad, women perpetually influence the people around them whether they intend to or not.

Let's look at snippets of stories in the Bible illustrating the fact that God made women to be influential. There will be a mix of the good, the bad, and the downright ugly.

Eve — Genesis 3:1-6

Of course, the first woman who influenced is actually the first woman: Eve. When Satan appeared as the serpent in the garden with a goal to get man to fall, he didn't even talk to Adam. No, who did he talk to? He talked to his wife. Satan knew that if he could get Adam's wife, she would get her husband. And it worked. She influenced him.

Sarah — Genesis 16:1-6; 21:8-12

After years of not being able to conceive, Sarai prevailed on her husband, Abram, to have a child by Hagar. Abram wasn't keen on the idea initially. If fact, it was his wife's idea, but Abram followed Sarai's wishes. Then after Hagar had the baby and her attitude toward Sarah changed, Sarah was distraught and told Abraham they had to leave. Abraham sent Hagar and Ishmael away for that reason.

Rebekah — Genesis 27:1-29

Rebekah had two sons: Esau and Jacob. She favored the younger son, Jacob, while Isaac favored the older son. Isaac's blessing was to go to Esau, the older son, when he died, but Rebekah wanted the blessing to go to her younger son when Isaac died. So, she connived and schemed to set up a plan.

She told Jacob, "This is what you do. Your brother has gone into the field to get an animal to make a special meal just like your father likes. Go ahead of him and bring me two fine goats. I know exactly how to fix that meat up like your brother makes it. Then you will take it in to your father and get the blessing."

Jacob told his mother, "You're going to get a curse on me instead of a blessing."

"No, you'll see!" she said.

Isaac couldn't see well. So he wasn't able to see the difference between his sons, but obviously, he was able to tell the difference by his other senses.

"This is what you're to do," Rebekah said. "You go in with the skins of the animal on your arms and the back of your neck, so when your father lays hands on you, you will feel like your brother." My, my! Esau wasn't hairy; he was furry! Don't you reckon?

Finally, he was to put on his brother's clothes, so he would smell like his brother. So, Jacob goes in according to his mother's plan (influence), and sure enough, the food tasted just like the food Esau made. The father said, "You sound like Jacob, but you smell like Esau." Esau must have had a very strong smell.

What ended up happening is that her child Jacob got the father's blessing because of this mother's influence. Actually, it was the will of God that it happened this way. I think it's quite interesting we think everything in God has to come about by people doing things in the most honest way.

Let me tell you, if God had to wait for everybody to do things right before He could use them, we would still be back in Genesis. Because God is all-knowing and knows how people will respond and do wrong things, God figures it in His plan. If He can't move through us because of our lack of responsiveness to Him, He will do a "bank shot" like in pool. He's so strategic. If we'll consecrate ourselves to God, He can even bounce off the negatives in our lives and get us in the pocket anyway! He did with Rebekah. The way she deceived her husband wasn't right, but the plan of God happened anyway.

Potiphar's Wife — Genesis 29:1-20

The story of Potiphar's wife provides us with another example of how even wicked and manipulating people don't thwart the plan of God. After her failed attempts to seduce Joseph, she lied to her husband about Joseph which landed him in prison. Nevertheless, through the gift of God in Joseph's life and God's favor on him, Joseph became the leader of Israel directly under Pharaoh.

Delilah — Judges16:4-31

You would never name a daughter you love *Delilah*. The very name is synonymous with deception, and Delilah was deceptive for sure. She leveraged Samson's affection for her to influence him to give up the secret of the purpose of his life. It cost him his eyes, and eventually, it cost him his life.

Abigail — 1 Samuel 25:2-42

Abigail, a benevolent, kind, and beautiful woman, was married to Nabal, a pretty awful man. In this true story, David and his mighty men were hungry, and they stopped by Nabal's farm and asked to buy animals and other food items to eat. Nabal blew David off, asking, "Who are you?" One thing about a man is that he may be pretty nice until he's hungry.

David had 300 mighty men, and they were all hungry. Nabal could have sold them whatever they needed because he had plenty, but he didn't even consider David's request. David went away angry and told his men, "We could have stolen this man's livestock anytime we wanted, but we didn't. We even protected him." The anger soon turned to fury, and David decided to take his army and raid Nabal's farm.

When the news got back to Abigail, she swung into action before David got there. She loaded up donkeys with food and went ahead to meet David. When she met up with him, she bowed and said, "My husband has not been wise or good to you. I'm so sorry. Here are gifts." Her benevolence saved her husband's life, saved the farm, saved the day, saved everything. That night, Nabal got drunk. The next morning when he was told about what happened the day before, the news shocked him into a stroke, and he died. David then married Abigail.

Bathsheba — 2 Samuel 11:1-5; 1 Kings 1:5-40

Then there is Bathsheba, who enters the story in a less than positive way. From the palace, David saw her bathing on her roof. Who does that? If your roof is the highest roof in the vicinity, it's one thing, but if there's anybody in a higher perspective than you, then you've made yourself a spectacle for sure.

David, who was not with the rest of his troops in battle, saw Bathsheba bathing and wanted her. In fact, he had her brought to him. He committed adultery with her, and Bathsheba became pregnant. Before the child was born, David brought the husband home from battle and arranged for him to go home to Bathsheba, hoping to cover his mistake. But the husband nobly refused to go home and slept outside. It was a mess. Worse yet, David had Bathsheba's husband killed. It's a terrible story.

The baby died soon after it was born. While Bathsheba was in mourning, David promised Bathsheba when she became pregnant again, her child would one day sit on the throne in his place. It's quite a promise to make before even knowing what kind of person the son will be, plus there were elder sons from other wives David could choose from. In spite of the sordid history, David made a promise to this mother that her son would sit on his throne.

THE REASON WHY SOLOMON BECAME KING IS BECAUSE HIS MOM NEVER FORGOT THE PROMISE DAVID MADE TO HER.

Years passed as we fast forward the story, and David was an old man. While he was bedridden, his son Adonijah was crowned king in another city. Trumpets were blown while Abiathar the priest and Joab, David's bodyguard, were there in a big celebration. Through Nathan the prophet, who David trusted, and Zadok the priest, the report got back to Bathsheba.

They told her, "You need to do something about this."

Bathsheba went to David's bedroom and says to him, "Do you remember when you told me my son would sit on the throne?"

"Yes," David said.

"Well, they've just crowned another one of your sons to be king. What are you going to do about it?"

The dear man had to get out of bed and fix it. I love that. So, David had Solomon crowned king. The reason why Solomon became king is because his mom never forgot the promise David made to her. I love that, too. Bathsheba used her influence tenaciously and persistently and refused to forget David's promise.

Solomon's Wives — 1 Kings 11:1-7 (NLT)

In addition to being famous for his wisdom and for building the beautiful temple that the glory of God filled, Solomon is also known for having had 700 wives and 300 concubines. Married guys, can you imagine?! What ended up happening to Solomon was very sad.

Think about it. It's crazy. Until Jesus came, Solomon was the wisest man who had ever lived on the earth. But most of the women Solomon married were from foreign nations who worshiped other gods, and those women actually influenced Solomon to turn his heart away from God and made him a fool. It's so sad.

Molech[2] was one of the gods for which he built a place of worship, and there the worshipers offered their children for burnt sacrifices. The Mount of Olives was the location of this horrible practice in Solomon's time. It's also the place that years later Jesus would consecrate to His Father to pay the price necessary to buy total redemption for humanity. This is where He began His passion.

Jezebel — 1 Kings 21:25

Jezebel's name is synonymous with evil and manipulation. She influenced her husband, King Ahab, toward the worship of Baal. Under Jezebel's control, King Ahab had the prophets of God killed in Israel and turned the people of God toward the worship of Baal.

Deborah — Judges 4-5

Deborah's influence was upon Barach, a reluctant leader, and through him, she influenced the nation toward victory over the cruel oppression of a Canaanite king.

Naaman's Wife's Maid — 2 Kings 5:1-4

Naaman's wife's maid discovered her master, Naaman, had leprosy. Being from Israel she knew of a prophet who could help. The wonderful story of how the great Syrian military commander, Naaman, was cleansed of leprosy after dipping in the River Jordan seven times wouldn't even be in the Bible if it had not been for Naaman's wife's maid. The Bible doesn't even record this lady's name, but she was quietly influential in the home where she lived—not as a queen but as a maid.

Esther — book of Esther

Esther's is one of the great stories of influence in the Bible. By God's amazing favor, Esther came to be Persia's queen. When she was chosen by the king to be his new queen, no one knew she was Jewish. Haman was the most powerful official to Queen Esther's husband, the king. Haman hatched a terrible plan for genocide of the entire Hebrew population, and through deception, he convinced the king to issue the edict.

This sinister plan came to Esther's attention through her cousin, Mordecai. Esther didn't think she could do anything to help because she couldn't approach the king uninvited. Her cousin challenged her, however, and said, "If you don't help the Hebrew people, help will arise from somebody else. Who knows but that you've come to the kingdom for such a time as this?" And "such a time as this" was a horrible time. It wasn't a time for fun, leisure, and frivolity; it was a time for pending genocide. That's why God had put her there.

Esther and her maids fasted and prayed, and she asked Mordecai to have the other Hebrew people fast as well. The Bible says she put on her garments and went in to see the king. What I see in this scripture is that the time of fasting was a time of spiritual adorning for Esther. What do I mean by that? There's something eternal and gorgeous about that kind of adorning that you can't buy in any store. Only in the presence of God can you find something so attractive. We'll talk more about what to put on and put off in Chapter 19.

We see the effect of her preparation when she comes to see the king uninvited. He looks at her and extends his sceptre, but he goes far beyond that. He offered her half of his kingdom. Now, there aren't any clothes anywhere that look so beautiful that even before a word is spoken a king says, "What do you want? I'll give you half of my kingdom." I reckon women revert to manipulation because they don't get something from God that gives them *divine influence.*

WOMEN REVERT TO MANIPULATION BECAUSE THEY DON'T GET SOMETHING FROM GOD THAT GIVES THEM DIVINE INFLUENCE.

God does want to use women to influence. But if we don't spend time in God's presence and get that influence from Him, then we default to List C with cunning and craftiness and manipulation and control and scheming. There's a better way! But the better way requires the right clothes, and we only get those in the presence of God.

Notice what did not happen when the king said, "What do you want?" At that moment, Esther did not fall in a heap right there on the floor hysterically, saying, "They're trying to kill us all!" Her lip didn't quiver, and she did not point an accusing finger at Haman. No, instead, she remained poised, because she was adorned in a garment that comes from time in God. She graciously answered, "I just want to invite you to a meal."

Interestingly enough, beauty and food are two things that tremendously influence men, and God used both of them here. Esther said, "I want you to come and bring Haman with you to a feast I want to make for you." Both came, and both were delighted. Haman was especially honored to be invited by the queen.

At the end of the meal, the king said, "What would you like me to do for you? Let me do something."

Esther said, "Just come tomorrow for another meal." At that point, you know the king was almost delirious with delight, thinking, *This woman is amazing!*

The next day the king and Haman returned to another feast prepared by Esther. After they had eaten, the king begged her, "What can I do for you? What do you want? I'll give it to you. I'll give you anything."

Esther said, "I simply request that you save my life and the lives of my people." The king was flabbergasted and asked, "Who's threatening you and your people?" Esther answered, "Him," as she pointed to Haman.

Esther was calm and cool. Nothing hysterical. Nothing out of control. Of course, hearing this made the king furious. He was livid! The king was so very angry he had to leave the room.

While he was gone, Haman began begging for mercy and for his life. He knew what was about to happen. As he was begging Esther in desperation, he fell on her. Right then, the king walked back in. Can you imagine? The guy who wants to kill his wife and her people is now lying on his wife.

It should be no surprise that Haman and all his sons ended up getting hanged. Do you know what he got hanged on? The very gallows Haman's wife influenced him to build in order to hang Esther's cousin. He got hanged on his wife's influence, so to speak.

Mary the Mother of Jesus — John 2:1-9

Jesus' mother was influential in Jesus beginning His ministry. Do you remember when they were at a wedding in Cana and the information came to Mary that the wedding party had run out of wine, which was a terrible shame in that culture?

What she did with that piece of information was so godly, definitely List A instead of List C. Mary took the situation straight to Jesus and said, "They've run out of wine."

Instead of telling her friends, "Do you know what I've just come to know? Don't tell anybody. Don't spread this. We don't want to ruin the wedding, but they just ran out of wine. I can't believe it. I feel so bad for them." Then moving on to the next friend, telling them, "I just hate that this has happened. Isn't it a shame?" No, Mary told Jesus instead of being a gossip.

Gossip is a classic List C characteristic and a sorry misuse of influence that destroys people's lives. Mary didn't do that. She went to Jesus and said, "They've run out of wine. What are you going to do about it?"

Jesus basically said, "I wasn't planning to do anything." Mary didn't even hear that.

She just turned immediately to His disciples and said, "Do whatever He says to do."

The next thing Jesus said was, "Go get water jugs!" Do you see how a woman can influence? It's amazing. And it was right. There was a sense of timing in Mary, and it was compelled by love. It was beautiful. She wasn't promoting her son as a child prodigy and selfishly making herself look like an amazing mother, saying, "See, I have this amazing son." It wasn't about that. It was about this: "We need to help this family. What are you going to do about it?"

The Woman at the Well — John 4:4-42

I love this story. Jesus was at the well by Himself until this woman came. She was a woman who was known in Samaria for all the wrong reasons. Jesus read her mail when He said that she had previously had five husbands, and the man she currently was living with wasn't even her husband.

Jesus gave this dear woman at the well the best teaching on the subject of worship, and through the conversation, her heart changed. She went into the city and told the men there, "Come and see a man who told me everything I did. This has got to be the Messiah!" You've got to wonder if some of the motivation for the men to go meet Jesus was curiosity of what Jesus might possibly have said about them.

Nevertheless, the men of the city came out, and after listening to Jesus, they were so moved they invited Jesus to stay a few days. Later on, the people of the city said, "Now we believe Jesus, not only because of your testimony, but also because we've heard Him ourselves." These men wouldn't even have heard Jesus if it had not been for the influence of this woman.

This is not an exhaustive list of the women of influence in the Bible, but it's definitely enough that we can observe women's God-given capability to influence. Even the serpent recognized these God-given capabilities in a woman to be able to influence. He saw these capabilities to influence and twisted them to get man to fall.

There are whole chunks of scripture in Proverbs written about the influence of a woman over a man to do a wrong thing. A good man going on a right road can be influenced to get on a wrong road by a woman.

MERCY AND COMPASSION WERE TO BE THE FIRST REALITY OF A TINY NEW LIFE.

Handcrafted

God not only handcrafted the body of the first human, but when He took a part of that human out to make a woman, He handcrafted her body as well. The Hebrew verb *râcham*[3] means *to have mercy,* and its corresponding *racham* translates to *mercy and compassion* as well as the word *womb.*[4] How remarkable!

The womb was designed as the safest environment and most nurturing room for a baby to get its start. Mercy and compassion were to be the first reality of a tiny new life. By contrast, the Greek word for womb is *hustera,* literally meaning *belly,* and any trouble or suffering in that area of the woman's body is *husterikos.* For instance, what do you have when you have your womb taken out? A hysterectomy.[5] Related words are *hysteria and hysterical,* which we find in the negative stereotypes of the post fall woman.

Motherhood

The natural God-given strong instinct of a mother actually has helped to preserve the human race. However, motherhood didn't even escape damage in the fall as we see indicated in this verse.

When my father *and* mother forsake me.

Psalms 27:10

Abandonment is less common with mothers, but it still happens. When it does, the effects are devastating. The fall's affect on this role has also resulted in controlling mothers, mothers who use their children to fill their own need and their own desire. It results in mothers who are not giving to their children but who take from them and manipulate them. There are also flat out mean moms. It's a scary thing when a mom is mean instead of nurturing. This next scripture is the extreme of mean.

56 The most tender and delicate woman among you—so delicate she would not so much as touch the ground with her foot—will be selfish toward the husband she loves and toward her own son or daughter. 57 She will hide from them the afterbirth and the new baby she has borne, so that she herself can secretly eat them. She will have nothing else to eat during the siege and terrible distress that your enemy will inflict on all your towns.

Deuteronomy 28:56-57 (NLT)

Okay, a woman eating her kids—now that's bad. That's absolutely debased. But, hey, there have been mothers who may not have eaten their own children, but they have devoured their children's lives with cruelty. So this role, even though it has very strong instinct, has also been critically damaged in the fall.

God's intention of women reflecting the personality of the Holy Spirit certainly won't happen through emotional, hysterical, controlling, condemning, fault-finding, manipulative, nagging, depressed, self-absorbed, materialistic, jealous, vain, catty, competitive women.

Could a woman with these characteristics represent the Holy Spirit? No way! In fact, she actually misrepresents the Holy Spirit and completely obscures and confuses the image that woman was designed and supposed to reflect of the unseen God.

Remember, in the last chapter, we saw that man was made to reflect God's glory. Let's look at that same verse again to see more about the woman.

A man should not wear anything on his head when worshipping for man is made in God's image and reflects God's glory and *woman reflects man's glory.*

1 Corinthians 11:7 (NLT)

Man is the glory of God; woman is the glory of man. Woman, in a real sense, was actually designed by God to reflect the glory of a man or be part of the glorious crown of a man. The fall certainly changed that (Psalm 8:5). Now with the fractures from the fall, woman became frustrating to man and frustrating to herself. Even worse, woman became the object of domination and cruelty.

> And I will cause hostility between you and the woman and between your offspring and her offspring. ...And you will desire to control your husband, but he will rule over you.
>
> Genesis 3:15-16 (NLT)

Notice how the New King James version words verse 16: "...your desire shall be for your husband, and he shall rule over you." We see in this verse that woman, who was created to be the glory of man and his glorious crown, is now under man's feet and his domineering treatment of her only adds to his shame. So instead of being his glory, she is degraded by him and degrading to him.

This was not a curse that God used to punish Adam and Eve. Instead, God is describing in these verses the collateral damage of the fall. God is describing the result or consequence of their choice to disobey Him in the garden long ago. God says to the serpent, the devil, that there will be hostility between him and the woman. As a result of this particular curse resulting from the fall, there is a special cruelty upon women. Essentially, anywhere you go in the world, you will find this to be the case.

Is there cruelty upon men too? Yes, but it is intensified on women—true to what God said in verse 15. Unfortunately, verse 15 also tells us that exceptional cruelty encompasses children as well. How tragic! Adam and Eve would not have imagined that responding to the serpent's temptation—choosing to disobey God—would result in such incomprehensible disaster and pain through untold generations.

Notes

1 Strong's Exhaustive Concordance: *brood* 7363. Genesis 1:2 HEB: מְרַחֶפֶת עַל־פְּנֵי הַמָּיִם וְרוּחַ אֱלֹהִים
NAS: *of God was moving over;* KJV: *of God moved upon;* INT: *and the Spirit of God was moving over the surface*
Deuteronomy 32:11 – HEB: עַל־גּוֹזָלָיו יְרַחֵף יִפְרֹשׂ כְּנָפָיו
NAS: *up its nest, that hovers over;* KJV: *her nest, fluttereth over her young;* INT: *over young hovers spread his wings.* http://biblehub.com/hebrew/7363.htm

2 *Molech* – King, the name of the national god of the Ammonites, to whom children were sacrificed by fire. He was the consuming and destroying, and [also at the same time] the purifying, fire. In Amos 5:26, "your Molech" of the Authorized Version is "your king" in the Revised Version (Comp. Acts 7:43). Solomon (1 Kings 11:7) erected a high place for this idol on the Mount of Olives. http://biblehub.com/topical/m/moloch.htm
Extra: http://biblehub.com/commentaries/1_kings/11-7.htm
Cambridge Bible for Schools and Colleges, and Matthew Poole's Commentary

3 *Racham - womb mercy* – Strong's #7356 – *racham* (pronounced rakh'-am)
from 7355; *compassion* (in the plural); *by extension, the womb (as cherishing the fetus); by implication, a maiden—bowels, compassion, damsel, tender love, (great, tender) mercy, pity, womb.*
https://www.bibletools.org/index.cfm/fuseaction/Lexicon.show/ID/H7356/racham.htm

4 English Root for *womb*. Word Origin and History for *womb*.
Old English *wamb, womb, belly, uterus* from Proto-Germanic **wambo* (cf. Old Norse *vomb*, Old Frisian *wambe*, Middle Dutch *wamme*, Dutch *wam*, Old High German *wamba*, German *Wamme, belly, paunch*, Gothic *wamba, belly, womb*, Old English *umbor*"child"), of unknown origin.
http://www.dictionary.com/browse/womb
hystericus (Latin) – From the Ancient Greek ὑστερικός (*husterikos*, "suffering in the womb, hysterical"), from ὑστερά (*hustera*, "womb") from the Greek belief that hysteria was caused by a disturbance in the uterus and that it belonged exclusively to women. Confer the English *hystero-* ("of or pertaining to the uterus or womb"), the Latin suffix *-icus* and the French *hystérie*. https://www.wordsense.eu/hystericus/

5 *Hysterectomy*: surgical removal of the uterus, via the Greek root *hystera—uterus, womb*; and yes, the word *hysteria* does derive from this root word because physicians once believed that a woman's womb could engender "extreme excitability or emotional overflow." Of course, this was around the same time that balancing humors was all the rage: medieval medicine taught that the body possessed four fluids or humors: black bile, yellow bile (choler), blood, and phlegm; the relative concentrations of these four humors, different for each person, determined mood, health, and general disposition. NB in time, the word *humor* became related simply to one's mood (as in a person being in a good or bad humor), and eventually evolved into the more specific meaning of *funniness*.
http://www.selfgrowth.com/articles/Medical_Vocabulary_from_the_Greek_Root_Word_Tomos.html

ENGENDERED

CHAPTER 11

The Creator's Intention for Marriage

Therefore a man shall leave his father and mother and be joined
to his wife, and they shall become one flesh.

Genesis 2:24

Many opinions exist about ideal marriage. There's the traditional thought of a monogamous "till death do you part" covenant between a man and a woman. There's the man with multiple wives. There's the casual connection between man and woman that allows them to change partners like changing shoes. There are husband and husband, wife and wife, multiple spouses, a business arrangement, and open swapping of partners with disregard of covenant or fidelity. Or, as bizarre as it may sound, some even consider marriage to an animal. Finally, there are those who don't believe in marriage at all; they're simply against it.

This book is not to argue any of those opinions. Instead, the goal of this book is to present the Creator's intention for man, woman and their roles, as well as marriage and family according to the Bible, which records God's will.

Jesus Himself made it clear that the words and teaching He presented were not His own. This is true even though He could have said, like we hear often in discussions everywhere, "I have a right to my opinion!" Jesus knew that ultimately His Father's opinion or will was the only one that was perfect, uncontaminated, and completely right (John 5:30; 6:38). Jesus' response when asked a question regarding divorce shows that His default opinion was always His Father's, which was one of the reasons He never sinned.

What Jesus Said about Marriage

3 Some Pharisees came and tried to trap him with this question: "Should a man be allowed to divorce his wife for just any reason?" 4 *"Haven't you read the Scriptures?"* Jesus replied. *"They record that from the beginning 'God made them male and female.'"* 5 And he said, "This explains why a man leaves his father and mother and is joined to his wife, and the two are united into one." 6 Since they are no longer two but one, let no one split apart what God has joined together.

Matthew 19:3-6 (NLT)

JESUS KNEW THAT ULTIMATELY HIS FATHER'S OPINION OR WILL WAS THE ONLY ONE THAT WAS PERFECT, UNCONTAMINATED, AND COMPLETELY RIGHT.

Notice how Jesus took them straight to the Word. He also referred the Pharisees all the way back to the beginning, stating how God made things pre-fall—before man, woman, marriage, or anything else was broken and contaminated.

Then in verse 7, the Pharisees quoted Moses and the law:

"Then why did *Moses say in the law* that a man could give his wife a written notice of divorce and send her away?" they asked (NLT).

Again, Jesus' answer in verse 8 models for us our approach on this whole subject. Jesus replied, "Moses permitted divorce only as a concession to your hard hearts, but it was not *what God had originally intended*"(NLT).

Jesus didn't disregard Moses, the Jew's most revered patriarch, the one who gave them the law. But Jesus went back further than Moses to what God originally intended at creation. And that is what we are doing page by page.

So, let's look again at the verse Jesus quoted.

Therefore a man shall leave his father and mother and be joined to his wife, and they shall become one flesh.

Genesis 2:34

What we can plainly see from this verse where the Creator first introduces marriage are these things:

- A man (husband) joins to his wife (woman). The Creator's intention in the beginning for marriage is that it's between a man and a woman.

- Marriage is one man to one woman. Even though there are many Old Testament examples of polygamy, God's original intention, shown in the beginning, was a marriage between one man and one woman.

- We also see in this verse that God intended a man to start a new home of his own after leaving his father and a mother. Before sin—before any fracture—God intended for a home with a father and mother to be the best place to raise a future husband for the next generation. Why?

What Marriage Reflects

Imagine a little boy raised in an environment where List A (page 278) is expressed through both father and mother. Getting to experience the characteristics of God every day in every situation and season of life would be the purest and most effective way to prepare this boy to be a man, husband, and father one day.

What other reason causes God to be so particular about these details regarding marriage?

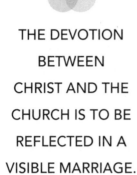

THE DEVOTION BETWEEN CHRIST AND THE CHURCH IS TO BE REFLECTED IN A VISIBLE MARRIAGE.

We find an answer in Ephesians 5 where marriage is talked about as being a picture of Christ and the Church. The Creator's intention was that by looking at a marriage, we could see an example of Christ and the Church. Christ is invisible to us. The Church also is invisible and almost incomprehensible in so far as its universality is made up of those in heaven and earth.

However, we are able to see a husband and a wife. The devotion between Christ and the Church is to be reflected in a visible marriage. When a marriage is as it's meant to be, it will reflect and portray this holy relationship. What a beautiful picture of commitment, love, faithfulness, and devotion is intended by the Creator.

In the same way, the devil despised God's image being expressed through a male and female, he also despised marriage—this picture and reflection of something so sacred to God. The one who steals, kills, and destroys marriages and breaks the home down is ultimately and purposely trying to destroy any kind of reflection of God in the earth.

Broken Marriage

An unhappy, broken, divided marriage ends up making a mockery of the unity between Christ and the Church. Clearly, we've recognized that the devil doesn't want the Father's heart, the nature of Jesus the Son, or the personality of the Holy Spirit reflected on the earth. He doesn't want Christ and the Church to be reflected in the world either.

CHAPTER 12

The Creator's Intention for Family

The family was intended to be a beautiful picture of the heavenly Father and His family. The loving interaction between the Father and each of His children, as well as their care and devotion to one another, was to be on display and portrayed through the family unit.

In the second prayer in Ephesians, Paul prayed, "I bow my knee unto the Father of the Lord Jesus Christ of whom *the whole family in heaven and earth* is named." The Amplified Bible, Classic Edition says, "from whom all fatherhood takes its title and derives its name" (Ephesians 3:14).

Broken Home

For this reason, the devil hates family. He never wants pure relationships mirrored in the world. He hates God's purpose and value of family. He hates your family. I'm talking about your immediate family and your extended family too. The devil viciously hates the very idea of family, and the fall accomplished a gross distortion to this divine image of the Father and His family.

THE DEVIL VICIOUSLY HATES THE VERY IDEA OF FAMILY

Would the expressions of love and a sense of belonging to the family of God ever be a reality? Would it only be like a movie or fairy tale? Would it always be something where we wish upon a star but never enjoy in real life?

In the broken family, the father may not be there at all, and if he is there, he may not image the characteristics of God as Father. The family may not even know God as a true Father. Their idea of God may be so confused they think He's mean and judgmental. They may never know what God will do or if He exists at all. All of this is a tragically cracked and fractured image.

Or, perhaps it is the mother who abandons the family. If the mother has the ability to make the Holy Spirit's characteristics tangible and then she disappears, a child could wonder if Jesus really meant what He said about the Holy Spirit *always* being with you and in you.

It's not hard to see that one of the devil's main targets is family. Recognizing what the devil hates, we can then recognize it must be important. In other words, if something is really valuable, the devil will attack it hard.

What did Jesus say about God's family?

> **21 That they all may be one, as You, Father, are in Me, and I in You; that they also may be one in Us, that the world may believe that You sent Me. 22 And the glory which You gave Me I have given them, that they may be one just as We are one: 23 I in them, and You in Me; that they may be made perfect in one, and that the world may know that You have sent Me, and have loved them as You have loved Me.**
>
> John 17:21-23

Jesus repeated a statement in both these verses, and He doesn't just repeat something because He forgot He said it. He repeats a statement because it bears such a strong message. In these verses, He prayed that they would be one, "So that the world would know that You sent Me." In essence, He's saying the reason why the world would know Jesus was sent to us from the bosom of the Father would be on display in a family situation, in a church family, and in us loving one another.

People in the world would wonder if God really did send His Son because of breakdown in the family or lack of unity in a family.

God sending Jesus, as John 3:16 states, could be in question because of strife and breakdown in family—the natural family and God's family as well. Just imagine how the devil just loves that. We don't want any part of his ugly devices.

Cruelty to Children

The atrocities against children would either rob them of dignity and value or make their value monetary. The truth be told, it was not only hostility or enmity between the serpent and the woman mentioned in Genesis 3:15 but also between his offspring and her offspring. Again, as a result of this part of the curse, we see not only cruelty against women but particular cruelty against children. Commonly, children who grow up to be abusers and perpetrators were themselves abused and damaged as children. This tragedy illustrates once again how horrible fractures continue down through generations.

ENGENDERED

CHAPTER 13

New Adam. New Image.

The male as man, husband, and father and the female as woman, wife, and mother were meant and designed to image and to reflect the unseen God. Marriage was to reflect Christ and the Church. Family was to reflect the Father and His family. Yet, as a result of the fall, all these roles failed to serve their purpose in imaging God and actually caused God to be obscured and misunderstood, feared, despised, and rejected.

Originally, we were made in God's glorious and beautiful image. Now, we reproduce after our broken image. The reason people think God is cruel, unloving, and uncaring is because they "learned" that about Him through His broken image in male and female.

First Adam vs. Last Adam

God had to make a new representative. He had to get a different, unfractured image on the earth. Although He didn't annihilate Adam's race with all of its mess and misery, He actually did start a new species in the human race. First Corinthians 15:45 says, "The Scriptures tell us,

"*The first man*, Adam, became a living person." But *the last Adam*—that is, Christ—is a life-giving Spirit" (NLT).

This verse identifies the Genesis Adam, as the first man, Adam, a "living being." It goes on to contrast the first Adam to the last Adam, the last being "a life-giving spirit." In other words, the first Adam was the original man, the first human. The last Adam is referring to Jesus Christ. Several other verses compare these two men: Romans 5:14, 19; 1 Corinthians 15:21-22.

These two Adams are unique from any other person who has ever lived. Why is this so, and what is it that makes them unique? Whatever these two men do influences the whole human race. For example, let's say you're a grandfather. What you do surely affects your kids and grandkids, friends, and close associates. Your actions and decisions—good or bad— affect the people you know and others you may not know.

In the case of a president or prime minister, their decisions don't just affect their families but whole nations. Some national leaders affect nations beyond their own, and a few of them impact the world with their policies and decisions.

Do you see the difference? The circle of influence that each person has is not the same. Then again, there have been people who have lived on the earth whose decisions don't just affect the people living in their time. Take for instance someone like Abraham Lincoln or William Wilberforce whose actions and decisions to abolish slavery didn't simply affect the people of their time, their family, or the countries of their time. Centuries later, their actions still affect us today, and they are still quoted today. That is extensive influence!

Then there is "an Adam." Adam was a person whose actions and choices didn't just affect himself and his family, community, country or other countries. His actions didn't even affect a chunk of society for years to come. No. *An Adam's* choices and decisions influenced, affected, and impacted every human born and yet to be born.

How many Adams have there been? Just two. A first and last. It wasn't the first and second, but the first and the last. There are no other Adams.

The first Adam through one act of disobedience took a plunge and fell from the glory of God. To understand this better, picture Adam as an elevator. What does that mean? An elevator moves people down and up in a building. There are small elevators that only two or three people can ride. However, there are large elevators that can accommodate a number of people. The "Adam elevator" had the whole human race in him. Wow!

So what did the first Adam do as an elevator? Through his act of disobedience, he took every one of us all the way to the bottom. Every one of us was separated from God.

When the last Adam—Jesus—came to the earth, He identified with man as a human. He further identified with every sin and every sinner when the Father made Him to be our sin. Through this action, the last Adam, whose spiritual journey began in heaven, went down past the earth all the way to the bottom. He had all of fallen humanity in Him—not only the good and the perfect.

The Father's plan was not only for Jesus to become man, but also to take sin and the curse for us and to be judged and separated from God because of those sins. The plan also had an upside. The Father would raise the last Adam from hell and the grave, past the earth, up, up, until He was seated at the Father's right hand. God raised Jesus to a place even better than from where the first Adam fell—a place of right-standing and wholeness.

GOD RAISED JESUS TO A PLACE EVEN BETTER THAN FROM WHERE THE FIRST ADAM FELL.

Jesus brought people up who could never climb the stairs through being perfect. Isn't that why we have elevators? For people who can't and don't want to climb the stairs? When Jesus came up, He brought us all the way to the top. Jesus—our Hero and our Elevator—brought us all the way back to our Creator.

High-Definition Image of the Father

Let's look at some verses that describe Jesus, the last Adam as the exact image of God.

…whose mind the god of this age has blinded, who did not believe, lest the light of the gospel of the glory of *Christ, who is the image of God.*…

2 Corinthians 4:4

Did you notice that phrase "Christ, who is the image of God"? There's that word *image*² again. This time it describes the last Adam. In addition to all that *image* meant in the Old Testament, this New Covenant Adam is even a more perfect image of God. He was, in fact, a "prototype" or a "high-definition projection" of God the Father.

THIS SON PERFECTLY MIRRORS GOD.

The word *image* is the Greek word *eikón* . Among the definitions that are the same as the first Adam image, *eikón* also adds these definitions: *what is very close in resemblance, mirror-like representation.* It can be defined as *a high-definition projection, of which it not merely resembles but from which it is drawn. Eikón* then is more than a *shadow*; rather, it is a replication.

He [Jesus] is the image of the invisible God, the firstborn over all creation.

Colossians 1:15

[Now] He is the exact likeness of the unseen God [the visible representation of the invisible]; He is the Firstborn of all creation.

Colossians 1:15 (AMPC)

What a powerful verse of scripture. You cannot see God; He's invisible. But as we see in this verse, when Jesus came as the last Adam, He came as a visible image, a representation, an exact reflection of the unseen God.

Who being the brightness of His glory and the *express image of His person,* and upholding all things by the word of His power, when He had by Himself purged our sins, sat down at the right hand of the Majesty on high.

Hebrews 1:3 (KJV)

…This Son perfectly mirrors God ….

Hebrews 1:3 (MSG)

> He reflects the brightness of God's glory and is the exact likeness of God's own being....
>
> Hebrews 1:3 (GNB)

> The Son is the radiance of God's glory and the exact representation of his being....
>
> Hebrews 1:3 (NIV)

> ...He is the perfect imprint and very image of [God's] nature.
>
> Hebrews 1:3 (AMPC)

"Philip said to Him, 'Lord, show us the Father, and it is sufficient for us.' Jesus said to him, 'Have I been with you so long, and yet you have not known Me, Philip? He who has seen Me has seen the Father; so how can you say, 'Show us the Father'?'" (John 14:8-9).

Have you ever heard someone say, "Don't put your eyes on me. Just keep them on the Lord"? Don't look at me. Only look at God." Those phrases sound spiritual and beautiful, don't they? The problem is, they aren't practical at all. People—your friends, family and those around you—*cannot* look at God. He's invisible.

Jesus actually didn't encourage people to only put their eyes on God the Father. He said, "If you've seen Me, you've seen God." How huge is that? Jesus is saying if you could see Him on any day of the week, you would be seeing God. You would see Him not just in the temple, but you could see at home and how He treated His mother and His brothers. You could see how He respected His stepdad. That's purely amazing.

HE SAID, "IF YOU'VE SEEN ME, YOU'VE SEEN GOD."

Man and Woman Can Image God Again

There was only one time that Jesus did not image the Father, but it was actually an intentional part of His substitutionary work for mankind that restored man and woman's ability to image and reflect Him. This prophetic verse concerning Jesus gave a glimmer of redeeming hope to the pathetically fractured man and woman.

Just as many were astonished at you, *So His visage was marred more than any man, and His form more than the sons of men.*

Isaiah 52:14

JESUS' VISAGE WAS MARRED SO THAT MAN AND WOMAN CAN ONCE AGAIN IMAGE OUR WONDERFUL CREATOR.

But many were amazed when they saw him. His face was so disfigured he seemed hardly human, and *from his appearance, one would scarcely know he was a man.*

Isaiah 52:14 (NLT)

As a result of both becoming sin and then being punished by God for our sins, Jesus' visage that had perfectly imaged the Father all through his life was marred and disfigured. Jesus' visage was marred *so that* man and woman can once again image our wonderful Creator as we were intended to do.

Notes

1 Jesus was sent to earth to be the image of the Father. Colossians 1:15, "Who is the image of the invisible God, the firstborn of every creature…" (2 Corinthians 4:4).

He was in fact a prototype or a high-definition projection of God the Father.

Image is the Greek word eikón (Strongs 1504) – eikón: an image, i.e. lit. statue, fig. representation

1504 eikón (from 1503 /eíkō, be like) – properly, mirror-like representation, referring to what is very close in resemblance (like a high-definition projection, as defined by the context). Image (1504 /eikón) then exactly reflects its source (what it directly corresponds to). For example, Christ is the very image (1504 /eikón, supreme expression) of the Godhead (see 2 Cor 4:4; Col 1:15). 1504 (eikón) "assumes a prototype, of which it not merely resembles, but from which it is drawn" (R. Trench). 1504(eikón) then is more than a shadow; rather it is a replication (F. F. Bruce, Hebrews, 226; see also Lightfoot at Col 3:10 and 2:21

Adam was created as a tselem—an image or shadow of his Creator – Original Word: צֶלֶם

New Adam. New Image.

An image or a likeness

From an unused root meaning to shade; a phantom, that is, (figuratively) illusion, resemblance; hence a representative figure, especially an idol: image, vain shew. We're also to be transformed into the image (*eikon*) of our Father, Colossians 3:10, "And have put on the new man, which is renewed in knowledge after the image (*eikon*) of him that created him." http://biblehub.com/greek/1504.htm

ENGENDERED

CHAPTER 14

Redeeming the Sexes

How brilliant of God to plan for the last Adam to be the model and prototype of a new species of recreated humans. However, Jesus didn't just "show up." The remarkable journey between God's first redemptive promise in Genesis 3:15 and John 3:16 was not brief but purposefully and intentionally included many generations of people.

The very plan for God's rescue of fallen mankind, while most holy, was not all spiritual and ethereal. No, instead, it even incorporated the male and female reproductive organs. In so doing, Jesus brought restoration and redemption to the function of the sexes and even how they express their gender roles, which we'll see in future chapters.

Think about it. What other part of the human body has been targeted, marketed, exploited, violated, degraded, and used as the focus of jokes as much as the male and female reproductive organs?

The brain is marvelous, and the body cannot live without the functioning of the heart. While the reproductive organs don't sustain your life, they do, however, give you the ability to make life. For this reason, these organs are highly valuable and highly dangerous if used wrongly. Recognizing this, the devil has harnessed the human reproductive organs for his purposes since the fall. By surrounding men and women with a minefield of shame and guilt, he's guarded them from the truth that could make them free.

JESUS BROUGHT RESTORATION AND REDEMPTION TO THE FUNCTION OF THE SEXES.

In church you can talk about most every doctrine from the pages of the Bible, but the devil has purposefully sought to keep matters of sex in the shadows. The armor of God in Ephesians 6 includes a girdle of truth. The area of the body protected intentionally by truth is the reproductive area. Without light and truth shining directly in this area, the devil continues his dastardly work.

God made the male and female sexes, and yet, this essential part of their identity was fractured in the fall until God's plan brought redemption's reality right to this place of impact. Instead of tiptoeing and timidly working around the male and female reproductive organs, God absolutely and shamelessly used them in fulfilling Genesis 3:15's promise. He sent His only begotten Son that whosoever believes on Him won't perish but have eternal life (John 3:16). Let's let the Word flood this topic with light!

CHAPTER 15

Redeeming the Male

Have you ever wondered why the Bible has so much to say about circumcision? If not, you may have been like many Bible readers who didn't highlight those verses and maybe even skipped over them. It would be rare to hear a sermon about it even though the word *circumcision* in some form is actually used more than one hundred times in the Old and New Testaments and is foundational to not only Judaism but also Christian theology.

The book of Romans, for example, uses some form of the word *circumcision* twelve times. Maybe we've skipped over these words because it's a little awkward in our context. Plus, we may be clueless as to why circumcision is spiritually important anyway, at least this was my experience. Paul, however, didn't mumble this word and neither did other writers of the Bible. Even Jesus didn't avoid speaking about it.

They intentionally spoke and wrote about circumcision. It was not an awkward subject to Paul or those of the Jewish nation. They spoke freely about circumcision, and when the word was used, they knew *exactly* what it meant. Circumcision, by its prominence in scripture, is a very important subject. In fact, we'll see it's actually vital to our redemption. So, for the sake of being able to study this subject, we will follow Paul's example and speak plainly.

Let's start at the beginning and consider how God sanctified and utilized the function of the male reproductive organs for His purpose.

And I will put enmity between you and the woman, and between your seed and *her Seed;* **He shall bruise your head, and you shall bruise His heel.**

Genesis 3:15

THE WORD WAS CLEAR THAT THE REDEEMER DEFINITELY WOULD BE A HUMAN.

Genesis 3:15 is the very first promise of the entire Bible, and it has to do with God's rescue of fallen mankind. In this first promise, we pick up a clue that the Redeemer will come as the seed of a woman or born from a woman. In other words, the Redeemer won't be a plant or animal, a force of nature, or an extra-terrestrial creature. No, the Word was clear that the Redeemer definitely would be a human.

What else can we learn from this promise? The scripture said the seed of a woman would crush the head of the serpent, so we know right away that the plan of redemption would crush the head of the one who tempted Eve and ultimately cause the fall of humans. We also know that in crushing the serpent's head, the Redeemer's heel would be bruised.

To fulfill this promise, God didn't just "speak it into existence" as He had done in creation. No, God used the humans He created, even though they had fallen, and He incorporated the first command He gave them which was to be fruitful and multiply. Obviously, this involved the act of sex—the very reason reproductive organs were creatively fashioned.

When God gave the promise in Genesis 3:15, Adam and Eve had no idea how many generations it would take to fulfill the promise. They may have thought it would happen right away, but it did not.

Safeguarding the Human Seed

In between the time God gave that promise and Genesis 9, the human race grew so morally gangrenous that God had to destroy, or we could say amputate, all those living at the time with the exception of one family. God had no choice so that He could accomplish His plan to redeem fallen man through a human redeemer.

We think the world is bad now, but it was actually much worse then. By the time the flood came, humanity was completely debased—except for Noah's family. Basically, the only way God could save this defiled human race was to save this one family.

God put this family in the ark that Noah had built, and the ark saved the family. It was an amazing act! Noah, his wife, and their sons and wives came out of the ark after the flood and began procreating again. Finally, we fast forward to Genesis 11 where Abram enters the story.

The flood and salvation of Noah's family was not the last time God had to sovereignly step in to safeguard redemption's plan. For instance, before Abraham had Isaac, he put Sarah into a harem two different times (Genesis 12:11-20; 20). In both instances, there was supernatural intervention so no one could have sex with her. God saved her reproductive organs so she would be able to carry Abraham's seed. While the Redeemer wasn't to be born through Sarah, God was particular about the one He wanted to start a nation through.

Finally, under Moses came some very strict laws regarding sex, and it wasn't just because God was a spoil sport and didn't want people to have "fun." One important reason for those laws had to do with the preservation of the line through which the seed would come. Those laws were meant to protect, and in a very real way, they *do* protect a person's body, family, and relationships. Those laws also protected the line bringing the seed that would save all the families of the earth and crush the serpent's head.

The redemptive plan was also being protected when the Israelites were instructed by God to destroy nations of people in the land of Canaan. Why? Didn't God love them? Yes, of course He did. The Redeemer would eventually provide salvation for *all* the people of the world. However, the religions of those nations around Israel were largely based on sex and fertility, and the risk of Israel being drawn in and given over to worshipping other gods was very real. The great redemption plan was vouchsafed to the nation of Israel, who was to serve as a safe place, a vault till God's perfect time.

The Making of a Nation

1 Now the LORD had said to Abram: "Get out of your country, from your family and from your father's house, to a land that I will show you. 2 I will make you a great nation; I will bless you and make your name great; and you shall be a blessing. 3 I will bless those who bless you, and I will curse him who curses you; and in you all the families of the earth shall be blessed."

Genesis 12:1-3

The first step toward making a nation was that God wanted Abram to get out of his country, his family, and his father's house. He didn't want any influence that had been passed down to him. He was starting something new and for a divine purpose. Through Abram and the nation that would come through him, all the families of the earth will be blessed.

Although God made this beautiful promise to Abram, it wasn't until Genesis 15 that He made the first part of His covenant with him. The entire covenant was given in two parts that we will call Part A and Part B. Part A is recorded in Genesis 15 and includes a brief promise about Abram's descendants, but the majority of Part A is about the land that God is giving to them.

Part A: God's Covenant with Abram

We just read in Genesis 12 where God first promised descendants to Abram. However, in Genesis 15, ten years later, Abram and Sarai were still childless. When Abram told God the only heir he had was a servant, this was God's response:

4 Then the Lord said to him, "No, your servant will not be your heir, for you will have a son of your own who will be your heir."

5 Then the Lord took Abram outside and said to him, "Look up into the sky and count the stars if you can. That's how many descendants you will have!" 6 And Abram believed the Lord, and the Lord counted him as righteous because of his faith.

Genesis 15:4-6 (NLT)

God reiterated His promise to Abram and gave him a visual of the stars to represent his descendants and then continued:

7 Then the Lord told him, "I am the Lord who brought you out of Ur of the Chaldeans to give you this land as your possession." 8 But Abram replied, "O Sovereign Lord, how can I be sure that I will actually possess it?"

Genesis 15:7-8 (NLT)

Descendants were part of the promises of the covenant, but we can see that land was also a significant part. What God did next made God's promise about the land ironclad.

4 Then the Lord said to him, "No, your servant will not be your heir, for you will have a son of your own who will be your heir." 5 Then the Lord took Abram outside and said to him, "Look up into the sky and count the stars if you can. That's how many descendants you will have!" 6 And Abram believed the Lord, and the Lord counted him as righteous because of his faith. 7 Then the Lord told him, "I am the Lord who brought you out of Ur of the Chaldeans to give you this land as your possession." 8 But Abram replied, "O Sovereign Lord, how can I be sure that I will actually possess it?" 9 The Lord told him, "Bring me a three-year-old heifer, a three-year-old female goat, a three-year-old ram, a turtledove, and a young pigeon." 10 So Abram presented all these to him and killed them. Then he cut each animal down the middle and laid the halves side by side; he did not, however, cut the birds in half. 11 Some vultures swooped down to eat the carcasses, but Abram chased them away. 12 As the sun was going down, Abram fell into a deep sleep, and a terrifying darkness came down over him. 13 Then the Lord said to Abram, "You can be sure that your descendants will be strangers in a foreign land, where they will be oppressed as slaves for 400 years. 14 But I will punish the nation

that enslaves them, and in the end they will come away with great wealth. 15 (As for you, you will die in peace and be buried at a ripe old age.) 16 After four generations your descendants will return here to this land, for the sins of the Amorites do not yet warrant their destruction." 17 After the sun went down and darkness fell, Abram saw a smoking firepot and a flaming torch pass between the halves of the carcasses.

Genesis 15:4-17 (NLT)

In this particular portion of the covenant God made with Abram, God details *His* part of that covenant. After bringing the animals and birds, dividing them in the middle and arranging them on the ground, Abram was only an audience to what happened next. Abram watched while a torch and a burning oven moved between all the halves of those animals. What an interesting sight that would have been to see!

On the same day the LORD made a covenant with Abram, saying: *"To your descendants* I have given this land, from the river of Egypt to the great river, the River Euphrates."

Genesis 15:18

Again, you can see that the covenant is quite detailed concerning God's promise for land, and that land was "to your descendants." That means that Abram most certainly would have a family.

Part A of God's covenant with Abram was *God's* part of that covenant. Abram believed in what God promised him about his descendants, and God counted it to him as righteousness (Romans 4:3; Genesis 15:6).

There was an amazing interaction and relationship with God that happened when the first part of the covenant was given to Abram. Notice that God didn't say, "Abram, here's a list of things you must do." No, it was God saying, "These are the things I promise to do for you," and then He walked between the pieces of the animals which speaks to us of the redemptive work of the Lord Jesus Christ. Similarly, we cannot redeem ourselves. All we can do is observe what Jesus did for us and believe it.

Part B: God's Covenant with Abram

In Genesis 17, we find Part B of God's covenant to Abram. Some years had passed since God made a covenant with Abram in chapter 15 regarding his descendants and the land they would live in. During this time Abram had a son, Ishmael, with Hagar, Sarai's maid.

1 When Abram was ninety-nine years old, the LORD appeared to Abram and said to him, "I am Almighty God; walk before Me and be blameless. 2 And I will make My covenant between Me and you, and will multiply you exceedingly. 3 Then Abram fell on his face, and God talked with him, saying: 4 'As for Me, behold, My covenant is with you, and you shall be a father of many nations. 5 No longer shall your name be called Abram, but your name shall be Abraham; for I have made you a father of many nations. 6 I will make you exceedingly fruitful; and I will make nations of you, and kings shall come from you. 7 And I will establish My covenant between Me and you and your descendants after you in their generations, for an everlasting covenant, to be God to you and your descendants after you. 8 Also I give to you and your descendants after you the land in which you are a stranger, all the land of Canaan, as an everlasting possession; and I will be their God."

Genesis 17:1-8

You can see that God's promise in Part B of this covenant is primarily about Abraham's descendants.

Notice below as Abraham's part of the covenant begins:

9 And God said to Abraham: "As for you, you shall keep My covenant, you and your descendants after you throughout their generations. 10 This is My covenant which you shall keep, between Me and you and your descendants after you: Every male child among you shall be circumcised; 11 and you shall be circumcised in the flesh of your foreskins, and it shall be a sign of the covenant between Me and you. 12 He who is eight days old among you shall be circumcised, every male child in your generations, he who is born in your house or bought with money from any foreigner

who is not your descendant. 13 He who is born in your house and he who is bought with your money must be circumcised, and My covenant shall be in your flesh for an everlasting covenant. 14 And the uncircumcised male child, who is not circumcised in the flesh of his foreskin, that person shall be cut off from his people; he has broken My covenant."

Genesis 17:9-14

After believing God's part of the covenant, God told Abraham what *he* was to do and what *his* part was. Abraham was to circumcise every male in his home. Circumcision was to be an outward sign of Abraham's faith and proof he had accepted the covenant.

Do you see how much weight God put in this act? In fact, it was so important that any male who wasn't circumcised was considered to have broken the covenant. It was obviously very crucial.

23 So Abraham took Ishmael his son, all who were born in his house and all who were bought with his money, every male among the men of Abraham's house, and circumcised the flesh of their foreskins that very same day, as God had said to him. 24 Abraham was ninety-nine years old when he was circumcised in the flesh of his foreskin. 25 And Ishmael his son was thirteen years old when he was circumcised in the flesh of his foreskin. 26 That very same day Abraham was circumcised, and his son Ishmael; 27 and all the men of his house, born in the house or bought with money from a foreigner, were circumcised with him.

Genesis 17:23-27

I love this about Abraham. When God told him what *His* part of the covenant was, he didn't take two years to think about it. No, he believed it. On the very same day Abraham came to know *his* part in the covenant was to walk before God and circumcise the males of his house, he had every one of them lined up to take the mark. Immediately, he responded. Quite remarkable!

On the day that Abraham and the males in his house lined up for circumcision, Ishmael did too. Arabs today still circumcise, and it started with Ishmael. However, when Ishmael himself was conceived thirteen years before, Abram was not yet circumcised. So, Ishmael was not a son conceived by someone with the mark of the covenant.

It's important here to emphasize that circumcision was not Abraham's first response to God's covenant with him. Faith was. And because of Abraham's faith, God credited righteousness to him, and he was able to walk with him as a righteous man.

CIRCUMCISION WAS NOT ABRAHAM'S FIRST RESPONSE TO GOD'S COVENANT WITH HIM. FAITH WAS.

9 Now, is this blessing (forgiveness of sins) only for the Jews, or is it also for uncircumcised Gentiles? Well, we have been saying that Abraham was counted as righteous by God because of his *faith*. 10 But how did this happen? Was he counted as righteous only after he was circumcised, or was it before he was circumcised? Clearly, God accepted Abraham before he was circumcised! 11 Circumcision was a sign that Abraham already had faith and that God had already accepted him and declared him to be righteous—even before he was circumcised. *So Abraham is the spiritual father of those who have faith but have not been circumcised.* They are counted as righteous because of their faith. 12 And Abraham is also the spiritual father of those who have been circumcised, but only if they have the same kind of faith Abraham had before he was circumcised.

Romans 4:9-12 (NLT)

Abraham demonstrated that faith is what appropriates God's promises—not works. Works, prompted by faith, follow as a demonstration of faith. In other words, circumcision didn't appropriate the covenant, faith did. If faith appropriates the covenant, then why, pray tell, did God choose this particular sign for His holy covenant with Abraham when covenants can be cut in so many other ways?

For example, marks of blood covenants[1] were sometimes put on the face, arms, or other parts of the body. But circumcision? Why is the covenant sign made on the male reproductive organ? To consider that question, let's first look at another question. What starts the next generation? Seed or sperm. And how does that happen? Through sex. Conception doesn't

GOD PUT THE MARK OF THE COVENANT EXACTLY WHERE THE SEED WOULD BE DISPENSED FROM.

happen over a cup of coffee or a good movie and a bag of popcorn. A couple won't have babies by building a house together or planting a garden together. They won't produce babies by riding together through the countryside.

Basically, we won't have another generation without the seed, and the dispenser of the seed is the male reproductive organ. God put the mark of the covenant exactly where the seed would be dispensed from. Essentially, the seed would have to pass by that mark to start each generation. To me that is just amazing. Only God would have thought of that!

When God promised Abraham that all the families of the earth would be blessed through him in Genesis 12:3, it didn't come to pass in the next moment. It was through the procreation of many generations that a new nation developed, and eventually the last Adam came. Through that last Adam's life, death, and resurrection, every single human was affected. Quite literally, when each generation initiated the next, that seed had to pass through the mark of God's covenant with Abraham because of circumcision.

Through circumcision:

- Every generation is initiated with the promise of redemption.
- Every generation exists because the seed came through the mark of circumcision, which was a sign of Abraham's belief and part in God's covenant with him.
- The male organ was sanctified and made sacred for God's purpose of redemption.
- Women were not circumcised, but because every person, male and female, in the nation of Israel had been *conceived* by seed that passed through the mark of circumcision, they were actually known by this.

In America people are known as Americans. In Italy people are known as Italians. In France people are known as French. In Africa people are known as Africans, and in Australia people are known as Aussies. Israel's people were known as the Hebrews, Israelites, and children of Abraham. Another name for them was The Circumcision. It was so essential to Israel's identity that they were actually called *The Circumcision*[2]. "What nationality are you?" "I'm The Circumcision." That's amazing!

Notes

1 Henry Stanley gives an account of the establishment of a "strong friendship" between himself and Mata Bwyki, an African chief: "Then a fetish-man came forward with his lancets, long pod, pinch of salt, and fresh green banana leaf. He held the staff of Kokoro's sword-bladed spear, [36] while one of my rifles was brought from the steamer. The shaft of the spear and the stock of the rifle were then scraped on the leaf, a pinch of salt was dropped on the wood, and finally a little dust from the long pod was scraped on the curious mixture. Then, our arms were crossed—the white arm over the brown arm—and an incision was made in each; and over the blood was dropped a few grains of the dusty compound; and the white arm was rubbed over the brown arm [in the intermingling of blood]."

"Now Mata Bwyki lifted his mighty form, and with his long giant's staff drove back the compressed crowd, clearing a wide circle, and then roaring out in his most magnificent style, leonine in its lung-force, kingly in its effect: 'People of Iboko! You by the river side, and you of inland. Men of the Bangala, listen to the words of Mata Bwyki. You see Tandelay before you. His other name is Bula Matari. He is the man with the many canoes, and has brought back strange smoke-boats. He has come to see Mata Bwyki. He has asked Mata Bwyki to be his friend. Mata Bwyki has taken him by the hand, and has become his blood-brother. Tandelay belongs to Iboko now." The Blood Covenant:A Primitive Rite and its Bearings on Scripture,
Author: H. Clay Trumbull

The Project Gutenberg EBook [EBook #48236] www.gutenberg.org.

Blood covenant marks on the stomach and cheeks: Observed by Dr David Livingstone in South Africa: Describing the rite of Kasendi: "It is accomplished thus: The hands of the parties are joined. Small incisions are made on the clasped hands, on the pits of the stomach of each, and on the right cheeks and foreheads. A small quantity of blood is taken off from these points, in both parties, by means of a stalk of grass. The blood from one person is put into a pot of beer, and that of the second into another; each then drinks the other's blood, and they are supposed to become perpetual friends, or relations." Missionary Travels and Research in South Africa, David Livingstone, Harper & Brothers Publisher, NY, 1858

2 The circumcision - Hebrews referred to in the New Testament. References: Acts 10:45; Acts 11:2; Romans 4:12, 15:8; Galatians 2:7, 2:8, 2:9, 2:12, Ephesians 2:11; Colossians 4:11; Titus 1:10.

CHAPTER 16

A New Covenant

Eight days after His birth, Jesus Himself was circumcised as the covenant required and also in fulfillment of the law. In fact, in His life Jesus fulfilled every requirement of the law perfectly so as a sinless person He would qualify to bear the sins of the whole world

On the night before His crucifixion, Jesus shared a last supper with His disciples. Look at what He says:

> After supper he took another cup of wine and said, "This cup is the new covenant between God and his people—an agreement confirmed with my blood, which is poured out as a sacrifice for you"
>
> Luke 22:20 (NLT)

Jesus speaks of a new covenant, and this new covenant doesn't require the blood of circumcision. Jesus' holy blood confirmed a new covenant between God and us.

Spiritual Circumcision

This new covenant brings a distinct shift to how we look at circumcision now, so let's consider this next verse:

> For when we place our faith in Christ Jesus, there is no benefit in being circumcised or being uncircumcised. What is important is faith expressing itself in love.
>
> Galatians 5:6

In the new covenant, circumcision is now spiritual, and it happens in the heart as these verses show:

> In Him you were also circumcised with a circumcision not made with hands....
>
> Colossians 2:11 (AMP)

> 28 For you are not a true Jew just because you were born of Jewish parents or because you have gone through the ceremony of circumcision. 29 No, a true Jew is one whose heart is right with God. And true circumcision is not merely obeying the letter of the law; rather, it is a change of heart produced by the Spirit. And a person with a changed heart seeks praise from God, not from people.
>
> Romans 2:28-29 (NLT)

By this verse I can know that even though I'm a gentile by birth, if I'm born again, spiritually speaking, I'm of The Circumcision. It's not a physical circumcision, but a spiritual one. Spiritual circumcision, which speaks of cutting away things of the flesh or of the world, is also known as sanctification. Sanctification is significant to the way the believer lives his or her life, separated from the ways of the first Adam.

In chapter 33, we'll look more closely at who we are as believers in Christ now and identify how to put off List B and C characteristics and put on List A characteristics. This process also can be considered as an aspect of sanctification.

We Are The Circumcision

In the Epistles, the Church has several names, each giving an aspect of our identity. Some of these names are bride of Christ, body of Christ, light in the Lord, family of God, chosen generation, royal priesthood, and holy nation. Do you know what else we're called? We are called The Circumcision.

> **For we are the circumcision, who worship by the Spirit of God and glory in Christ Jesus and put no confidence in the flesh….**
> Philippians 3:3 (ESV)

Spiritual circumcision is so important to our identity as representatives of Christ that it is actually one of the names for the Church. In the same way, circumcision was an identifying mark to the Jews, and now spiritual circumcision or sanctification is to us as believers. If we are in Christ, our lifestyles are empowered to look like it! Anything of first Adam's actions and reactions are cut away. We are in Christ! Everything is new, including how we express our sex and gender roles.

WE ARE IN CHRIST! EVERYTHING IS NEW, INCLUDING HOW WE EXPRESS OUR SEX AND GENDER ROLES.

Natural circumcision holds no spiritual value in the New Covenant. The Promise has come. Physical circumcision can happen for health or other reasons now, but it doesn't have any spiritual implication for us as Christians. The cycle has been completed in Christ.

What an amazing plan!

ENGENDERED

CHAPTER 17

Redeeming the Female

But when the time arrived that was set by God the Father, God sent his Son,
born among us of a woman, **born under the conditions**
of the law so that he might redeem those
of us who have been kidnapped by the law.

Galatians 4:4 (MSG)

What took so long? Why did the time set by God the Father, or the "fullness of time" as it says in the New King James, take so long? And why were generations of circumcised males needed to participate? Through these circumcised males, a nation developed called The Circumcision. Literally every person—male and female—had been conceived with the "signature" of the covenant.

Finally, the prophecy in Genesis 3:15, given 4,000 years before, about the woman whose seed would be the "crusher of the serpent's head" was ready for fulfillment. She was ready. Generally, we know the woman prophesied about was Mary, and every year at Christmastime we rehearse her story in song, poems, plays, sermons, and movies. We're familiar with her encounter with the angel, the trip to Bethlehem, the birth of Jesus, the shepherds, the wise men, and more.

ULTIMATELY, THE WHOLE CIRCLE FINISHES WITH A WOMAN GIVING BIRTH TO THE GREAT ANSWER TO THE PROBLEM THE FIRST WOMAN STARTED!

Yet, let's look a bit closer at the part she played as female in this great plan. Remember, the whole problem in the beginning started with Eve being tempted and deceived and then influencing her husband to knowingly act against God. Ultimately, the whole circle finishes with a woman giving birth to the Great Answer to the problem the first woman started!

The verse that follows was included in Gabriel's message to Mary about the baby who would be conceived in her:

He will be great, and will be called the Son of the Highest; and the Lord God will give Him the throne of His father David.

Luke 1:32

The nation of Israel was made up of families in twelve different tribes. This verse identifies that the "Son of the Highest" came from King David's line, which was the tribe of Judah.

Joseph, who was chosen to be Jesus' stepfather, was from the tribe of Judah, as we can see from the genealogy of Matthew. However, Jesus obviously did not come through Joseph's seed or any other man's seed. Jesus was conceived by the Holy Spirit in Mary, a female who had been conceived through that mark of circumcision and from the tribe of Judah as well (Psalm 132:11; Hebrews 7:14a).

Pictured is a circle with God's covenant with Abraham marking the beginning point.

God started with one man, Abraham, who was circumcised as a sign of his faith in God's covenant. His son of promise, Isaac, had a son, Jacob, whose name was changed to Israel. Israel had a family of twelve sons who developed into twelve tribes that grew to be a nation. This nation that served as a safeguard for the seed was referred to as *The Circumcision*. Generations later, and in the fullness of time, from those twelve tribes was chosen the tribe of Judah. Through the tribe of Judah came a family, and from the father of that family, Heili, came one young, virgin woman, Mary (Luke 1:26-27, 34; Isaiah 7:14; Matthew 1:23).

The part of God's covenant with Abraham promising that through him all the families of the earth would be blessed began with one man and was completed with one woman.

Incarnate

GOD'S COVENANT WITH ABRAHAM, PROMISING THAT THROUGH HIM ALL THE FAMILIES OF THE EARTH WOULD BE BLESSED, BEGAN WITH ONE MAN AND WAS COMPLETED WITH ONE WOMAN.

Remember back in Genesis 2:7 we were told that God formed the first Adam from the dust. Yet, think about this. When Mary became pregnant by the Holy Spirit, she was a representative of the first Adam line carrying the seed of God, the *last Adam*. The last Adam was a unique combination—from the dust came His humanity that He received from His mother, but His Father was God.

14 Since the children, as he calls them, are people of flesh and blood, Jesus himself became like them and shared their human nature. He did this so that through his death he might destroy the Devil, who has the power over death, 17 This means that he had to become like his people in every way, in order to be their faithful and merciful High Priest in his service to God, so that people's sins would be forgiven.

Hebrews 2:14,17 (GNT)

What a Plan! What a Planner!

Although Jesus' birth is totally supernatural, it is not an unfamiliar truth to Christians. What else can we learn about this part of the plan involving Mary? The difference between Mary's pregnancy and every other one since the beginning of time is that it was not instigated by sexual intercourse and human seed. When Jesus was born, his dear mother was still a virgin.

Commonly, the hymen in a woman's vagina is broken the first time she has sexual intercourse, and there is blood. In some cultures, the blood was and still is an essential part of the marriage ceremony[1]. It's so important that traditionally the couple was actually asked to produce the bloody sheet as evidence of the wife's virginity—proof that her hymen was broken during the very first time of sex with her husband. This sealed the promises the couple had made as valid and sacred. Their covenant was sealed by blood—not the husband's but the wife's. We can hardly imagine such a thing in this day and age because sex has become common; couples rarely enter their covenant of marriage as virgins. But this part of making the marriage covenant used to be precious, and still is to some.

Consider this then. When Abraham was circumcised as a sign that he believed God and as his part in the covenant, naturally the male reproductive organ bled. So, by circumcision the male organ was sanctified from what Joshua 5:9 refers to as the "reproach of Egypt" and was dedicated to God's holy plan to redeem mankind.

What about the female reproductive organs? When Jesus was born from Mary's virgin womb, there was also blood. God purposefully used these organs to bring into the world the Seed that He had promised in His covenant to Abraham.

Has there ever been a birth more purposeful than the birth of the Lord Jesus? It didn't just happen, however. Angels didn't bring Him to earth. No, He was born, and His birth naturally utilized the very human organs that the devil had dominated.

Notes

1 https://www.sbs.com.au/topics/life/relationships/article/2018/01/10/historic-tradition-wedding-night-virginity-testing

ENGENDERED

CHAPTER 18

Jesus in the Flesh

Through an amazing plan spanning centuries, and involving a nation called The Circumcision and finally culminating with Jesus' birth from His virgin mother, God gave us a new Adam—a new prototype, a new model, a new imager. We see that this last Adam is the exact reflection of the Father. He lived thirty-three years on the earth in every scenario of life and never ever misrepresented His Father. That's truly amazing!

Even the physical body of the last Adam had particular significance. Do you remember the first promise in the Bible (Genesis 3:15)? God promised the devil that the seed of a woman would bruise his head. Right there, we get an important picture. What will bruise our enemy's head won't fall out of the sky. It won't emerge out of the sea. It won't blow in with the wind. No, what will crush the serpent's head will be human. Our Redeemer is a human! That's significant.

> So the Word became human and made his home among us. He was full of unfailing love and faithfulness. And we have seen his glory, the glory of the Father's one and only Son.
>
> John 1:14 (NLT)

The Word, Jesus, became human. Other translations say He became flesh. God in a human or in flesh, either way we say it, gives us a powerful truth: the incarnation. God came in human flesh.

Since the children, as he calls them, are people of flesh and blood, Jesus himself became like them and shared their human nature....
Hebrews 2:14a (GNT)

Wasn't there a different way that humanity's problems could be fixed? Couldn't there have been a different way to redeem us from this heinous fracturing other than for the One who redeemed us to be like us and identify with us?

Verse 14 continues:

...He did this so that through his death he might destroy the Devil, who has the power over death.
Hebrews 2:14b (GNT)

Verse 17 goes on to say:

This means that he had to become like his people in every way, in order to be their faithful and merciful High Priest in his service to God, so that the people's sins would be forgiven.
Hebrews 2:17 (GNT)

There is no way to miss this. The Word, Jesus, had to partake of flesh and blood—He had to—so He could die. Think about it. He's God, so in order for Him to redeem us, He had to die. Love alone didn't fix this. God didn't just love us so much that our condition was automatically fixed. No. God's fury and judgment on sin was required to fix the dilemma. The price of sin had to be paid. However, love is what sent Jesus to the cross, and the torture He went through was God's judgment on our sin. The work of redemption was literally compelled by love.

God has always loved the world. But nothing could change our fallen, broken condition until God's redemptive plan was complete. His redemption of us included Jesus' life, torture, crucifixion, death, burial, resurrection, and ascension. Without a doubt, it was love that compelled Jesus to come in a human body to identify with broken, fractured, sinful humanity. At the end of His life, a perfect life as a human, Jesus took those fractures and became the sin of all of us. He was judged and cursed by God, and as a result, He died. That's our story, and we never get tired of telling it. It's beautiful and amazing.

I often find myself singing this old song, written in 1876 about our Redeemer:

"I will sing of my Redeemer, And His wondrous love to me; On the cruel cross He suffered, From the curse to set me free.

Refrain

Sing, oh sing, of my Redeemer, With His blood, He purchased me. On the cross, He sealed my pardon, Paid the debt, and made me free.

I will tell the wondrous story, How my lost estate to save, In His bound-less love and mercy, He the ransom freely gave.

Refrain

I will praise my dear Redeemer, His triumphant power I'll tell, How the victory He giveth Over sin, and death, and hell.

Refrain

I will sing of my Redeemer, And His heav'nly love to me; He from death to life hath brought me, Son of God with Him to be.

P. P. Bliss[1]

Identification

Therefore, when He came into the world, He said: "Sacrifice and offering You did not desire, but a body you have prepared for Me."
Hebrews 10:5

In this messianic prophecy, God is saying it wasn't sacrifice and offerings He desired. The sacrifices He's referring to are the animals slaughtered on Passover and the Day of Atonement along with the Levitical offerings and sacrifices prescribed by the law. They weren't satisfying to Him. They covered the sins of the people and gave us a picture of Jesus' future sacrifice of Himself, but the sacrifices didn't redeem anyone. They atoned and covered the sins of the people from year to year, but animal blood was not sufficient to redeem or return humanity to the unbroken condition in which God created us.

If He wasn't satisfied with sacrifice and offerings, what did He desire? What would satisfy Him? And what did God prepare? He prepared a body for Jesus. Why is that such a big deal? Why is that so vitally important to God? In addition to the sacrifice His body became, it was through that body He was able to identify with us. Jesus couldn't redeem us unless He identified with us.

JESUS HAD TO IDENTIFY WITH ADAM'S FRACTURED RACE.

In addition to the sacrifice His body became, Jesus had to identify with Adam's fractured race, including everything and more that we've identified on Lists B and C. I recommend taking a moment to look again at Lists B and C on page 279, so you can see practically how Jesus identified. Identify the problem areas that you or someone you know face. Remember, it was only by His identification with Adam that Jesus could redeem him. In fact, only to the degree that Jesus identified with us could He radically change us.

Think about this. Jesus didn't come merely to teach Adam. He didn't come to say, "You need to be more like List A. Or, here's a way that you can learn to cope with your problem, so you can navigate around that fracture. Or, what you need to do is use this mental glue to repair that ugly fracture." No! That's not what Jesus came to do. Jesus came to identify with Lists B and C, take sin on Himself, receive God's judgment for it, die, be buried, be raised from the dead, and put His blood on heaven's mercy seat. All that was necessary for Him to redeem us back to God. What a hero!

> **2 By this you know the Spirit of God: Every spirit that confesses that Jesus Christ has come in the flesh is of God, 3 and every spirit that does not confess that Jesus Christ is come in the flesh is not of God. And this is the spirit of the Antichrist, which you have heard was coming, and is now already in the world.**
>
> **1 John 4:2-3**

What is the spirit of the antichrist? Someone with the number 666? Revelation 13:18 does say that 666 is the number of the man, the Antichrist. But 1 John explains that the spirit of the antichrist denies that God came in the flesh. Why does that describe the spirit of the antichrist?

It's like this. If you deprive the story of redemption of the fact that God—the Word—came in the flesh, mankind cannot have total redemption because total redemption requires total identification. We would be left as we are with good teachings in the Bible encouraging us to do better. We would be left trying hard to love more, be kinder, and get over it. We would be left trying not to be broken. Yet, God's plan wasn't about behavior modification but about redemption and reconciling us to God.

The spirit of the antichrist denies this even happened. Gnosticism[2] was a prominent heretical movement of the second-century Christian Church, partly of pre-Christian origin. Gnosticism presents the teaching that in a mystical kind of way all things spiritual are wonderful, but anything flesh is bad and inferior. This demeans God's value on the body and demeans that God lived in the flesh.

For many deceivers have gone out into the world who do not confess Jesus Christ as coming in the flesh. This is a deceiver and an antichrist.

2 John 1:7

The spirit of the antichrist that was in the world way back when John wrote this letter and is still in the world today, denies that God came in the flesh. Let's go one step further. If this teaching denies God came in Jesus' flesh, then it also denies God is in *your* flesh.

How much difference does that make for us? It makes a massive difference! Most Christians believe that Almighty God can do anything, and He reigns in heaven above. However, if they never identify that the same Almighty God moved into *their* flesh when they were born again, then their thinking and perspective is pre-Cross. Perhaps unknowingly, those believers believe and act as though the cross never happened except for the fact that they are going to heaven.

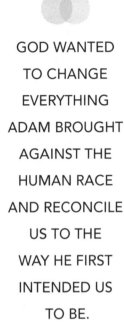

GOD WANTED TO CHANGE EVERYTHING ADAM BROUGHT AGAINST THE HUMAN RACE AND RECONCILE US TO THE WAY HE FIRST INTENDED US TO BE.

Think about it. People in the Old Testament and Gospels believed that God was almighty and reigned in heaven. These people experienced healings and enjoyed some of the most amazing miracles recorded in the Bible. They didn't need what Jesus did on the cross in order to experience those miraculous testimonies.

So, in addition to being able to go to heaven, what was the cross for if we're just living from miracle to miracle and intervention from God to intervention from God? Why did we need the cross? God wanted to do something about the condition of fallen Adam's race. God wanted to do more than a miracle to fix an area of our life so we can have a wonderful experience, a blessed event until the next crisis. No. God wanted to change everything Adam brought against the human race and reconcile us to the way He first intended us to be. And the price was incredible to do that.

Say this about yourself: "God is in me!" Look in the mirror and declare it because the devil hates it. He'll work every day to try to put space between you and God. It's fine with the devil for you to recognize God in that amazing minister on TV or the Internet or in a great meeting somewhere. But he never wants you to realize that God has come to live in YOU. Christians easily say, "Oh, God's in heaven" or "The presence of God is in this room or in that anointed minister." But what about the One who's in *your* heart? In *you?* Do you see what I mean?

Born Again

Jesus answered and said to him [Nicodemus], "Verily, verily I say to you, except a man be born again he cannot see the kingdom of God."

John 3:3

Every human to ever live on earth was born the first time. But those who have put their faith in Jesus Christ have been "born again." Because that's a term often used in church, it can lose its simple but powerful significance. What was Jesus actually saying? He was saying that a person literally can be born *again* with a new life in Jesus Christ.

The weight of the term *born again* can dissolve if we don't see how it practically impacts us. To help identify the notable contrast between the realities of the first birth and the second birth, let's look at what Jesus told Nicodemus using other translations.

> Jesus answered and said to him, "Verily, verily, I say to thee, If any one may not be *born from above*, he is not able to see the reign of God."
>
> John 3:3 (YLT)

> You shouldn't be amazed by my statement, "You all must be *born from above!*"
>
> John 3:7 (TPT)

Spiritually speaking, not only can we have a second birth, but this second one is *from above*. The first is earthly, natural.

Notice below:

> Jesus was not born by the joining of human parents or from natural means, or by a man's desire, but he was born of God.
>
> John 1:13 (TPT)

THE WEIGHT OF THE TERM BORN AGAIN CAN DISSOLVE IF WE DON'T SEE HOW IT PRACTICALLY IMPACTS US.

The first birth comes as a result of natural parents producing a body that is influenced by both family lines and is mortal. Race and citizenship are associated with this birth.

In the second birth, we are literally born of God (1 John 5:4) and with that comes a different reality. This reality includes the fact that He really is our Father, and we have a spiritual family. We receive our Father's life, His List A nature, and heaven is where our citizenship is.

One of the greatest delights as a parent is when your children identify with their heavenly Father. There's not a jealousy issue when they do. It's actually a relief and blessing because you know you can't be with them all the time, but He can. You can't do everything for them they will need in life to be a victor, but He can. You can't protect them at every turn, but He can. You can't strengthen them on the inside, but He can. They may buck and fight against your advice and want to get away from you, but they can't get away from Him.

Every person has natural parents, and Jesus Himself had a natural mother and an earthly stepfather. Yet, let's observe Jesus' response when people said to Him, "Look, Your mother and Your brothers are standing outside, seeking to speak with You" (Matthew 12:47).

Jesus responded, "Who is My mother and who are My brothers?" (Matthew 12:48). Was Jesus being disrespectful? Could Jesus have fulfilled the law if He dishonored His parents? No. Fulfilling the law meant that Jesus always honored His parents. So why did Jesus say this?

Using this occasion as an opportunity to teach, Jesus answered His own question: "Anyone who does the will of My Father is my mother, my sisters, and my brothers" (Matthew 12:46-50). Basically, He was saying that the people He regards as His family are the people who obey God.

If you're ricocheting from the higher-birth realities to the lower-birth realities depending on what day of the week it is and who you're around, then you're living most of your Christian life from the first-birth level. From this lower reality, you're hitting every bump, every stump, and every hole in the road. Your actual Christian life may not look a lot different than someone who is not even born again. Lists B and C include words that describe you.

CLAIM YOUR BORN-AGAIN SELF—THE SELF THAT WAS BORN FROM ABOVE—AND SAY, "THIS IS ME!"

But listen! Christianity is not meant to be lived from Lists B and C. It's meant to be lived with the godly characteristics of List A. So, claim your born-again self—the self that was born from above—and say, "This is me!"

The devil will forever try to minimize Christ's victory and his own defeat. He tried to keep both from ever happening. He inspired the mass murder of little boys on two separate occasions trying to get to the one Seed (Exodus 1:22 AMP; Matt 2:16 AMP). He was radically trying to thwart God's redemption plan from happening, but he failed. Christ's victory—and the devil's defeat—happened all right. Then the devil falls back to his second-line of defense, which is to prevent people from finding out about it. He doesn't want people to know the gospel. If you find out the gospel—the truth—he'll try to convince you not to believe it. If you do believe it, he drops back, yet again, to his next line of defense and tries to get you to diminish portions of God's Word.

If you believe even a chunk of God's Word, he'll try to minimize it. He'll say, "Well, you know, Jesus did die, and He was raised from the dead, but...." He minimizes the impact of the redemptive gospel in your life, so you live like hell on the earth on your way to heaven. You may have a horrible life physically or a horrible life mentally. You may have a horrible life financially, emotionally, and relationship-wise all the while saying, "My life is terrible now, but one day I'll go to heaven where it will all be nice."

Do you see how he tries to minimize the impact of his bruising? He implies, "It wasn't really *that* bad. Jesus didn't really bruise me *that* bad. Okay, yes, you can go to heaven. But Jesus didn't bruise me so badly that it will make a difference in your life. I still will make you miserable every day till you go to heaven."

No!

The Redeemer thoroughly bruised his head. We're finding out about the brilliant plan and the extent of the work the Lord Jesus Christ accomplished for us, and by the help of the Holy Spirit, we're going to spread the news. We'll tell it, preach it, sing it, declare it, prophesy it, and live it.

God is not only in heaven to watch us and intervene miraculously as He did all through the Old Testament and Gospels before the cross, but also because of the cross and resurrection, He's also living *in us*. That's powerful!

Now thanks be to God who always leads us in triumph in Christ, and through us diffuses the fragrance of His knowledge in every place.

2 Corinthians 2:14

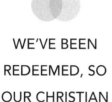

WE'VE BEEN REDEEMED, SO OUR CHRISTIAN EXPERIENCE— OUR REAL LIFE CHRISTIAN EXPERIENCE— IS IN THE LAST ADAM.

The "triumph of Christ" is reduced to Christianese when we don't know what it meant when Jesus defeated death, hell, and the grave. Death never happened until there was sin, and Jesus triumphed over sin, death, hell, and the grave. Yet, what does that mean practically for us? Among other things, it means we don't have to live our lives in Lists B and C any more. We've been redeemed, so our Christian experience—our real life Christian experience—is in the last Adam.

Look at Lists B and C (page 279) again to see exactly what you do not have to look like. Then look at List A once again. That's who we are in Christ. Look at that list, and claim it by saying, "That is me!" Before Jesus came, the characteristics and qualities of List A only described God the Father, God the Son, and God the Holy Spirit. But through Jesus' work of redemption, List A is now you and me as well. Keep looking at List A and saying, "That's me! I'm a new creature." Say it! Believe it! Live it!

Don't we look good in Christ?

Notes

1 *I Will Sing of My Redeemer*, P.P. Bliss 1876, Public Domain

2 The majority of Gnostics accepted the fact that the flesh was evil and the spirit was good, and therefore, took great pains to supplant all fleshly desires, even to the point of renouncing women and marriage. There were other groups, however, who believed that since the flesh was inferior to the spirit, the deeds of the flesh were irrelevant as long as the spirit aimed for higher knowledge. This group was, therefore, known for its wide-

spread immorality. The philosophy of Gnosticism existed before Christianity, dating back to the last centuries before Christ, as a philosophy incorporating the Greek philosophy of Plato and others along with the Persian philosophy of Zoroaster. It did not take long after the Hellenistic world was exposed to Christianity for many groups of Gnostics to begin to incorporate Christ into their philosophy. The first such example may have been in the church of Colossae, to which Paul writes the following in Colossians 2:8-9: "Take heed lest there shall be any one that maketh spoil of you through his philosophy and vain deceit, after the tradition of men, after the rudiments of the world, and not after Christ: for in him dwelleth all the fulness of the Godhead bodily." This text would demonstrate to us that a form of Gnosticism, probably a proto-Gnosticism, had come forth in the church of Colossae, for Paul does give a hint of what this "philosophy" entails: the concept that Christ did not come in the flesh. Many Gnostic groups, following after the dualism of flesh and spirit of Plato, accepted the idea of Christ but not that He came to Earth in the form of a man. They believed that He came in the appearance of a man, what we would call today a hologram, but could not have possibly humiliated Himself to the point of becoming human. We see, however, that Paul affirms this very thing, here and also in other places, especially Philippians 2:5-10. http://www.astudyofdenominations.com/history/gnosticism/

ENGENDERED

CHAPTER 19

Celebrating Your Death

I died!

Celebrating the day someone is born is common in most places of the world. Yet, celebrating the day you die is not so common. For those who have a strong consciousness of heaven and the reality that it's better to be with the Lord, celebrating their home going is not strange. Yet, there's also another death that's not physical that we will focus on in this chapter, and it's really worth celebrating.

Jesus crushed the devil's head, indeed, but that was only a part of His triumph. The other part of the triumph was achieved when Jesus' heel was bruised in the process of crushing the serpent's head. It was Jesus' brutal torture and finally His death that fulfilled the prophecy of Genesis 3:15. How did that bruised heel contribute toward the triumph of Christ and our redemption?

Remember, Christ identified with Adam's race and carried all our sin and all the collateral damage of sin to the cross where He died. Because of His identification with us, His death became ours. Or we could say, when

He died, so did we. Actually, the Bible says exactly that in Romans 6. Look at a few verses in that mighty chapter.

> **6 We know that our old sinful selves were crucified with Christ so that sin might lose its power in our lives. We are no longer slaves to sin. 7 For when we died with Christ we were set free from the power of sin. 8 And since we died with Christ, we know we will also live with him."**
>
> Romans 6:6-8 (NLT)

BECAUSE OF HIS IDENTIFICATION WITH US, HIS DEATH BECAME OURS.

When you were born the first time, you were born with a natural birth, a birth from natural parents and bloodline. You were born into Adam's race as a human, of course. However, do you know what happened when you declared Jesus to be the Lord of your life? You died. Your body didn't die, but the spiritual person you were when you were born, died.

And, at the same time, you were born again.

We've seen that the term *born again* is more than just church jargon, it's what Jesus told Nicodemus would happen if anyone would believe in Him. The person's spirit would literally be born again into Christ, the last Adam's race. This new species is very human, but the difference is that Christ actually lives *in* each born-again Christian.

On our own, the damage done to us in Adam can only be cosmetically dealt with and covered. The fractures can perhaps be filled in, but not gone. We would have to learn to tolerate and cope with them because the human spirit was separated from the life of God by sin, which is what created the fractures in the first place. The only thing that could stop the fractures from dominating us was for us to die. After all, people in cemeteries don't have a problem with crime, and not one of them struggles with depression, anger, unfaithfulness,

CHRIST ACTUALLY LIVES IN EACH BORN-AGAIN CHRISTIAN.

manipulation, selfishness, or any of the other characteristics on Lists B and C.

Jesus' death supplied us with a spiritual disconnect from Adam's line. And Jesus' resurrection supplied a new birth for anyone who would believe in Him.

> **10 When he died, he died once to break the power of sin. But now that he lives, he lives for the glory of God. 11 So *you also should consider yourselves to be dead to the power of sin* and alive to God through Christ Jesus."**
>
> **Romans 6:10-11 (NLT)**

JESUS' RESURRECTION SUPPLIED A NEW BIRTH FOR ANYONE WHO WOULD BELIEVE IN HIM.

Verse 11 says to consider yourself to be dead to the first Adam and power of sin in his line—dead to the things on Lists B and C. Acknowledge your death or separation from those things specifically, and celebrate that you're dead to them.

Are you born again? If so, look at what this verse says about you.

> **17 Therefore, if anyone is in Christ he is a new creation; old things have passed away; behold, all things have become new. 18 Now all things are of God, who has reconciled us to Himself through Jesus Christ, and has given us the ministry of reconciliation."**
>
> **2 Corinthians 5:17-18**

These translations[1] of verse 17 below will help you soak in the truth of who you are in Jesus Christ:

- The Twentieth Century New Testament – "Therefore, if anyone is in union with Christ, he is a new being! His old life has passed away; a new life has begun!"

- The Amplified Bible, Classic Edition – "Therefore if any person is [ingrafted] in Christ, (the Messiah) he is a new creation (a new creature altogether); the old [previous moral and spiritual condition] has passed away. Behold, the fresh and new has come!"

- Today's Living Bible – "When someone becomes a Christian, he becomes a brand new person inside. He is not the same any more. A new life has begun!"

- The Inspired Letters in Clearest English – (Laubach) The Inspired Letters in Clearest English – "If a man is in Christ, he is created new. The man he was has passed away, and, behold, a new man has been created!"

- J.B. Phillips New Testament – "...he becomes a new person altogether—the past is finished and gone, everything has become fresh and new...."

- (Shuttle) Paraphrasic Translation of the Apostolic Epistles – "...the deadliness of our former condition is passed away...."

- (Dean) Paul and his letters – "...and the true Christian is not merely a man altered but a man re-made..."

Think about the words, *"If any man be in Christ...."* Are you in Christ? If so, identify yourself in Him, and every opportunity you can, claim it. Going to heaven isn't the only blessing that comes from being in Christ. The verse says if you are in Christ, you are a new creation, a new being. It's important that the potency of this statement doesn't get watered down into religious terminology. It's real.

When you were born the first time, you were born into Adam's race; that was your reality, your identity. Things on Lists B and C used to be your identity because those fractures came with Adam's race. When you were born again, the scripture says that old things or the ugly Lists B and C stereotypes of male and female passed away, and everything becomes new and from God. List A is the new you. Why don't you look again at the new you on page 278.

When you're born again, even though you still have the body that came from your parents, your spirit is regenerated—not just cleaned up. It's this new spirit that puts you in the last Adam race or the in-Christ race. In the same way that death worked out of the first Adam's spirit to affect the rest of his person, now life works out of your regenerated spirit to affect the rest of your person.

The last Adam/in-Christ race is a human race. In other words, a person who is in-Christ is absolutely human, but he or she is not in the old Adam's race. He or she is a new Adam species. That's pretty radical!

We really do believe the radical things the Epistles teach us. If we don't believe them, we may as well tear out Romans 6 from the Bible. While we're at it, we might as well tear out most of the book of Romans, the first three chapters of Ephesians, and all of Galatians. We just plain don't need them if we refuse to embrace what's revealed in them. *NO!* I believe before Jesus comes we can actually believe these truths and live by them. We can believe that when any man is in Christ, he is literally a new creature. Everything on Lists B and C passed away. Everything became new, and everything in this new race is from God. List A is your new reality as a man or woman.

Identifying with the Heavenly You

And as we have borne the image of the man of dust we shall also bear the image of the heavenly man. Just as we are now like the earthly man we will someday be like the heavenly man.
1 Corinthians 15:49 (NLT)

As surely as we have born the image of the man of dust—Adam—we will bear the image of the man from heaven—Jesus. In context, this portion of scripture refers to the resurrection. It's saying there will come a time when we receive new bodies and are glorified so that we won't die. In other words, we will be completely transfigured (1 John 3:1-2).

Yet, even now before we see Him and before we're resurrected with new immortal bodies, we can begin to experience the first fruits and blessings of redemption and bear the image of the heavenly One (Romans 8:23). If you identify mostly with the dust or your first birth, that will be the reality you live by. Instead, identify with Jesus and His identity.

Consider Jesus' example. Some people said He was from Galilee, and other people said He was from Nazareth. In scripture, did Jesus ever say where He was from? You don't see Him ever claiming a town for a part of His identity. That's interesting, isn't it? I'm not suggesting that if people ask you where you're from you say, "Heaven." You don't have to go weird on us. My point is that there were reasons Jesus lived the way He did. One is that He claimed His heavenly origin first and foremost because it was real to Him. If we embrace and claim the dust, then we have to deal with the dust.

As we've already pointed out, Jesus identified more strongly with His spiritual family than His natural one when He said, "Who is my family? Everybody who obeys the will of God, that's my family" (Matthew 12:46-50). Was He being rude? No, He couldn't have been rude because He always responded perfectly. He said it in the greatest respect. He was not demeaning His family but elevating the fact that anybody who does the will of God (2 Peter 3:9) is family, and there are definite family traits in this new race. As a child of God, you have a right to reject what's on Lists B and C as your identity. Instead, because God is your Father, you have a right and a privilege to claim the qualities of List A.

Jesus talked often about His Father. In the book of John, He referred to God as His Father more than 100 times. Not one of those times was He referring to Joseph. Is it wrong for you to talk about your family? Of course not! I'm not saying that at all. But if you refer to your heavenly Father only when you're in church or someone else encourages you to, then the rest of the time your identity will be with the elements of your first birth. The weight of your identity and the way you think will come from your first birth. You'll live as a male or female with the characteristics of your first birth, which will include the fractures of Lists B and C.

> **For those whom He foreknew [of whom He was aware and loved beforehand], He also destined from the beginning [foreordaining them] to be molded into the image of His Son [and share inwardly His likeness], that He might become the firstborn among many brethren.**
>
> **Romans 8:29 (AMPC)**

Jesus was the firstborn, or the first person, the head, or the prototype of this new race, this last Adam race. And part of our destiny is to look like Him. We are ordained to bear His image. That's the plan! It's not just because we wear a bracelet on our arm that says, "What Would Jesus Do?" It's not just because there are external rules from the outside to guide

Christian behavior with do's and don'ts. No, it's actually and in reality *who we are.*

It's who *you* are! *You* are in this new race, and what you look like now includes the characteristics of the Father, the Son, and the Holy Spirit in List A (page 278).

> **To whom God was pleased to make known how great for the Gentiles are the riches of the glory of this mystery, which is Christ within and among you, the Hope of [realizing the] glory.**
>
> Colossians 1:27 (AMPC)

Is Christ in heaven, seated at the right hand of the throne of God? Yes, absolutely. But the profound mystery is that by the Holy Spirit, this Exalted One is also in you.

God is in *you.*

> **[You] "…have put on the new man who is renewed in knowledge according to the image of Him who created him."**
>
> Colossians 3:10

You have put on the new man who was created after what? Created after "…the image of Him who created him." Highlight that phrase in your Bible, so you'll remember your image. When it says you're a new creature created in Christ Jesus, you were created after what image? *His image!* Whether you're male or female, you look like God.

We've already said List A includes characteristics of His nature and His image, and because you're created after this image, these qualities are now *in you.* This is how we're supposed to believe and think.

THE CROSS WAS GREATER THAN A GOOD EFFORT. IT WORKED!

Now, here's how we're *not* supposed to think: *Oh God, You're so wonderful, but I'm such a pathetic Lists B and C person. Even though I'll always be broken and disgraceful like my natural family, I worship You because You're a faithful, loving, merciful, and forgiving God.* Oh, no! No, no, no. That thinking squashes, demeans, and diminishes the power of the cross to practically impact your characteristics. It's like saying the cross was only a good effort, a good run, a good go. "You gave it your best shot, God." No! A thousand times no! The cross was greater than a good effort. It worked!

Jesus said, "It's finished!" What He meant, included, and provided was a death from the first Adam's race and a new birth into the last Adam's race where Christ's nature would become ours. That goes for both man and woman.

Seeing You in the Mirror

What we do through personal devotions and throughout the day is to identify in ourselves the in-Christ image or List A. We do the same with others. People who are truly effective in preaching, ministering, or even simply sharing the Word with other believers, no matter their age, help Christians find their true identities in Christ. Lists B and C may be how other people identify them, but our job is to hold up to them their true identities shown in the Bible. Our job is to say, "Let me show you who you are. This is you!"

As it clearly states in 2 Corinthians 3:6 "who also made us sufficient as ministers of the new covenant, not of the letter but of the Spirit; for the letter kills, but the Spirit gives life." An Old Covenant-oriented minister condemns and reminds believers of their first Adam characteristics, but an effective minister of the New Covenant doesn't do that.

> **But we all, with unveiled face, beholding as in the mirror the glory of the Lord, are being transformed into the same image from glory to glory, just as by the Spirit of the Lord.**
>
> **2 Corinthians 3:18**

In addition to what the veil represents in this context, it can also represent the realities of the past. When you look at what God says you are, take the veil off by looking away from your past (Lists B and C), and believe and accept your new image. Believe the mirror of the Word of God. When we look with an unveiled face into that image like looking into a mirror, we're supernaturally changed to match the beautiful image of Christ!

When you look into the mirror of the Word, you're seeing Jesus in His perfection, true. But what is amazing is that you're also seeing *you* because *you are in Him.*

When you look in the mirror each morning, you don't see somebody else, do you? Of course not. You see you. The verse of scripture above says that when you look into His Word, you're looking in a mirror that shows you, your real self. Embrace it! Especially embrace areas where you have experienced more Lists B and C characteristics.

For example, if you've been uncompassionate, if you've been selfish, if you've been unfaithful, etc., acknowledge that those characteristics have passed away. Call them dead. Bury them. Secondly, acknowledge the contrasting godly characteristics that are a part of your nature in Him. Identify them. Worship those qualities in Him but also identify them in you, because everything *He is, He is in you.*

You may say, "What does this have to do with being a husband or a mother?" Everything! It affects how each gender expresses God's characteristics through each of our roles.

The Hulk

...The yoke shall be destroyed because of fatness [which prevents it from going around your neck].

Isaiah 10:27 (AMPC)

This verse was a part of Isaiah's prophecy that Judah would indeed be cruelly oppressed by Assyria, though not forever. Instead, the yoke of Assyrian bondage would be destroyed by the presence and power of the Holy Spirit, represented by the anointing oil. There were different purposes for the use of anointing oil that still apply to us today because of the ministry of the Holy Spirit. The anointing of the Holy Spirit is effective to break the yoke anywhere and anytime there is oppression and bondage.

Isaiah 10:27 paints a picture of you actually breaking out of the yoke. Commonly, we think of the anointing being external and breaking the yoke of bondage off people, and it does. I don't disagree with that because it's certainly true, but that's not how this verse of scripture reads. This scripture doesn't mean the yoke is broken off by an external outside force. Instead, it's saying because of the fatness of your neck, the yoke is broken off from the *inside out*. In other words, you break out of restrictions from the inside out.

It reminds me of the superhero character the Hulk. He's just a regular guy. He's not really buff but more of a nerd guy. He turns green and gets bigger and bigger and bigger until he finally breaks out of his clothes. In the same way, Isaiah 10:27 refers to an internal anointing that helps you get bigger and bigger and bigger with the reality of who you are until you break out of what you used to be.

There's a woman in our church family we love to pieces. She's powerful in prayer. When we first became pastors of the church, she came to Tony and I after a couple of months and said, "I just want you to know about a problem I have. I must be honest. I love the church, and I want only to be a blessing here. So, it's okay if I need to leave after telling you this. I've already prepared myself for you to tell me that it's better that I go." She continued in tears, saying, "I have an addiction that I can't quit. I don't want to quit, but I don't want to bring reproach on God."

"You know what?" we said. "You're exactly where you need to be. You just keep coming and keep feasting on the Word of God—on the Truth— and you will outgrow your need for that addiction." Sure enough, she kept coming, and after spending extra time in the presence of God, the fatness of the anointing broke her out of chemical dependence. This is only one of scores of similar examples I could share.

Not understanding New Testament ministry causes us to hurt struggling believers. We say, "Stay away from church until you deal with that problem." Yet, when believers are struggling, it's time to embrace and surround them with the truth about their in-Christ characteristics. That's where the power is that will change them from the inside out—not from the outside in.

In John 11, we read the story of how Jesus' friend Lazarus was sick and died. After being in the tomb four days, Jesus stood in front of the tomb and said, "Lazarus come forth!" And here he came! Lazarus was alive, but he was still wrapped in his grave clothes. Can you imagine Lazarus walking out of the tomb looking like a mummy? That would have been something to see for sure.

Jesus said, "Loose him, and let him go!" Those words can apply to a lot of Christians. There are Christians all around us who are alive spiritually but still wrapped in grave clothes. Isn't that interesting? They're wrapped in clothes characteristic of their old dead men or those who are still spiritually dead. They are wrapped in Lists B and C. Like Lazarus, these believers need to be loosed.

"Loose him, and let him go! Jesus said. Yet, what the Church has done a lot of times is tell Lazarus to go back in the tomb. Too often the Church has said, "Don't you come out of that tomb until you get rid of those old clothes." How wrong! True New Covenant-ministry is effective at getting those grave clothes off people. You don't condemn grave clothes off nor do you leave them on, assuring and lying to people that they are okay the way they are. *No!*

When you show people who they are in Christ—whether man or woman—the fatness of who they are has the "Hulk effect" and breaks them out of those awful grave clothes.

Fathers break out of anger, and mothers break out of manipulation. Unfaithful people break out of unfaithfulness and become faithful; they manifest what's on the inside. There is faithfulness on the inside, and it grows so big that faithfulness comes out. Instead of being impatient, unkind, and selfish, Christ grows in them, and they break out until love and kindness prevail in a home.

The mind must be transformed by a revelation of the new you. Romans 12:2 says to be transformed by the renewing of your mind. Don't be conformed to this world. Don't be conformed not only to the world in general but also to your own world, your first Adam world. Don't let it define and confine you. Be transformed by the renewing of your mind so you can prove what is that good and acceptable and perfect will of God. Find yourself in God as revealed in His Word and by His Spirit. Identify with your new identity.

I like to read the great stories of people who knew and worked with God during their lifetime. I've had the privilege to know some great men and women of God, and I've been able to easily identify Christ in them. That's what made them great. First of all, the reason people are able to clearly see Christ in an individual is because that individual saw Christ in himself or herself. You can do the same. Everything Jesus is, He is in you.

IT'S ALSO A BEAUTIFUL THING TO COME TO KNOW YOU— THE NEW AND REAL YOU WHO WAS RECREATED IN THE IMAGE OF GOD.

Jesus came to show us the Father, and He accomplished that. But Jesus also came to show us, us. Remember in Matthew 16 when Jesus asked his disciples who they said He was? (Matthew 16:15-18 KJV). Peter made the famous declaration, "Thou art the Christ the Son of the living God," Then Jesus said, "Blessed are you, Simon Barjona because flesh and blood has not revealed this to you but my Father which is in Heaven."

However, that wasn't the end of the story. Jesus went on to say, "And I tell you, you are *Peter*[2] [Greek, *Petros*—a large piece of rock], and on this rock [Greek, *petra*–a huge rock like Gibraltar] I will build My church, and the gates of Hades (the powers of the infernal region) shall not overpower it [or be strong to its detriment or hold out against it]" (Matthew 16:18 AMPC).

On what rock will the Church be built that hell won't be able to overcome? Is Peter the rock? No. The rock the Church is built on is the revelation of Jesus' identity *and* the revelation of *your* identity according to Him. Do you get it? It's a beautiful thing to come to know Jesus. It's also a beautiful thing to come to know you—*the new and real you who was recreated in the image of God*. It will transform your world and the world around you when you find out who you are in Christ.

The truth about God makes you free from the deceit of the devil designed to put you under his influence. Yet, if you know the truth about God but are confused about your identity or your in-Christ characteristics, you will end up misrepresenting God in your life.

For example, imagine how glorious it is to God when you speak of His love, image it, and represent it in your life, rather than speaking of His love while demonstrating anger and holding a grudge. All the characteristics you find to be true about Him have direct impact on you when you embrace them as who *you* are in Him. Lists B and C pass away, and List A begins to describe *you!*

> **Don't be overcome with evil, but overcome evil with good.**
>
> Romans 12:21

Don't try to outrun evil. Don't try to overcome what's on Lists B and C with, "I've got to do better. I've got to be a better man. I've got to be a better dad. I've got to be a better father. I've got to be a better wife and mom." No. You overcome Lists B and C characteristics with List A characteristics.

You're Just Putting That On

It's possible to alter who you *were* by putting on who you *are*. You can alter your actions the same way. There are a number of scriptures that refer to putting on and off ways of acting much like you can put on and off clothing.

For example:

> 8 But now you yourselves are to *put off* all these: anger, wrath, malice, blasphemy, filthy language out of your mouth. 9 Do not lie to one another, since you have *put off* the old man with his deeds, 10 and have *put on* the new *man* who is renewed in knowledge according to the image of Him who created him, 12 Therefore, as *the* elect of God, holy and beloved, put on tender mercies, kindness, humility, meekness, longsuffering; 14 But above all these things *put on* love, which is the bond of perfection.
>
> Colossians 3:8-10, 12, 14

Spiritually speaking, the Holy Spirit through Paul is telling us what to wear and what not to wear. Trust Him! He knows best!

If you're being nice and somebody says, "Oh, you're just putting that on." You can say "Yes, I'm putting that on. I'm putting on kindness!" But you cannot put on something you don't have in your closet. Your spirit is your spiritual closet, and you've got gorgeous things in there that you may

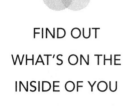

FIND OUT
WHAT'S ON THE
INSIDE OF YOU
AND PUT IT ON.

not know you have. It's packed with the nature and characteristics of God. Find out what's on the inside of you and put it on.

These scriptures also say you can put off things that you shouldn't be wearing. "Do I have a choice? I mean everybody in my family is a prime example of Lists B and C!" The Bible says you can take off Lists B and C and put on List A. Yes! You have a choice what your life will wear. The Scriptures repeatedly show you how to put off the characteristics from Lists B and C and put on the characteristics from List A.

Can you tell family, friends, and co-workers, "If you see me, you see the Father?" That might be a little bit of a stretch right now because of the wrong "Lists B and C clothes" you're still wearing. But it's not impossible, and it's actually the plan. It was the mystery that was hidden from ages and generations, but now is revealed to us. What is this amazing mystery that Paul's ministry was dedicated to revealing? Is it Christ up in heaven? No, it's Christ *in us* the hope of glory. The hope of being glorious and the hope of a life that gives glory to God is Christ *in us*.

Let's begin looking at the primary roles of men and women now that we've thoroughly looked at both man's problem and God's solution to it. In Christ, in this last Adam race, we're absolutely able to represent our Creator and reflect characteristics of His invisible Person.

For me as a woman, wife, and mom, it's not quite enough to say, "I hope I can be a good person. No. That people can recognize and identify the nature of God in me *is* God's purpose for my life.

I was *made* to make visible the invisible God.

So are *you!*

In the first three chapters of Ephesians and first two chapters of Colossians, Paul helps believers identify themselves spiritually in Christ. However, in the last half of both of these books, Paul was inspired to write very practically describing how the roles should look in this new race of inChrist men and women.

If Paul would have started his letter in the last half of Ephesians and Colossians, it would have looked a lot like a rule book. Yet, because he started with the core of our spiritual identity and moves outward, the last half of both these books serves as a manual of how we function and reflect the indwelling Christ.

Notes

1 Excerpt from *Spirit Filled Scripture Study Guide,* Mark Hankins, Mark Hankins Ministry, 2004
https://itunes.apple.com/us/book/spirit-filled-scripture-study-guide/id1161767074?mt=11
Used by permission.

2 *Petros* for *Peter* in the Greek is in the masculine gender and the word *petra* for the rock is in the feminine gender. *Petros* and *petra* are two distinct words in the Greek. *Petros is a shifting, rolling, or insecure stone,* while *petra is a solid, immovable rock.* http://www.trustingodamerica.com/Petra.htm

ENGENDERED

CHAPTER 20

InChrist Man

We've considered what redemption means to man and woman generally, but let's consider the inChrist man specifically. Do men have a significant role with God as they do in many religions? I haven't observed all of the religions in the world, but I have been exposed to several of them in the parts of the world where we've lived and traveled. What I found to be remarkable is that men are actively and conspicuously involved in the religions I've seen.

Tony and I were guests at the home of one of our student's during the Chinese New Year, and we were able to observe a Buddhist ceremony. The student's brother-in-law, as the man of the house, invited a Buddhist priest to usher a Chinese dragon through every room in his house, making declarations and prayers. He said, "Come in this room," and the Buddhist priest would enter that room carrying out the same prayers and incantations. He said, "Now, come in my child's room," and here came the Buddhist priest to pray and pronounce various blessings.

This raises a question: Why in Christianity have men been so stereotypically non-dominant? I'll tell you why: The devil knows that something amazing and authoritative happens when a man believes and acts on the truth. I'm all for women; I *am* a woman. But there is a unique splendor that comes from a man who images God. Men walking in who they are in Christ are something that hell fights.

WHEN A MAN WALKS IN HIS GOD-GIVEN PLACE OF DOMINION AND MANIFESTS THE NATURE OF THE INDWELLING CHRIST, HE'S THE MOST MAGNIFICENT OF GOD'S CREATURES.

Every revival that's ever affected or shaken a city or region can be traced back to and associated with a man who took his place in Christ. Preceding this, it's not uncommon to find a prayer force largely composed of women, and the results of that prayer activates carriers of revival fire. After all, to start a fire, you don't strike a match and put it directly on a log. No, you gather kindling and purposefully position it under the logs. It seems to me that generally women are like kindling and catch fire easily. Men are more like logs, and it may take some time for the fire to catch on. But when it does, look out. That log is on fire!

When a man walks in his God-given place of dominion and manifests the nature of the indwelling Christ, he's the most magnificent of God's creatures. I believe that. That's why it's good to not feed on thoughts and entertainment that diminish men and mock and disrespect manhood. Man is the glory of God.

The standard that God has given to men as fathers and husbands is not their dads, not their grandpas, not their mates. Look at the standard! The pattern according to the Creator and His Word is nothing less than God the Father and Christ Himself. That's extraordinary!

In Adam, man was unfaithful and irresponsible to God, his wife, his home, and himself. He wasn't faithful or responsible to the command God gave him to guard and protect the garden. When an intruder came into the garden, he didn't respond. The intruder was talking to his wife, and he was present with her. But man didn't take his place of authority. He didn't guard. He didn't protect.

First Timothy 2:14 says, Eve was deceived, but Adam was not. He saw what was happening, and he just didn't do anything. He was detached, absent, unfaithful, and irresponsible. And so began List B.

But the inChrist man is faithful. He is faithful in all His house just like Jesus (Hebrews 3:2). Faithfulness is core. Our first Adam wasn't faithful to God and wasn't obedient. The last Adam was perfectly faithful and obedient. Do you see how Jesus began reversing everything in the way that He lived? Jesus redefined manhood.

ENGENDERED

CHAPTER 21

InChrist Husband

There are specific truths from the Bible that make the intentions of the Creator crystal clear and apply practically to husbands. As we highlight these characteristics of God, we'll gain a clear picture of who God says the inChrist husband is and how he looks. God's definition of a husband is far greater than whatever images we've previously gathered from our family, our culture, our past, and whatever is portrayed through the media.

Just Like Christ

The husband is the head of the wife *as also* [Greek word: *hoce*, meaning *in that manner*] Christ is the head of the church and He is the savior of the body.

Ephesians 5:23

Being the head in the marriage is clearly the husband's position. However, being the head is not only his position, but the manner in which he carries out this position is to represent Christ. So, the position of the head in a marriage is not domineering or tyrannical, because that's not what we see as the example in Christ. He is to be the head *hoce*[1] (*even as* or *in the same manner in which Christ is the head of the body*).

Without dispute, Jesus is the King and the Lord. But when we see how He personally imaged His Father, we also see how Jesus was void of an authoritarian, arrogant "serve me" attitude. We don't see that attitude in the example of Jesus, do we? No. In fact, the opposite is true. So, it doesn't matter what our example or experience has been naturally. An inChrist Husband must get his example from Christ.

In the same manner as Jesus is the head of the Church, a husband is the head of his marriage. But the verse straightaway includes that Jesus is also the Savior of the body. So, the manner in which the husband is to be the head is to help, to protect, to save, and to nourish. He can do all of that from that place of headship.

> **For husbands, this means love your wives, *just as* Christ loved the church. He gave up his life for her.**
>
> **Ephesians 5:25 (NLT)**

There it is again. *Just as* is the same Greek word *hoce*,[1] which means *in the same manner as*. Husbands are to love their wives in the same way Christ loved the church and gave Himself up for her. In other words, a husband cannot be saying, "She's my ol' gal. She's my old battle axe" or equally unflattering statements. A husband is the head, but the purpose of his headship is to be the savior by loving and giving of himself. Why? Because that's the manner that Christ takes headship toward the Church. Any way other than a husband loving and giving himself to the wife misrepresents Christ.

HUSBANDS ARE TO LOVE THEIR WIVES IN THE SAME WAY CHRIST LOVED THE CHURCH.

Anything you've learned of Christ—His giving, His attitude, His demeanor and more—is not weak. Jesus isn't a pushover or a mouse of a man. He is strong, but He is also tender. Everything that a husband learns of Christ can be applied to himself. An inChrist husband can rightfully and personally claim these characteristics for himself.

This is bigger than culture or environment. Practical ways of how a husband loves and gives of himself can be manifested in different and unique ways in different cultures. Yet, without a doubt, Christ is to be imaged by husbands everywhere in the world. The truth and reality of this word must be flesh and dwell among us—in our homes, in our marriages.

There's more. Notice what Ephesians 5 goes on to say in the next few verses:

> 28 So husbands ought to love their own wives as their own bodies; he who loves his wife loves himself. 29 For no one ever hated his own flesh, but nourishes and cherishes it, *just as* the Lord does the church.
>
> Ephesians 5:28-29

There it is yet again. The husband is to love his wife *just as* or the word *hoce —in the same manner*—a man nourishes and cherishes his body. We know that Jesus does that with the Church. So that's what a husband, as the head of a marriage and the one that gives of himself, must always do. The inChrist husband must nourish and cherish his wife in the same way Jesus does the Church.

Look at Adam's first words regarding the one that God made from his side:

> 22 Then the rib which the Lord God had taken from man He made into a woman, and He brought her to the man. 23 And Adam said: "This is now bone of my bones and flesh of my flesh; she shall be called Woman, because she was taken out of Man." 24 Therefore a man shall leave his father and mother and be joined to his wife, and they shall become one flesh.
>
> Genesis 2:22-24

Husband and wife are one flesh. That's why God designed for a husband to take care of his wife because she is one with his own flesh. He does not treat her differently or lower than himself. If he demeans his wife, he demeans himself. If he dishonors her, he dishonors himself. If he abuses his wife, he abuses himself.

Paul was quoting the Genesis account of the first man and woman in his connection with these words:

We are members of His body, of His flesh and His bones.

Ephesians 5:30

This was in the original intent, purpose, and image in the beginning, embedded in the reason why God even created man and woman. God's original design and pattern is that by looking at the way a man treats his wife, we would know how Jesus treats the Church. The invisible is again imaged by the visible.

For this reason a man shall leave his father and mother and be joined to his wife, and the two shall become one flesh.

Ephesians 5:31

Notice, it does not say *one spirit*. When you're born again you're one spirit with the Lord, 1 Corinthians 6:17 tell us. However, when you get married, you're not one spirit with your mate, but you do become one flesh. At this point, you've got double flesh to work with! (Actually, you become one flesh with anyone/thing you have sex with according to 1 Corinthians 6:16 GNT).

Paul repeats the instruction to the inChrist husband:

Nevertheless, let each one of you in particular so love his own wife as himself.

Ephesians 5:33

In other words, inChrist husband, you take care of yourself. Now, take care of the person that is your wife, even as your own flesh. You would never hurt your own flesh, so don't ever hurt her.

Let's look at what husbands are to do *even as (hoce—in the same manner)* Jesus would do.

- Be the head of the marriage
- Be the savior – protect and supply
- Love
- Give himself for his wife

- Nourish and cherish his wife

Because a husband's relationship to his wife personally represents and images (or misrepresents) Christ, there's significant instruction to the inChrist husband. Let's look again at Ephesians 5.

Divine Equation

25 Husbands, love your wives, just as Christ also loved the church and gave Himself for her, 26 that He might sanctify and cleanse her with the washing of water by the word, 27 that He might present her to Himself a glorious church, not having spot or wrinkle or any such thing, but that she should be holy and without blemish.

Ephesians 5:25-27

It's important that the truth of this verse is applicable. Something for us not just to know but actually to *do!* The blessing is in the doing. So, let's break it down a bit.

Every husband desires his wife to be pleasing to him. It's important to him that she does certain things or behaves in a certain way. I surely discovered right away that Tony had personal preferences and desires for me as a wife.

For example, I never locked doors. Being from a small farm community, none of us ever locked doors. Plus, we left the car keys in the ignition. Oh my! Did that ever have to change! Tony wanted doors locked and keys not left in the car. Similarly, it's true that each husband has personal preferences regarding his wife that make her "glorious to him."

Let's paraphrase verse 27 with the thought in mind that the husband is to represent Christ and the wife is to represent the Church: "That the husband might be able to look upon his wife and see that she is glorious and perfect for him; not being contrary or doing the things that bug him but doing the things that he likes and prefers, and that she really be completely his and does what is pleasing to him" (Patsy's Paraphrase).

Okay, in what world does this exist? Remember, this verse is describing God's description of an inChrist husband and an inChrist wife. We'll get to the wife's part later, but first let's continue with the husband.

What we just paraphrased is verse 27—not verse 25. Let's examine this carefully. Verse 27 comes after verse 26, which comes after verse 25. I call attention to this because what happened in the fall is that the order was mixed up with the expectation of verse 27 coming first. In other words, a man wants his wife to be what he wants: "Do that, be that, and I will love you." No! God designed it the other way around. The first Adam mixed it up.

Notice carefully the divine order Ephesians 5 lays out:

1. *"Husbands, love your wives, just as Christ also loved the church...."* Who loved first and best? The Church or Christ? When did Christ love us? Before we were lovable. Why do we now love Christ? Because He first loved us. Why will your wife want to lavish you with love years into marriage? Because her mother told her that's what she's supposed to do and it's her duty? No! Do you see that kind of love would be so much less than the best?

You love first **before** the wife gets it right, **before** she is pleasing, **before** she is doing all that you like and not doing the things that are troublesome. InChrist husbands love their wives in the same manner as Christ did the Church. Aren't you glad that He loves *us* before *we* get it all right?

An inChrist husband is to love even as (*hoce*) his dad? His grandfathers? His mates or uncles? No. While these examples may or may not be good, the inChrist husband's standard is Christ. Christ loves **first**.

2. *"...and gave himself for her,* **that** *He might sanctify and cleanse it with the washing of water by the word...."*

Anytime the word *that* appears in the Bible, it's good to read it with the word *so* in front of it. Let's read the phrase above that way: Jesus loved the Church, gave Himself for her, **so that** or in order that—keep going—He might sanctify and cleanse her with the washing of the water of the Word.

Paul said to Timothy:

16 All Scripture *is* given by inspiration of God, and *is* profitable for doctrine, for *reproof,* for *correction,* for *instruction* in righteousness, 17 that the man of God may be complete, thoroughly equipped for every good work.

2 Timothy 3:16-17

Besides correction and instruction, how else does the Lord speak to us? The Word also says that prophecy, or God-inspired words, or words that build the Church, are words of edification, exhortation, and comfort (1 Corinthians 14:3). In the same way, an inChrist husband will talk to his wife like Jesus talks to the Church and will build his wife up with words that encourage, advise, and comfort.

So, we see the words of Jesus aren't correction only. Think about churches where all the people ever hear is correction and condemnation. What happens to those kinds of people? Those believers become pathetic and hopeless, thinking, *I can never do anything right.* They doubt God loves them because hearing only correction implies that love is conditional and must be earned.

Husbands are to love just as or even as Christ loves. So, the way in which Christ loves and gives of Himself is not saying, "I'm the head. Do what I tell you to do, and then I'll treat you nice." No, that kind of thinking is definitely first Adam's race. It is fractured, and it definitely misrepresents Christ.

GOD INTENDED FOR UNCONDITIONAL LOVE TO BE VISIBLE AND TANGIBLE BY WATCHING HOW A HUSBAND TREATS AND TALKS TO HIS WIFE.

On the other hand, it would be totally untrue for a wife to think that an inChrist husband only speaks encouraging and affirming words that never correct her. Why? Because we see in Hebrews 12:6 that the Lord corrects those He loves. Correction can be motivated by agitation, or it can be motivated by pure love. The way to know the difference between these motivations is that Jesus is loving *even before* He corrects.

God intended for unconditional love to be visible and tangible by watching how a husband treats and talks to his wife—*before* she does anything that pleases him.

If loving this way came naturally, the instruction wouldn't have to be repeated so much. What is natural to the flesh is that a man will wait until his wife is glorious to him, without spot or wrinkle, and love her for that. Yet, it's the opposite in Christ. The inChrist husband must love his wife before she deserves it. He must love her despite the spots and the wrinkles.

Of course, Jesus desires to present the Church to Himself as glorious, not having spot or wrinkle or any such thing. He desires that the Church be holy and without blemish. Yet, the words Jesus uses to make you glorious are edifying, exhorting, and comforting as well as instructional, correctional, and reproving. Jesus uses words that are love inspired—and so must the inChrist husband. Love on purpose because it sets you up to be able to say the corrective things you need to say.

Words that come from Christ or the inChrist husband will be instructive or even corrective. But when the husband loves with the selfless kind of love and gives of himself, he can give instruction and even correction with more success (verse 26). If his instruction and correction follow verse 25, his wife will have an attitude of "What do you want me to do?"

Here's the divine order and equation straight from Ephesians 5: **verse 25 + verse 26 = verse 27.**

Loving your wife and giving of yourself to her using words that edify and comfort + words inspired by love that correct, instruct, reprove, and exhort = a wife who is glorious to the husband. InChrist husband, if you're not getting what you want, you're probably not doing it in that order. Love on purpose!

The Bottom Line

Husbands love your wives and do not be *bitter* towards them.
Colossians 3:19

Actually, this word *bitter* also is translated *harsh*. That's one of the first Adam characteristics; harshness is in List B. But it's not a last Adam characteristic, is it?

Bitter also means *sharp, cruel, severe, as bitter enmity, sharp with words, reproachful, and sarcastic.*

According to the Creator, the bottom line to a husband is to love and give of himself, and women are to respect and submit (We'll look at that later!). The fall really broke that pattern, and men became dominant as God said they would. In response to that dominance, a woman pulls back, resists, and bucks. And God knew that as well.

When a wife doesn't do what the husband says to do, the husband often becomes harder and harder: "Did you hear what I said?" "Are you stupid?" "What's wrong with you?" When that happens, even if there is momentary compliance, something withdraws in a woman, because God didn't hardwire her to respond to dominance. He hardwired a woman to be like the Church responding to Christ and His love.

So, even though there may be seeming compliance, a husband who uses force and dominance to present his wife to himself as he wants her to be actually robs himself of glory. Why? A woman who does not submit from her heart cannot truly be glorious to her husband.

The husband then feels uncovered and unglorified, so he demands more, which makes the wife more resistant or defensive, which makes him yet again harsher, which makes her yet again more resistant. This cycle is an effective plan from the devil because it's an ugly picture that would never ever properly reflect Christ and the Church.

This reality that non-submissiveness incites bitterness and harshness in the husband, which incites more non-submissiveness in the wife, is a relevant point in any nationality because it's from Holy Scripture. This is not a cultural issue, and it's not man made. Yet, the results are commonly an awful stand-off or full on strife. It's the reason why there's so much separation and divorce because it all comes down to irreconcilable differences.

What's the bottom line? Love.

THE CHRIST-KIND OF LOVE IS NOT A FEELING; IT'S SOMETHING YOU DO.

Does that mean you'll feel loving all the time? No. In fact, the Christ-kind of love is not a feeling; it's something you do.

When Colossians 3:19 instructs husbands, "…love your wives and do not be bitter toward them," it gives an indication there will be things wives do that make their husbands feel bitter. One way to love your wife is *to choose* not to be bitter. Remember, love is something you do!

For the instruction not to be bitter to make it into the Bible, means it's pretty much what husbands may experience at some point in marriage. Face it, in every marriage there will be things that are agitating and hurtful. Are there husbands who enjoy glorious exceptions to this rule? Sure. But it's not uncommon for husbands to deal with bitterness.

Get Smart

Peter also gives husbands instructions for living in the new inChrist race.

> In the same way, you husbands must give honor to your wives. Treat your wife with understanding as you live together. She may be weaker than you are, but she is your equal partner in God's gift of new life. Treat her as you should so your prayers will not be hindered.
>
> 1 Peter 3:7 (NLT)

The King James Version says it like this, "…husbands…dwell with them [wives] according to knowledge…."

In *Sparkling Gems*, author Rick Renner points out that the words *dwell with your wife* comes from the Greek word *sunoikeo*[2] and carries the idea of *partnership and cooperation*. So, to dwell with your wife is to seek a partnership and cooperation. A partnership amounts to walking with your wife according to knowledge. Not only is it important to acquire knowledge about your wife, but also it's important to live by the knowledge you acquire. A husband who wants to find out more about what is important to his wife will ask questions.

People express and receive love uniquely. My husband and I have different ways we give and interpret love, and he had to learn my love language to him just as I had to interpret his love language to me. Make it a quest to learn about one another and how each receives love. By the same token, make it a quest to learn how you interpret love and live accordingly. Ask the Lord to help you express love. He's good at it. I also highly recommend reading after people whom God has blessed with insight on the topic.

In the same way your knowledge of God can increase and become sweeter and sweeter as the years go by, you can also increase in your knowledge about your wife. This applies also for the wife knowing more and more about her husband. Because we're spirits, there's no end to a person. So, if you become bored with your spouse, it's because you've quit seeking to know him or her. Don't just know a person by his or her face, know what's behind the face. Know what the person does, his or her personal history—know the whole person. Ask the Lord to show you secrets about your spouse that He knows and loves. Seek to learn him or her.

IF YOU BECOME BORED WITH YOUR SPOUSE, IT'S BECAUSE YOU'VE QUIT SEEKING TO KNOW HIM OR HER.

Tony and I got married in 1989, and I just learned some things about him this past year that I sure wish I had known a long time ago. But I had to seek to know it, and actually I went to the One who knows Tony best to find out about him. Tony just found out some things about me that have enhanced our relationship, making it better than ever. Seek and ye shall find!

For many years, I had the privilege of serving the late Kenneth E. Hagin, a great man of God and a well-known Bible teacher. One thing I respected about him was that even though he was greatly used of God and knowledgeable in so many areas, he would read books on marriage. He always wanted to improve his marriage and seek to know things about his wife so he could keep their relationship sweet. This dear man of God based this practice on 1 Peter 3:7. Keep learning about God your whole life. But if you're married, learn also about your wife. She's complex, but rather than just writing her off, seek to learn and acquire knowledge and live by it.

"Giving honor to the woman as the weaker vessel" – *giving honor*[3] means *to esteem, especially to the highest degree, dignity itself, honor, precious prize, cherish treasure, valuable and very dear*. Interestingly enough, *weaker vessel* does not mean inferior or substandard. It carries the meaning in the Greek of *something fragile and of great value to be treasured and handled with special care*. In other words, the weaker vessel is extra precious.

Consider this phrase also from 1 Peter 3:7: "...that your prayers may not be hindered." One reason this would be the case is because it's such a misrepresentation of the head of the Church to disrespect your wife. It affects your ability to receive things from God as it affects the grip of your faith.

A great preacher, one who can absolutely preach brilliantly but disrespects his wife, misrepresents God. He may accurately and powerfully present the scripture, but if he misrepresents God by the way he treats his wife, in the end, he sabotages his ministry.

On the other hand, the husband who loves his wife as these verses instruct can reflect, represent, and image the head of the Church more powerfully than a sermon. In seeing the inChrist husband, people can visibly see how Christ is. Now that's glorious!

Notes

1 *Hoce* – Strong's Concordance 5613: *hós: as, like as, even as, when, since, as long as*
Original Word: ὡς
Definition: *as, like as, about, as it were, according as, how, when, while, as soon as, so that.*

2 Strong's G4924 – συνοικέω – *sunoikeō* – *soon-oy-key'-o*

From G4862 and G3611; *to reside together (as a family): dwell together.*

2b Rick Renner – *Sunoikio*
Husband, You Need To 'Dwell' With Your Wife! (October 8, 2016 entry).
This is precisely why Peter in 1 Peter 3:7 told husbands that they are to *dwell* with their wives. The word *dwell* is the Greek word *sunoikeo*, a compound of the word *sun* and *oikos*. The word *sun* always carries the idea of *partnership* and *cooperation*. When the word *sun* is used in the New Testament, it always *connects two or more people into a very vital union*. The second part of the word, *oikos*, is the Greek word for *a house*. When these words are linked together as they are in 1 Peter 3:7, it means *to share a house together* or *to dwell together in one residence.*
Because the first part of the word *sunoikos (dwell)* is the word *sun*, which always conveys the idea of *partnership* and *cooperation*, this lets us know that Peter is urging husbands to *share* their lives with their wives. This is a great challenge to men, who often want to be quiet when they come home after a busy day at work. Many men would rather sit down in front of the television and flip the channels all evening rather than communicate with their wives.
Sparkling Gems from the Greek, Rick Renner, Harrison House 2003, Tulsa, OK
https://renner.org/husbands-dwell-with-your-wife/

3 Strong's G5092: τιμή – *timē – tee-may'*
From G5099; *a value, that is, money paid, or (concretely and collectively) valuables; by analogy esteem (especially of the highest degree), or the dignity itself: honour, precious, price, some.*

ENGENDERED

CHAPTER 22

InChrist Father

Father is one of God's names, and human fathers are the only ones among all of God's creation who have the privilege of sharing a name with God. The honor of that role is staggering just because of the name itself. There's nothing like it: *father*. This role is the most threatening to the devil because it essentially reveals and represents to the next generation the heart and character of the heavenly Father. You can imagine why the devil couldn't have that. It would seem the impact of the fall hit the *father* harder than any other role, and the ripple effect was disastrous to every other role.

HUMAN FATHERS ARE THE ONLY ONES AMONG ALL OF GOD'S CREATION WHO HAVE GOTTEN TO SHARE A NAME WITH GOD.

Even among the great patriarchs of the Old Testament, it's a challenge to find glowing examples of fatherhood. The Bible is very transparent in revealing not only the great feats, but also the tragedies and weaknesses in the lives of Bible dads. Even though Noah saved his family, the remnant of the human race, one of his sons discovered him naked and drunk. Mighty David didn't shine so well as a father with Tamar, Amnon, and Absalom although he greatly influenced Solomon. Does the Bible say anything about the next generations after Joshua, Daniel, Shadrach, Meshach and Abednego, Gideon, Samuel, and Solomon doing the kinds of exploits their fathers did? Sadly, no.

My Father, Your Father

If the role of fatherhood was the epicenter of the fall affecting all the other roles, then the redemption Jesus brought to this role can effectively reverse the tragedy. Fatherhood can be redefined in Jesus. How? He wasn't a father. Let's look at what Isaiah prophesied generations before Jesus was even born:

> For unto us a child is born, unto us a son is given, and the government will be upon His shoulder and His name will be called wonderful, counsellor, mighty God, *everlasting father,* prince of peace.
>
> Isaiah 9:6

This verse is most commonly used during the Christmas season because it prophetically tells of the Messiah. We can see that Jesus' humanity is referred to in "a child being born." We can also see His divinity identified with "a son is given" (John 3:16).

Then Jesus is characterized in this most beautiful list of names: Wonderful, Counselor, Mighty God, Everlasting Father, and Prince of Peace. I can understand every one of these wonderfully descriptive names for Jesus, but what about everlasting Father? Why is one of His names everlasting Father when Jesus is the Son? Don't you find that interesting? Did Jesus image and represent His Father so perfectly that He is actually called by His name? How impressive would that be!

We must first note that God is rarely referred to as Father in the Old Testament. He was referred to as God Almighty, Jehovah, Lord God, and other such names, but the term Father was not associated with God except for a handful of occasions.

I want to emphasize that in the Old Testament, pre-last Adam and pre-new birth, it was uncommon to address God as Father, expressing a warm father/son relationship. However, there were men like Enoch, Noah, Abraham, Moses, David, the prophets and others who experienced a strong working and worshipful relationship with God.

Yet, could it be that we take calling God Father and the invitation for a very personal relationship with Him for granted? There had to be a whole new race established to make God our Father. In the Old Testament, the word father generally indicated a person's natural lineage, and genealogies in the Bible were often traced all the way back to David or even to Adam, identifying each person's dad. The Jews of Jesus' time spoke freely of their identification of Abraham as their father (John 8:39).

When Jesus came as the new Adam, He defined the realities of a new race, beginning with the fact that His relationship with God is noticeably different. It's intimate. He calls God Father. Jesus didn't throw that name around in a "daddy-o"-disrespectful sort of way but with the ultimate honor. He spoke about or addressed God as Father numerous times all through the Gospels and more than 100 times in the book of John alone. Religious leaders were shocked at what this implied.

> **17 But Jesus replied, "My Father is always working, and so am I."**
> **18 So the Jewish leaders tried all the harder to find a way to kill him. For he not only broke the Sabbath, he called God his Father, thereby making himself equal with God.**
> **John 5:17-18 (NLT)**

Your Father or *our Father* was terminology Jesus used in His teaching (Matthew 5:16, 45, 48; 6:1, 4, 6; 7:21; 10:32-33). This showed that the relationship He had with His Father was not exclusive, and it was generally extended to others. For example, heartfelt prayers prayed in the Old Testament by Hannah, Jehoshaphat, Isaiah, and Daniel began with "Lord God, Lord of Hosts, etc." But Jesus began His prayers with *Father*, and He taught others to do the same. What we call the Lord's Prayer begins with "Our Father, Who art in heaven…."

Yet, the most significant of Jesus' introductions of the Father to a follower was in the garden after He rose from the dead. Jesus said to Mary in John 20:17, "…'Do not cling to Me, for I have not yet ascended to My *Father and your Father*, and to My God and your God." Until Jesus came, no one had been given the right to call the Great and Almighty God *Father.*

In the first conversation after Jesus arose from the dead, He announced: "He's *Your* Father." In His resurrection, Jesus became the firstborn of many brethren (Romans 8:29; Hebrews 2:11).

Those of us who are born again are not just servants, but we're sons. We've been adopted and chosen by the Father (Romans 8:15; Galatians 4:5). Not only have we been adopted and belong to God the Father generally, but also we're born spiritually of this wonderful Father to which all these amazing List A characteristics belong.

12 But as many as received Him, to them He gave the right to become children of God, to those who believe in His name: 13 *who were born, not of blood, nor of the will of the flesh, nor of the will of man, but of God.*

John 1:12-13

That which is born of the flesh is flesh, *and that which is born of the Spirit is spirit.*

John 3:6

Our bodies were "fathered" by a human. But God is a spirit, and as such, He is not of the male sex. God is literally our spiritual Father—not just metaphorically or symbolically. Jesus provided a spiritual birth into the family of God, with God as our Father and Jesus as our eldest brother.

In Acts, the Epistles, and Revelation it's not uncommon for the writers to often refer to God as Father. Ephesians 3:14-21 is one of most prominent Epistle prayers we pray. Look how the prayer begins:

14 For this reason I bow my knees to the *Father of our Lord Jesus Christ,* 15 from whom the whole family in heaven and earth is named....

Ephesians 3:14-15

It would bless you to get out of your chair when you pray this prayer and actually get on your knees and acknowledge His fatherhood as the apostle Paul did. It does something! It positions your spirit in respect and honor. Bow your knee to Him, to the Father of the Lord Jesus Christ.

The Amplified Bible, Classic Edition says:

...[that Father from Whom all fatherhood takes its title and derives its name].

Ephesians 3:15b (AMPC)

God designed and defined fatherhood. It originated in Him and came up out of Him. Yet, the title and role of father has been defiled and fractured in various degrees. The fall did not contaminate all characteristics of godly fathers, but there are varying degrees of fracture in different families. Obviously, not every father represents every fracture. There are many fathers who have characteristics that nobly represent godly fatherhood.

Watch Me

God intended that the child would grow up learning love and respect through experiencing and observing his or her father. His presence, voice, actions, and reactions were to demonstrate protection, provision, and all the other characteristics included in List A. Obviously, the opposite happened in the broken father of Adam's race.

In Christ, God's plan is for a child to observe and experience His reality through the natural father. What does an inChrist father look like? List A is what a child is meant to see. A child who grows up witnessing List A characteristics (page 278) in his or her father can transition seamlessly into a relationship with the Father God. How amazing! How beautiful!

Ephesians 5:1 says, "Be ye therefore followers of God, as dear children." The most natural and simple way a child learns to imitate the Father God is initially by imitating his or her dad. An inChrist father will say, "Do what I say and do what I do," instead of "Do as I say, not as I do." An inChrist father says, "Come here. Let me show you what to do. Let me show you how it looks." He is a visible image of the unseen Father.

Remember, you're looking back to the pattern, the image God wanted and created. If God's original intention for fatherhood is not what you're currently expressing as a father, don't despair. Keep looking at God's original intention and His pattern in Jesus because there's hope. In fact, more than hope, there's actually transforming power in looking at the pattern.

To Correct or Not to Correct

I have singled him out so that he will direct his sons and their families to keep the way of the Lord by doing what is right and just. Then I will do for Abraham all that I have promised.

Genesis 18:19 (NLT)

One of the things that can be learned from this verse is that when a dad determines to eliminate the negative List B characteristics he experienced from his own abusive or absent father, he may go to another extreme and refuse to correct his children at all. That's the other extreme and doesn't represent God either.

Clearly, being a mean dad is wrong, but a godly father actually does give direction and correction to his children. Good fathers don't timidly tolerate and weakly facilitate all of their children's whims. Remember, fathers are to represent the Father, who by the Holy Spirit through the Word helps us to know His way and will that's best for each area of our lives. This is what the inChrist father does.

The Father doesn't say, "Whatever you all want to do on earth is fine with Me." No, then we would hurt ourselves and others. The Father is not out to win a popularity contest. He is nice. He is strong, and He knows what's right. He's just, and He has a purpose and plan that is best. Representing Him, a father will say, "Come on, we'll do this. This is where we're going." And His children follow Him.

Fathers, do not irritate and provoke your children to anger [do not exasperate them to resentment], but rear them [tenderly] in the training and discipline and the counsel and admonition of the Lord.

Ephesians 6:4 (AMPC)

Admonition means *general reproof, counseling against a fault, instruction in duties, caution, and direction.* It's important that we don't abuse our children in anger, but we do purposefully correct. Why? Because God corrects us in love. To abuse and overcorrect misrepresents God, but again, not to correct at all misrepresents Him as well.

Proverbs has much to say about instruction, reproof, and correction. It would be a worthwhile study for you to go through that book and highlight every time you come across these words: *Only a fool hates correction; a wise person actually craves it and loves it.* Why? Because a fool will defend his or her actions and doesn't want anybody to tell him or her anything different. A wise person says, "Tell me. Give it to me." Unless someone is broken, that person doesn't crave abuse, but correction, yes!

GODLY CORRECTION DEVELOPS KIDS TO LOVE CORRECTION.

Godly correction develops kids to love correction. This will help them esteem teachers, supervisors, and bosses and enable them to even turn negative criticism into productive correction and instruction. Ultimately, we must raise our children to cherish and respond to God the Father's correction.

Fathers, do not provoke your children lest they become discouraged.

Colossians 3:21

Discouraged means to be *disheartened, deprived of courage or confidence, depressed in spirit, dejected.* The instruction to fathers to not provoke their children is in both Ephesians and Colossians. The Holy Spirit made sure this was in the Bible, didn't He?

Crossing the Line

Teasing kids can be fun—fun for the father and the kids too. It makes for good and healthy bonding. However, there's a line that can be crossed when teasing isn't fun anymore. That line is when the teasing makes children mad or feel hopeless. Scriptures instruct fathers not to do that

YOUR GOAL AS A VISIBLE FATHER IS TO CONNECT YOUR CHILDREN WITH THE INVISIBLE FATHER.

because it will discourage their children and misrepresent God because He doesn't do that. Jesus was anointed with joy above all His companions, and as the Father's representative, this gives us a picture of the Father that's different than just being stern and austere. He's joyful!

A godly father loves his children and doesn't want to hurt them physically or emotionally. Children can be provoked and become discouraged with themselves and disillusioned with God through berating. Remember, your goal as a visible father is to connect your children with the invisible Father who loves them. Misrepresenting the Father will necessitate your children learn that God the Father is not like you, and it might require special ministry and anointing to restore them. But it doesn't have to be that way.

Frankly, it takes only a few minutes for a man to be a father. However, it takes the rest of that man's life to *be the father God wants to represent and image Him.* Representing Father God is an enormous responsibility and privilege! There's no way to accomplish this unless you know and remember that you are in Christ and part of what became new at your moment of salvation is the way you father. The old List B dad has passed away, and you are empowered from the inside as a father who represents and images God. That's who you are!

God's hand is not abusive, but neither is He "hands off." His voice to His children is not cruel, but neither is He silent. His eyes do not condemn, but neither are His eyes closed or distracted. No, God the Father instructs, trains, holds, embraces, and encourages. Look again at List A (page 278) that shows characteristics of God the Father—and the inChrist Father. This is God's intention, that by knowing and seeing you, your kids will see the Father.

A dad who continues to be Fathered by God and keeps learning from His example will speak as He speaks, correct as He corrects, and love as He loves.

CHAPTER 23

InChrist Woman

E ve, the first woman, ate of the fruit in the garden and then "helped" her husband fall by giving him the fruit and influencing him to eat it. Today, the inChrist woman helps and influences her husband, family, friends, and others to stand strong. Instead of bringing people down or making them fall, the inChrist woman is empowered to help people get up and be what God has made them to be.

God Values Women

Jesus taught about marriage, but women were never the subject of any of His teaching or comments. When He talked and interacted with women, He talked with them as individuals rather than a different gender. The way Jesus respected and showed compassion to women showed that God esteems them no less than men. Remember Jesus said, "If you've seen Me you've seen the Father." So, when we watch how Jesus interacted and spoke with women in the Gospels, we see the way God thinks and interacts with women dignifies them.

Here are some examples of Jesus' interactions with women that demonstrate how God values them.

The Woman at the Well – John 4

In Chapter 10, the woman at the well was one of the examples we considered of women in the Bible who influenced. Yet, we also see from this interaction that Jesus values women. Jesus talked to women, and in this case, He even talked to a woman with a terrible reputation. That's amazing! Think what the disciples must have thought when they came back from town and saw Jesus talking with this particular woman.

What is He doing? they wondered. This woman's life journey would have left her pretty degraded, so what was Jesus demonstrating when He entrusted her with one of the most revealing scriptures about God and how He wants to be worshipped? He is saying that she's not stupid or incapable of such enlightenment. He's saying that she is valuable—and valuable for more than just her body.

The woman who washed Jesus' feet with her tears – Luke 7:36-50

Jesus accepted extravagant worship expressed through two women who anointed him. A woman came to Him having an alabaster flask of very costly fragrant oil and poured it on His head as He sat at the table (Matthew 26:6-13). Jesus was anointed a second time by a "sinner" woman, who used her tears and ointment to wash his feet and dried them with her hair.

To understand the significance of what happened, picture the scene in your mind. This woman was "known" by men as immoral, and she came into a setting with only men, probably lounging around on cushions. Suddenly, she fell down at Jesus' feet and started kissing and crying over them. I think we all know there isn't anything that makes men more uncomfortable than crying women. So, here in the company of only men, a woman was crying over Jesus' feet. And it didn't get better—it got worse. The woman used her hair to dry His feet.

What Jesus did next was so amazing to me! This event happened in a company of men with all of them, no doubt, watching. It was common for servants to wash a guest's feet, but the woman was doing it in an uncommon way. Don't you know there would've been a temptation for Jesus to pull in His feet and say, "Go away! Somebody get her out of here." Or, I'm sure Jesus was tempted to look at some of the guys and roll his eyes to indicate, "This is so embarrassing!" Instead, Jesus defended the woman's actions, forgave her sins, and honored her publically.

God made women to be responsive to love, and women can be quite demonstrative in their worship in His presence, perhaps crying or dancing and whirling about. Men may be bold and demonstrative, too, like David dancing in the streets when the ark was brought to Jerusalem. Worship that is demonstrative makes other people uncomfortable if they're not also worshipping. Michel despised and was embarrassed by David's worship (2 Samuel 6:14-23).

But for this dear woman who attended to Jesus' feet, I love how Jesus dignified the moment and did not pull in His feet. He honored what she did and received her worship.

Tony and I have some women in our church who sometimes come up to the front in services to worship. Before Jesus came into their lives, they were so messed up. But now, they whirl about to give Jesus honor and glory, not caring what anyone thinks. No one else helped them when they were in their messes except Jesus. So if they want to dance about, I'm shouting, "Go girls! Go! You just dance. Jesus is receiving it." It's very precious in His eyes.

Woman caught in adultery – John 8:1-11

The Bible also tells of the woman caught in the act of adultery. Jesus didn't side with those who were about to stone her, but He perfectly represented God's thoughts and God's actions toward this woman. He did not accuse her nor did He excuse her. But His forgiveness lifted her above what she had done so she didn't have to continue in it or be defined by it.

First evangelists – Matthew 28:10

After Jesus was raised from the dead, the first people He commissioned were women. If you want an amazing event to be talked about, a woman typically won't disappoint. I say this humorously, but I still believe it's an accurate statement. Jesus knew He could count on these women who first saw Him and said, "Go tell My brethren you've seen Me."

A woman can keep a secret, but if you don't tell her it's a secret, it's probably one of the least expensive ways of publishing. Tell a woman! Praise God. We claim that. God made us ladies this way, but we just want to keep our mouths in List A and not List C.

CHAPTER 24

InChrist Wife

And the LORD God said, "It is not good that man should be alone;
I will make him a helper comparable to him."
Genesis 2:18

So Adam gave names to all cattle, to the birds of the air,
and to every beast of the field.

But for Adam there was not found a helper comparable to him.
Genesis 2:20

A Comparable Helper

After Adam had seen and named all of the creatures, it was apparent that none of them were comparable to him. In fact, in both these verses of scripture, it refers to woman as a *comparable helper*. Let's break that down so we can see what God intended in the wife.

A *comparable helper* comes from two Hebrew words, *ezer*[1] *k'negdo*, and actually has nothing to do with domestic things, although wives commonly function in that capacity. A wife who fits the description of e*zer kenegdo* is a *corresponding helper who has the strength to protect, to surround, to aid, help* and *support*. A wife is her husband's partner and counterpart,[2] his opposite and his mirror that reflects how he looks.

Let's look in particular at her unique design to mirror her husband—to reflect[3] him.

Mirror Mirror in My Arms

But we all with unveiled face beholding as in a mirror the glory of the Lord are being transformed into the same image from glory to glory just as by the Spirit of the Lord.

2 Corinthians 3:18

A WIFE IS HER HUSBAND'S PARTNER AND COUNTERPART, HIS OPPOSITE AND HIS MIRROR THAT REFLECTS HOW HE LOOKS.

This verse says we are being transformed by looking in the mirror of the glory of the Lord. What an amazing reality! You're transformed into what you're looking at, or in other words, you look like what you look at. This is very important as we bear in mind that God, the Creator, from the beginning made a woman to be a mirror to her husband. She was made to show him what he looks like, which at the time, were the gorgeous qualities of List A.

The tragedy is that both of them fell from the glory of God. How did this affect Eve, the wife? The woman still functions as a mirror because God made her for that purpose. But now she reflects what's broken. Remember, as we established earlier, he's cracked and so is she. She's a cracked mirror, reflecting a fractured man. Oh dear! As she reflects what's broken, it sounds more like this, "Adam, you're being arrogant and mean. You're so self-absorbed. You never listen." What's she doing? She's mirroring. What is she mirroring? The fractures.

Adam then sees himself through what Eve says, which keeps on confirming and re-confirming his faults. A woman's desire and intention when she says, "You're insensitive. You're being irresponsible. Can't you be more affectionate?" is to make the man stop demonstrating List B but instead demonstrate List A. But that's not the way to do it. All that does is reflect to him how terrible he is: *Yeah, that's horrible me. That's who I am. My help-mate is showing me how bad I am. I'm pretty much rubbish. That's who I am, all right. I'm just no good.*

Do you see that? Pretty sad, isn't it? Do you see that this is a cruel plan of the devil is to get a woman to sabotage her marriage and hurt the one she loves? What ends up happening is that he becomes bitter at the "mirror" who keeps telling him his faults even though she's telling him those things for the purpose of making him better. Of course, her being fractured herself makes it worse yet.

Nag Drag

Then he said to the woman, "...And you will desire to control your husband...."

Genesis 3:16 (NLT)

Remember, in this portion of scripture, God was describing to the serpent and Adam and Eve the particular curses each of them would experience as a result of their part in the transgression. For Eve, the tendency to nag, fault find, and control would be a curse to her—and Adam also. This is not the only tendency that started as a result of the fall. There's more.

Genesis 3:16b gives us another way this can be interpreted, *"To the woman he said, '...your desire shall be to your husband and he shall rule over you.'"* Part of how Eve would be affected is that her husband would have rule over her. That's not a blessing—but a curse and something else that resulted from the fall.

But why is the woman's "desire to her husband" a curse? Wouldn't that be a good thing? Part of the damage Eve sustained in the fall is that she "needs." She *needs* reassurance, she *needs* help, she *needs* comfort, and she *needs* to be lifted up, and she looks to Adam to give her what she *needs*. Her desire for fulfillment is on Adam to supply, so she begins pulling on him, "I need! I want!" Then if he doesn't give what she needs, she demands more.

This tendency isn't experienced in only one culture, but it's common the world over. But here's the weird thing. This "need for more" often begins even before a couple marries. A woman will start demanding more and more of a man to be what she needs. Actually, she will demand that the man be *all* she needs—to be what only God could be. How suffocating and frustrating!

Think about it. If you're walking along and someone hangs heavily on your arm, what do you want to do after a while? Honestly? You probably will have an urge to push that person's hand away, but when you do, it gets even worse. The person grabs on and drags even harder. If you're trying to walk forward, that person hanging on is *not* a blessing. It's not helping. It's hanging. Get it?

The woman's "desire toward her husband" is also that she looks to him to be the image that she was created to reflect. There is something hard-wired in her to reflect God, and originally, that image was visible in Adam. Post fall that's no longer the case. So, the woman starts demanding and demanding more. She begins nagging.

This odd and wearisome tendency is a part of the curse of the fall. It's not a curse that God pronounced like, "Now, I curse you." No. God identified that this tendency and fracture would be a curse in the dynamic of marriage, and is that *ever* the case.

In order to deal with a woman's continual nagging, it's common for the husband to ignore her or put her down under His control. And the more that happens, the more she demands. This only incites bitterness in the man. At this point, the woman needs her husband but refuses to submit to him. We've already described this ugly cycle in Chapter 21.

Is there hope? Yes! A wife's ability to help her husband was sabotaged in the fall but it's restored in Christ. Ladies, identify yourself by saying, "I'm an inChrist wife. Instead of nagging my husband, I freely give to him, because I freely receive God's strength." I don't have to give my husband what Eve gave Adam—the fruit of the knowledge of what's wrong and what's right. Instead, because the roots of my life are in Christ, the fruit of the Spirit are all available to my husband.

Submit as to Christ

Our hope for breaking out of this cycle is not found in Adam but found in Christ. The Bible provides specific instruction for the inChrist wife. Let's see what it says.

Ephesians 5:22 says, "Wives, *submit* to your own husbands *as to the Lord.*" Notice the words *as* or *hoce,* which mean *in the same way or manner* you would submit to the Lord, you should submit to your own husbands.

Ephesians 5:24 "Therefore, just *as the church* is to *submit* to Christ so let the wives be to their own husbands in everything." Encouragement to submit appears once again.

Ephesians 5:25b "...let the wife see that she *respects* her husband." This verse doesn't use the word *submit.* Instead, it says a wife is to see that she respects her husband (we will return to this point.)

Colossians 3:18 says, "Wives, *submit* yourselves unto your own husbands as it is fit in the Lord." The instruction to submit is the same in this sister book of Colossians.

GOD'S KIND OF LOVE CAN LOVE WHEN THERE'S NO FEELING AT ALL.

Titus 2:4 says, "So that they will wisely train the young women to be sane and sober of mind, temperate and disciplined *to love* their husbands and their children." Here in the verse, younger wives are to be taught to love their husbands. Really? Does this actually have to be *taught?* Obviously, this scripture must not be referring to a gushy feeling or twitterpated-type of love. No, this is talking about teaching a wife how to love like God created her to love her husband. God's kind of love can love when there's no feeling at all.

You must be taught to love this way. It doesn't come by hormones and chemistry. It doesn't come by sentiment. And it doesn't come as a reaction to flowers or perfume. You must be taught in the Lord how to love as an inChrist wife. The Holy Spirit can help you learn. The apostle Paul was also saying that women who have learned how to love like this are to teach younger wives the art of this love.

Here's yet another scripture instructing wives to submit. Titus 2:5 says "to live wisely and be pure, to work in their homes, to do good, and to be *submissive* to their husbands. Then they will not bring shame on the word of God" (NLT). Read the last phrase of that verse again: "*Then they will not bring shame on the word of God.*" Wow. It doesn't matter how super spiritual a woman is with spiritual gifts, speaking ability, prayer, and ministry to people. A woman who does not respect and honor her husband sets up the Word of God to be blasphemed. That's awful. It's an honor to the Word and to God Himself for a wife to be subject to her husband and respectful to him.

Here's the deal. It may not be easy for a husband to love his wife when she is not the way he wants her to be. He may think, *If she would just do this or that. I'd like her to look a certain way. I don't like the way she talks. She needs to stop doing this and do that. If she'll do this better, then I'll love her.*" No! That's a List B characteristic—it's certainly not in Christ.

The inChrist man loves. Period. He loves and gives Himself. He pours out his love even before he gives any kind of correction or direction at all—love, love, love. Why? Because that's the way Jesus does it. That's the way Jesus loves the Church—that's the way Jesus loves. In the same way that love is the bottom line for men, being subject and submissive is the bottom line for women. The truth is, being submissive wouldn't have been repeated so much in the Scriptures if it came easily to women. I don't know a woman on the planet who believes this always comes naturally.

There may be subservient women who just do what they must do because they are slaves, but that kind of woman is so inglorious to a man. When a man treats his wife like a slave, it's pathetically ugly. There's no glory for that man. He may look arrogant and powerful but not at all glorious.

My husband, Tony, had an uncle who would tell his wife to walk behind him. That was the culture of the town he came from in Italy years ago. So, sometimes when I'm with Tony in the mall, he tells me to walk behind him in an Italian accent. It makes me laugh, because I know he's teasing me by imitating his uncle. But in cases where it's not a joke but reality, the man who degrades and diminishes a woman is never glorious. He's robbed himself of his own glory by acting like that.

On the other hand, not honoring and submitting to a husband makes a woman inglorious as well. Why is submitting so difficult for a woman to do? One reason is fear—fear of being controlled, fear of being misrepresented to other people, and fear of never getting what she wants and needs. In fact, fear is the basis for a woman's desire to control, which isn't confined to her husband. It goes beyond that, directed to her children, friends, and others.

Look at this translation of *Genesis 3:16b* where we see the beginning of control and manipulation: "...and you will desire to control your husband, but he will rule over you" (NLT).

Perfect love is found in Christ, and what does perfect love do? It casts out fear. In other words, when a man gives perfect love—not conditional but unconditional love—it will cast out the fear of submitting, and his wife will be freer to submit. Yet, when a husband acts like List B, it can be scary to submit to him.

Breaking the Cycle

Why would God give direction to women to submit to their husbands if it's so difficult and scary to do? Because submission has the ability to break the cycle.

When a man gets his love from God to love his wife—even when she's not doing, looking, and being what is needed to merit his love—that God-given love will help her submit, which will make her more loveable.

In the same way, where will the woman get the perfect love that casts out the fear of submitting to a man who has serious fractures and isn't loving to her? If she waits until everything is lovely, nothing will ever change. She will have to stop reflecting her husband's List B characteristics. That's a time waster. Instead, she must trust and draw on the perfect love that comes from God and reflect what God says about her husband.

Faith in God, not her husband's perfections, enables a wife to submit. God watches over that kind of trust. He personally works with that woman, not to submit like a degraded slave, but to submit as an expression of her trust in God. God can work with a woman like that.

Aren't we thankful for redemption? It is not just about heaven and healing; redemption also restores the sexes and the roles those genders play.

Notes

1 *Ezer kenegdo* is a *corresponding helper* who has the *power* and *strength to protect, to surround, to aid, to help to support and to succor.* She is his match, an equal partner a counterpart to man, his opposite and his mirror that reflects who he is and how he looks like. *Woman, God's Undercover Agent Vol 1*, Margaret Kamuwanga, BookVenture Publishing LLC, Ishpeming, MI 2017.

2 In the Hebrew language the word *neged* literally refers to *something in from of or in the presence of another.* The root word *neged...refers to rulers and leaders in the Old Testament.* The word in Genesis, however, is altered by the prefix *k*, which refers to *some type of similarity or comparison.* So, the word appears to refer *to someone similar to, yet in front of ha-adam*, almost as if the earth being is looking into a mirror image of itself. The phrase indicates that God intends to fashion another creature who will not be inferior or superior to *ha-adam*, but rather one with whom *ha-adam* can share a relationship of total equality. *Kenegdo* is the Hebrew phrase for *helpmeet* or *helper fit for* in Genesis is *Ezer Kenegdo*, which means *help, a power, or a force...*the second part of *kenegdo* implies opposite. The impression is a mirror image. *A Blessing for the Heart: God's Beautiful Plan for Marital Intimacy*, James E Sheridan Marriage Done Right Publisher, 2004. Used with Permission.

3 With the creation of Eve, Adam had a mirror in which to see himself, a creature with whom to compare and complete himself. To be fully human, thereafter, Adam and Eve needed each other. That is what was signified in the phrase *one-flesh union* between and man and a woman...
The Hebrew phrase *ezer kenegdo* is usually translated as *someone suitable*, a *help meet* or even a *help mate*. But properly it means that the woman is a helper who is like the man, who corresponds to him, who is suitable for and needed by him. *From Sacrament to Contract, Second Edition: Marriage, Religion and Law in the Western Tradition,* John Witte Jr, Westminster John Knox Press, Louisville, KY, 2012, pp 33-34. Used with permission.

CHAPTER 25

Without Words

1 In like manner, you married women, be submissive to your own husbands [subordinate yourselves as being secondary to and dependent on them, and adapt yourselves to them], so that even if any do not obey the Word [of God], they may be won over not by discussion but by the [godly] lives of their wives, 2 When they observe the pure and modest way in which you conduct yourselves, together with your reverence [for your husband; you are to feel for him all that reverence includes: to respect, defer to, revere him—to honor, esteem, appreciate, prize, and, in the human sense, to adore him, that is, to admire, praise, be devoted to, deeply love, and enjoy your husband].³ Let not yours be the [merely] external adorning with [elaborate] interweaving and knotting of the hair, the wearing of jewelry, or changes of clothes;⁴ But let it be the inward adorning and beauty of the hidden person of the heart, with the incorruptible and unfading charm of a gentle and peaceful spirit, which [is not anxious or wrought up, but] is very precious in the sight of God.⁵ For it was thus that the pious women of old who hoped in God were [accustomed] to beautify themselves and were submissive to their husbands [adapting themselves to them as themselves secondary and dependent upon them].⁶ It was thus that Sarah obeyed Abraham [following his guidance and

acknowledging his headship over her by] calling him lord (master, leader, authority). And you are now her true daughters if you do right and let nothing terrify you [not giving way to hysterical fears or letting anxieties unnerve you].

1 Peter 3:1-6 (AMPC)

A WIFE WILL NEVER REALLY CHANGE HER HUSBAND'S HEART BY NAGGING.

This passage is usually considered to be written to wives regarding husbands who are not yet born again, but because it says, "if *any* refuse to obey the Good News" the scope of application is broader. This can also be applied to husbands who are born again, but who just aren't obeying the Word in an area.

What should a wife do? Should she nag her husband, tell him what he's doing wrong, what to do to be right, and reflect his ugly List B characteristics to him? No, that is a default first-Adam reaction. What makes a woman even more dangerously problematic is when she knows from God's Word the way things are supposed to be and uses these truths to nag her husband. Instead of submitting, she preaches: "Now that is really ugly!" and gets terrible results. What should she do instead?

These verses in 1 Peter 3 explain plainly what an inChrist wife is to do instead of nagging. Verse 1 says "…so that even if any do not obey the Word [of God], they may be won over *not by discussion* but by the [godly] lives of their wives…."

A wife will never really change her husband's heart by nagging and preaching to him what he must do, so put less time there. It would be better for the wife to put time toward getting something from God that enables her to move into a meek and quiet spirit. Remember Eve "helped" Adam to fall through her influence. Now, in Christ we help "our Adam" stand but not by telling him what he should and shouldn't do.

Notice the instruction again from verse 2: "When they observe the pure and modest way in which you conduct yourself." Let me just expose a common train of thought here that a wife might have: *Okay, I won't say anything. I'll just do what's right, and my husband will see my example and "get it."* So, she goes her way setting a good example while watching to see if her husband notices. She thinks, *Husband, I'm not saying anything, but notice what I'm doing. Learn something!* Wives, I've got bad news! Guys are onto that. They're smart. Tony told me one time, "I know what you're doing." I thought I was being so clever and godly, but he saw it as manipulative. And it was.

InChrist wives, we've got to use the entire 1 Peter 3 recipe if we're going to get it to work. It says, "That they may be won over, not by discussion, but by the godly lives of the wives when they observe the pure and modest way in which you conduct yourselves...." Keep reading because there's still more in the recipe! "...together with your reverence" (verse 2). The godly way that you live alone is not enough, like flour alone doesn't make a cake. No. Your godliness must be combined with reverence for your husband as well.

Verse 2 in The Amplified Bible, Classic Edition describes what reverence looks like. "...You are to feel for him all that reverence includes: to respect, defer to, revere him—to honor, esteem, appreciate, prize, and, in the human sense, to adore him, that is, to admire, praise, be devoted to, deeply love, and enjoy your husband]." I think a man wrote the Amplified Bible, at least this portion of it. Don't you reckon?

Why in the world is a woman to do this? God made a man to respond to being esteemed and adored. Why? Because *He* does. Heartfelt worship moves Him. A man responds to respect. There is a similar list in Ephesians 5:33 (AMP) that we looked at earlier. Showing our husbands respect in this way is what inChrist wives do.

Initially, this kind of respect may not be easy, especially if you honestly don't see qualities in your husband to respect. Don't hesitate to ask God. He will show you something true about your husband that you aren't seeing on your own. There may be a gift or quality buried in your husband that you've never yet seen, but God will show it to you so you can honor and respect it. The accuser of the brethren, the devil, will only show you things on List B. But the Holy Spirit will show you what List A characteristics you are to look at and respectfully reflect.

Don't limit your sweet words of honor and respect to generic remarks like, "Honey, I love you. I respect you." Worship becomes more intimate and less generic to God when, like David, we specifically identify what it is we're worshipping about God. Wives, we are to interact with our husband as we do with the Lord. In the same way, communicate the specific things you respect about your husband.

POUR PRAISE ON YOUR HUSBAND LIKE THE WOMAN POURED OIL ON JESUS.

The same goes for admiring your husband. Identifying each quality allows you to name them and what he genuinely is to you is far more meaningful than a cliché remark. Don't just think it. Speak it in the same way powerful worship is expressed in word and action to the Lord. Give it. Pour praise on your husband like the woman poured oil on Jesus. Don't offer up "ice cube" praise. Be fervent with your praise and turn it up.

The Right Clothes

3 Don't be concerned about the outward beauty of fancy hairstyles, expensive jewelry, or beautiful clothes. 4 You should clothe yourselves instead with the beauty that comes from within, the unfading beauty of a gentle and quiet spirit, which is so precious to God. 5 This is how the holy women of old made themselves beautiful. They trusted God and accepted the authority of their husbands.

1 Peter 3:3-5 (NLT)

This is a powerful portion of scripture: *"You should clothe yourselves from the beauty that comes from within."* Doesn't this remind you of what we looked at in Chapter 19 concerning what the Bible tells us to puff off and put on? These scriptures make abundantly clear what to put off and what to put on, in case you don't know what to wear.

Something I miss with my daughters living away from us is that they would tell me what to wear and not to wear. I'd have an outfit on and ask them, "What do you think?"

"No, don't wear that. That doesn't look good. Put this on instead. That looks right!" they would say. So, I would always check with them. Even now on Facetime I can still check with them, because when I ask their father what he thinks, he most of the time says, "Ask the girls!"

But when it comes to spiritual things in your own life, you can check the "put on, put off verses" for quick reference[1]. Or, you may also ask the Holy Spirit what to put on and put off. He tells you the truth about the spiritual clothes you're wearing. If you've got something on that is not becoming to you and does not glorify Him, He'll tell you the truth. You may call it something else because you've worn it so long, but He'll tell you the actual truth. He will tell you, "Put that off! Actually, I've put something in your closet (your heart) that would really be nice for you to wear."

Look at the New King James translation of these verses:

3 Do not let your adornment be merely outward—arranging the hair, wearing gold, or putting on fine apparel— 4 rather let it be the hidden person of the heart, with the incorruptible beauty of a gentle and quiet spirit, which is very precious in the sight of God. 5 For in this manner, in former times, the holy women who trusted in God also adorned themselves, being submissive to their own husbands.

1 Peter 3:3-5

Notice the wording of verse 4 again, "…rather let it be the hidden person of the heart," which is what you want to put on. This hidden person, the inChrist woman or inChrist wife, is one who knows what to wear and, on purpose, adorns herself. She takes time to get dressed. Any of us can throw something on, but if we're going to look right, we must choose what we will wear and put it on purposefully.

This verse goes on to describe exactly what a woman is to choose to put on:

"…a gentle and quiet spirit." Different translations will give different words here, so let's look at the original words in Greek to see exactly what these clothes look like.

Gentle[2] – Greek – *praus* - *warm, forbearing, patient, kind, and gentle; opposite of angry, temperamental or exploding with anger*

Beautiful gentleness would be perfect for anybody, men or women.

Quiet³ – Greek – *hesuchios* – *depicts a person who knows how to calm herself and maintain a state of peace and tranquility*

You definitely have to get peace and tranquility from God, and then put it on. You can't get this quality from friends. You don't get it from a peaceful environment. You don't get this quality from having a perfect husband. And you don't get it from perfect surroundings.

Most people can be calm if their situation is calm and peaceful. But if you get a wrinkle in your situation, and you don't have these godly "clothes" on, you will get plenty wrinkled yourself. You will end up mirroring your situation rather than changing your situation.

As we described earlier, before Esther went in to see the king, she and her maids fasted and prayed. She asked Mordecai to have all the Jews pray for her as well. Then, after praying three days, Esther 5:1 says she put on her royal robes. But what Esther received from God during the time of prayer made her so exquisitely attractive that without a word spoken, the king offered her one half of his kingdom.

What's interesting is that these verses of scripture say these qualities are valuable in the sight of God. What could be valuable to God when He paves heaven's streets with gold? Each of the twelve gates of the city is a massive pearl. What would be valuable and precious to God that you could possibly give to Him?

What is absolutely valuable to God is a woman with a quiet and gentle spirit, because He can work with this person. This woman can be in a really negative situation, but she knows how to calm herself. There's something from within that keeps her calm, and she doesn't get hysterical and break down. God says "I don't have to work around this woman and the collateral damage she creates. She is helping Me help her husband."

Let me tell you something important! It's impossible to wear these "clothes" if you don't spend time with God. Because of the way women are made up, if you don't make time to put on these clothes, you'll end up mirroring the people around you. That can be chaotic. But if you get into the presence of God and start reflecting Him, His reflection will overshadow and bring something bright into every environment and relationship you touch. Make a difference. Bring God in.

I love what this passage goes on to say in verse 5, "This is how, long ago, holy women who put their hope in God made themselves beautiful: by respecting the authority of their husbands" (Voice). By trusting God, holy women in the Old Testament beautified themselves with a gentle and quiet spirit. If we don't have these two qualities, it means we're not trusting God and are probably in fear, anger, or frustration. But there's a rest when you're absolutely trusting God (Hebrews 4:3a, 10).

Don't you find it interesting that these verses don't instruct you to trust your husband? What if trusting your husband is a problem because he has lied, disappointed, or was unfaithful to you or in some way hasn't been reliable?

Then notice, the Bible doesn't call on you to trust your husband. It calls on you to trust God, and He is worthy of that trust. Submission to your husband is leveraged on your trust of God, not your husband. Listen to this! Your ability to submit is your part in creating a gorgeous marriage. Even if your husband isn't loving to you, you can still break the vicious cycle by trusting God.

Trust activates the hand of God in your husband's life, but your manipulation hinders God's hand. If you want God to talk into his life, then shut up. Shut the manipulation and nagging down and talk to God instead. Trust God, and He will talk to your husband. You're not the first woman to have to do this. Holy women all the way back in the Old Testament who trusted God walked this way.

First Peter 2:24 is one of the great healing verses of the Bible, but let's look at the context this verse is in:

> 18 You who are slaves must submit to your masters with all respect. Do what they tell you—not only if they are kind and reasonable, but even if they are cruel. 19 For God is pleased when, conscious of his will, you patiently endure unjust treatment. 20 Of course, you get no credit for being patient if you are beaten for doing wrong. But if you suffer for doing good and endure it patiently, God is pleased with you. 21 For God called you to do good, even if it means suffering, just as Christ suffered for you. He is your example, and you must follow in his steps. 22 He never sinned, nor ever deceived anyone. 23 He did not retaliate when he was

insulted, nor threaten revenge when he suffered. He left his case in the hands of God, who always judges fairly. 24 He personally carried our sins in his body on the cross so that we can be dead to sin and live for what is right. By his wounds you are healed. 25 Once you were like sheep who wandered away. But now you have turned to your Shepherd, the Guardian of your souls....

1 Peter 2:18-24 (NLT)

Peter wasn't finished, so let's keep reading into the next chapter:

In the same way, wives, you should patiently accept the authority of your husbands.

1 Peter 3:1-2 (NLT)

It's all in the same breath. In the same way that Jesus committed Himself to God who judges righteously, he tells wives to submit to husbands. So, let me just ask a question: How has it turned out for Jesus? Did God leave Jesus in hell? Did God leave Jesus in His situation to rot? No. Who raised Jesus from the dead? *God* raised Jesus from the dead by the glory of the Holy Spirit.

But the reason why Jesus was poised and positioned to be raised from the dead is because He committed Himself in trust to God. Jesus didn't trust the Roman soldiers. Jesus didn't trust His disciples, and He didn't put His trust in His family at the foot of the cross. No, He said, "Into *Your* hands I commit my spirit." God went to work for Him. And when Jesus was raised and purchased our redemption, even the ones who deserted Him, the ones who mocked Him, and the ones who crucified Him were included.

TRUST GIVES THRUST TO THE PLAN OF GOD.

What would happen if you didn't seek to achieve justice for yourself? What would happen if you trusted and leaned into God, saying, "Okay, God. This isn't going to be right unless you fix it. I'm trusting You." I want to go to my grave having a banner on my life saying, 'I trusted God.'" Trust activates the hand of God. Trust gives thrust to the plan of God.

In the end, you don't want your husband to do just whatever you want. "Honey, do this. Honey, stop doing that." You'll make him a mouse. That's not glorious. He's supposed to be the most magnificent of all God's creatures. You don't want to be ordering him around, so he spends his life taking orders, do you? You don't want that! You want him to be the glory of God—a man of God.

InChrist wife, you'll need to back out and work *with* God—instead of trying to *be* God. Talk when He wants you to talk. Zip it when He doesn't. Why you do that isn't because you're so under the boot in fear. Why you do that is because you trust God. God will turn up the heat and amplify His voice in your situation. Your faith in God—not your husband—activates God's hand regarding your husband. Isn't that better? It connects that man with God.

Do you know what happens then? Your husband starts looking glorious! When you see that start happening, your heart goes, "Oooh, I love my husband! He is amazing and looking good!" Then a new cycle begins because that kind of reverence unlocks a heart of love from a man, and it's easier for him to love with a heart that's been opened by respect.

A husband can love anyway if he gets that love from God, and a woman can submit even before her husband is loving. It's just easier when the husband is loving and the wife is submitting and respecting. Do you see how it's *supposed* to be? But we don't have to wait on, "Well, if my husband would just…." Or, "Well, if my wife would just…." Don't wait on one or the other. You do your part, and it begins changing the perpetual cycle.

First Peter 3:5 says that she's in subjection. Peter is saying the same thing Paul said. So, in the same way, that love from the husband can break the cycle, the wife's submission can also stop the vicious cycle that sabotages a glorious marriage.

How is that? Neither spouse has to wait on the other one to act first. If you're the man in a situation and you want to break the ugly cycle, *love!* If you're the woman in an ugly situation, *respect and submit!* Isn't that amazing? Both the inChrist husband and inChrist wife require connection with God to be able to do what God intended and create a marriage that reflects Christ and the Church.

Don't Lose Your Keys

There are two essential keys that God has given to a wife. One key opens her husband's heart, and the other opens his emotions.

God made reverence to be the key that opens a man's heart and that's where his purpose is. You don't want anyone else with this key. As a wife, you want to be the one who most reverences your husband. You want to be able to say, "People love and appreciate my husband, but I have the key." Don't you lose your key and let somebody else pick it up. Don't leave your key around. Use your key! Reverence your husband and open his heart.

The other key is actually the sexual relationship. You be the one who has this key and uses it. Don't lose this key either! While respect opens his heart, sex is a key that opens the emotions—the soul. Obviously, you don't want anybody else to have that key. Sometimes men will close up in different ways. If you want them to open up in their soul more, then give to them in that area. It will help them be open in the soul.

Keys are very personal, so keep them in a safe place, and *use* them!

Notes

1 Romans 13:12; 1 Corinthians 15:53-54; Galatians 3:27; Ephesians 4:24; 6:11

2 *Praus* – Vine's Expository Dictionary of New Testament Words – G4239 "…It must be clearly understood, therefore, that the meekness manifested by the Lord and commended to the believer is the fruit of power. The common assumption is that when a man is meek it is because he cannot help himself; but the Lord was 'meek' because he had the infinite resources of God at His command. …It is one of the most power-filled words in the entire Bible."

3 *Hesuchios* – Strong's Concordance 2272 – *hésuchios: tranquil* – Original Word: ἡσύχιος, α, ον
Definition: *quiet, tranquil, peaceful.*

CHAPTER 26

InChrist Mother

The role of motherhood in its creative design is beautiful and strong. Even in the animal kingdom, the instinct of a mother is notable. And yet, as we've already established, every role including this one was fractured in the fall. What does an inChrist mother look like? What instruction is given so this role represents and images God? Let's see.

Taught to Love

That they may admonish the young women…to love their children.

Titus 2:4

Why would the Bible say that mothers need to be taught to love their children? Wouldn't that just be her instinct? You don't have to tell a mother, generally, to love her children. But a mother's own love can also be selfish, and she can put selfish expectations on her child to fulfill her own desires, dreams, and needs. This hurts and confuses her child. That's why this verse of scripture tells older women who have learned the difference between their love and God's love to teach younger mothers how to love their children.

As strong as a mother's love is, divine love is stronger yet. Here's a powerful prayer to increase in this kind of love:

1 Paul and Timothy, bond servants of Christ Jesus (the Messiah), to all the saints (God's consecrated people) in Christ Jesus who are at Philippi, with the bishops (overseers) and deacons (assistants): 2 Grace (favor and blessing) to you and [heart] peace from God our Father and the Lord Jesus Christ (the Messiah). 3 I thank my God in all my remembrance of you. 4 In every prayer of mine I always make my entreaty and petition for you all with joy (delight). 5 [I thank my God] for your fellowship (your sympathetic cooperation and contributions and partnership) in advancing the good news (the Gospel) from the first day [you heard it] until now. 6 And I am convinced and sure of this very thing, that He Who began a good work in you will continue until the day of Jesus Christ [right up to the time of His return], developing [that good work] and perfecting and bringing it to full completion in you. 7 It is right and appropriate for me to have this confidence and feel this way about you all, because you have me in your heart and I hold you in my heart as partakers and sharers, one and all with me, of grace (God's unmerited favor and spiritual blessing). [This is true] both when I am shut up in prison and when I am out in the defense and confirmation of the good news (the Gospel). 8 For God is my witness how I long for and pursue you all with love, in the tender mercy of Christ Jesus [Himself]! 9 And this I pray: that your love may abound yet more and more and extend to its fullest development in knowledge and all keen insight [that your love may display itself in greater depth of acquaintance and more comprehensive discernment], 10 So that you may surely learn to sense what is vital, and approve and prize what is excellent and of real value [recognizing the highest and the best, and distinguishing the moral differences], and that you may be untainted and pure and unerring and blameless [so that with hearts sincere and certain and unsullied, you may approach] the day of Christ [not stumbling nor causing others to stumble]. 11 May you abound in and be filled with the fruits of righteousness (of right standing

194

with God and right doing) which come through Jesus Christ (the Anointed One), to the honor and praise of God [that His glory may be both manifested and recognized].

Philippians 1:9-11 (AMPC)

God's love helps you make right and unselfish choices in your words to your kids, the way that you interact, your facial expressions, and other reactions. Love governs you.

A MOTHER IS MUCH LIKE A THERMOSTAT ON THE WALL OF A HOME.

Thermostat

A mother is much like a thermostat on the wall of a home. Her temperament or the "temperature" of her soul will set and establish the atmosphere of the home. For instance, if the mother is a cold and cranky person, that house will have a cold and cranky atmosphere. Or, she can let the peace of God rule her, and when it does, it will rule the house. Basically, whatever influences the mother[1] will be an influence in the house.

Lois and Eunice's Faith

I remember your genuine faith, for you share the faith that first filled your grandmother Lois and your mother, Eunice. And I know that same faith continues strong in you.

2 Timothy 1:5 (NLT)

Paul apparently knew Eunice and Lois, Timothy's grandma and mother. He observed that the same quality of faith he saw in his grandmother and mother was also in him. This faith was not something passed down in Adam or in the natural bloodline. No, it was something they lived personally and were purposeful in transmitting to Timothy. One of the obvious ways to communicate something to someone is verbally, but there can be other ways to transmit things, such as touch and example. For sure this mother and grandmother influenced Timothy's life with their own faith, and it impacted who he became.

Dominion

A woman's house is "her garden." Along with the natural cleaning and the settling of the home, a mother can maintain the right and peaceful spiritual climate too. Jesus has restored authority to the inChrist mother for her to make sure unseen, devilish influences are unwelcome. Taking authority over the devil doesn't need to be done in front of everybody, because they aren't who she's talking to anyway. After everyone's gone or in bed, mom can put her foot down and say, "Let me just tell you what it's going to be like, Mr. Devil. This is my house, and you're not welcome here."

Preparing Children for the Future

From meals to major moves, it's common for a mother to be thinking and preparing ahead of time. Her body is even made to be a safe place for the body of a baby to be prepared for birth into this world.

The Holy Spirit is a Great Preparer, and the mother was made to image His qualities. He works ahead of time on all the details, and everyone involved in all of God's plans. One of the most important and fulfilling things an inChrist mother can do is work together with the Holy Spirit to prepare her children for their future.

Look how Hannah's prayer illustrates this:

And she made this vow: "O Lord of Heaven's Armies, if you will look upon my sorrow and answer my prayer and give me a son, then I will give him back to you. He will be yours for his entire lifetime, and as a sign that he has been dedicated to the Lord, his hair will never be cut."

1 Samuel 1:11 (NLT)

Wow, you can really give your child to the Lord? Yes, that's what dedicating a baby means. I believe if a parent really means it when they have their baby dedicated, God puts a claim on that child and shows them how to work in collaboration for the rearing and training of that child for His purposes. By way of dedication, God is given the right to say how that babe is raised and exposed, so they hit their mark. Dedication is not a religious ritual, but it's an absolutely real transaction when a child is dedicated to the Lord like Samuel was.

Hannah wanted a son, and God needed a prophet. God hadn't had one in a while, and He had no prophetic voice on the earth at the time. God did have a priest, Eli, who didn't serve Him responsibly. Eli's sons, who also were priests, consistently misrepresented God. So, when God needed a prophet and this mother desired a man child, their desires were both met in Samuel.

Yet, Hannah gave Samuel back to the Lord. In a sense she gave him to eternity. There are many people who have lived and died on the earth making very little eternal impact at all. They came and went. But Samuel was given to the Lord, and we're still affected by the fact that he anointed King David. Amazing!

HANNAH GAVE HER SON TO THE WILL OF GOD.

Hannah gave her son to the will of God. Her aspirations for him were only to fulfill God's will. By releasing a child to God's purposes, should the child stay or return will be a choice between the child and God and not because of obligation, fear, or manipulation.

My mother gave all five of her children to God and knew that the calls on our lives would require each of us to live away from her. What a champion she is to me of a mom with no whinge and whine in her voice at all—none—zero. She's only full of happiness and curiosity of what God is doing in all her family's lives. I'd say she's a very rich woman—rich because her children belong to God.

When my mother had opportunities to feel as though her heart was being torn out, but she would go to God. His grace would enable her to be an inChrist mother for God, and her example is helping me now as my own girls are grown and must be free to follow God.

Strength and dignity are her clothing and her position is strong and secure; she rejoices over the future [the latter day or time to come, knowing that *she and her family are in readiness for it*]!
Proverbs 31:25 (AMPC)

Notes

1 The Hebrew word for *mother* אֵם *(em)* is the same as the word *if* אִם *(im)*. If the mother is pious, in all probability, the children will take after her. The mother is the big "if" of family life. In her hands is the future fate of her children.

In religious law, the child takes after the identity of his or her mother. For the child to be considered Jewish, it is the maternal genealogy that is primary. As the mother goes, so goes the child." *The Secrets of Hebrew Words,* Rabbi Benjamin Blech, Rowman & Littlefield Publishers, Lanham, Maryland 1991, p160. Used by permission.

CHAPTER 27

InChrist Marriage

Like every role we've looked at so far that was broken in the fall, God's intention for marriage is to image the faithful and loving Christ as the responsive and glorifying Church does as well. Redemption addressed everything that broke, including marriage.

> **Two are better than one because they have a good reward for their labor.**
>
> **Ecclesiastes 4:9**

When I was in my early 20s, I set out on a missions trip to India. I got as far as Rome, and due to some complications, I ended up staying in Europe by myself to minister in a few churches. There was a dear Italian couple who could hardly speak English, and they would drop me off to look at various famous sites. So, there I was, by myself, at the Colosseum and Venice and other amazing places. By the time that trip was over, I made a vow to myself I would never come back there alone. You need somebody to experience it with; Italy should never be viewed alone.

I did go back to Italy on my honeymoon with Tony. We went to the same places I had gone to by myself, and yes, two are definitely better than one! In other words, you have somebody to "ooh and ah" with, because good and joy are sweeter when shared.

If challenges of life come, and they do, to have someone to share them with means you can encourage one another toward triumph. And when the triumph comes, you can rejoice together.

The book of Proverbs put it this way:

Whoever finds a wife finds a good thing and obtains favor of the Lord.

Proverbs 18:22

Husband, have you ever told your wife, "You are my good thing!"?

This verse does not only say you, husbands, find a good thing, it goes on to say you find favor with the Lord. You already have favor, but when you find a wife, you get extra favor from God. There may be times when the relationship doesn't look like God's favor, especially if your mirror (wife) is reflecting all your faults. You're thinking, *Is this woman a good thing or a bad thing?* But, praise the Lord, by breaking the cycle we discussed in previous chapters, she can become the mirror you need her to be and really magnify the favor of the Lord in your life.

Husbands, start calling your wife a good thing. Claim it! "My wife's a good thing, and I have favor through her." Your faith will activate this truth, and you can respond in love to that truth rather than her actions.

The Greek word *agape* refers most often to the God-kind of love. I actually love the Hebrew as well, which is *ahava*[1]. It's based on the word *hav* which means *to give*. It's so completely different than emotional feelings of "He's got the most gorgeous eyes, and he gave me perfume. I love him." Or, "I love the way she cooks," or "I love the way she looks," or anything superficial like that. God's love isn't about what the other person gives you. That's not love in the Hebrew meaning of the word. Love isn't what you *get* from somebody; love is what you *give them*. I think that's so powerful.

Think about this. Jewish marriages have the lowest divorce rate[2]. Could this Hebrew meaning for love actually give Jewish couples an advantage? When they go into marriage and pledge their love to one another, it doesn't have to do with feelings or expectations of what that spouse will give to them. No! Pledging to love your spouse for the rest of their life means pledging to *give* to that person. Do you see the difference it makes? Wow.

Imagine how glorious a couple would be when both individuals are not taking but giving. Glorious indeed! You may say, "Well, I don't have that. It seems like I'm always the one giving, and my spouse is always the one taking." Yet, if you'll give according to being the inChrist wife and the inChrist husband, it's not just a giving of yourself, but it's a giving of God. It infuses God into the relationship, and it's the way to break a cycle of taking.

If you go into marriage looking for "something that I need," it's so pathetic. You're going in the wrong way. You're going into marriage already all crippled up and setting yourself up for disappointment.

I was talking to a lady recently as she cut my hair. She told me she had become engaged, and I said, "So, you've found somebody you want to live with the rest of your life?"

She stopped working with my hair and said thoughtfully, "I don't know about that. We just want to get married and see what happens." Do you see how people enter marriage? They go in to see what they will get? Yet, *ahava* presents a whole different possibility!

God gives and gives and gives. God so loved that He gave. Marriage is a perfect opportunity for this kind and quality of love to "become flesh."

Guard Your Marriage

Let us look at three ways of guarding your inChrist marriage so it images what God intended. Does it have to be guarded? Let me answer this way: The quality of guarding must match and be appropriate to what is being guarded. Things with enormous value are enormously guarded. And because marriage is more valuable to God than the crown jewels, the devil wants to steal it, mar it, and obscure the image of Christ and the Church in it. So, yes, you must guard it!

1. Kindness

8 Finally, all [of you] should be of one and the same mind (united in spirit), sympathizing [with one another], loving [each other] as

brethren [of one household], compassionate and courteous (tenderhearted and humble). 9 Never return evil for evil or insult for insult (scolding, tongue-lashing, berating), but on the contrary blessing [praying for their welfare, happiness, and protection, and truly pitying and loving them]. For know that to this you have been called, that you may yourselves inherit a blessing [from God—that you may obtain a blessing as heirs, bringing welfare and happiness and protection]. 10 For let him who wants to enjoy life and see good days [good—whether apparent or not] keep his tongue free from evil and his lips from guile (treachery, deceit). 11 Let him turn away from wickedness and shun it, and let him do right. Let him search for peace (harmony; undisturbedness from fears, agitating passions, and moral conflicts) and seek it eagerly. [Do not merely desire peaceful relations with God, with your fellowmen, and with yourself, but pursue, go after them!]

1 Peter 3:8-11(AMPC)

Notice the first phrase of the passage, "Finally, all of you...." Who is Peter addressing? Remember 1 Peter 3:1 begins with, "Likewise, wives...." Then verse 7 begins, "Husbands, likewise...." So, when verse 8 begins above and says "...all of you...", Peter could be writing to the whole church family. Or, it also can be interpreted to speak to both husbands and wives. In other words, he could be saying, "Wives this is what you need to do. Husbands this is what you need to do. Now, finally, this goes for both of you. Be nice!"

I wish I could tell you I've always been kind to Tony, but alas, I cannot. Thankfully, both the Lord and my husband are merciful! It's possible to be kind all through the day to friends, co-workers, people, passers-by, people who need help. But after you give, give, give to others, when you finally come home, is the tone of your voice cranky with your spouse? At times, mine has been pretty cranky. Are your words short and demanding? Or, do you talk really nice to God, saying, "I worship You, Jesus. O Lord, You're so wonderful and awesome?" but lambaste and degrade your spouse?

To be perfectly honest with you, I remember one of my daughters spoke really sharply to her father one time. There was a sound in her voice that was not good, and I didn't like it. I said, "Hey, don't be talking like that to your father." During my next time of prayer, I brought this up to the Lord, saying, "Lord, help me to know how to help my daughter along that line." He said, "She's learned to talk to him from listening to you. The tone of your voice, even though you're not saying mean things, is lacking respect." Oh my! Did that ever correct me, and I'm thankful it did.

No, of course I didn't want that in my child, but that's what I was modeling. I didn't even know I was. This is a perfect example of when it's important to practice what was in Chapter 19 and ask the Lord if He's okay with the "clothes you've put on," how you're looking. The Lord might say, "There's something harsh in your voice." Or, "Your facial expression is conveying something disrespectful." Or, "Okay, you're not saying anything mean, but you're rolling your eyes and huffing. Stop it. Take that off and put something else on that's kind."

Kids don't just end up respecting father and mother by accident. They must be taught respect. Don't just tell them, "You've got to respect me!" No. No. Model it. Kindness should be what we do. We should practice everything with kindness, putting on kindness, wearing kindness. It's one of the lovely fruit of the Spirit. If you're not naturally inclined to do so yet, drink it in from Jesus. Drink it until you get so full of it that you start putting on fruit of kindness because Jesus sure is kind.

What a funny way to guard something of extraordinary value—with kindness. Yet, kindness guards your marriage. It's like putting Gurkha soldiers around your marriage, so be sure to guard it with kindness. Keep a lot of kindness in your voice. There are collars for dogs to keep them from barking. What if there were collars for people that give an electric jolt whenever unkind words are spoken? Hmm. That could be pretty shocking! Guard your voice to speak kindly.

2. Honesty

But, speaking the truth in love, may grow up in all things into Him who is the head—Christ

Ephesians 4:15

We simply should not lie to the person we married. Lying breaks trust, so we must speak the truth. Keeping honesty in your marriage guards it and protects it.

Yet, how does it look and sound to speak the truth in love? First Peter 3:2 instructed wives not to correct their husbands with words, but does this mean you never communicate honestly about how your husband's actions affect you? No! You don't have to correct your husband, but he needs to know. This also goes for husbands explaining to their wives how her actions affect him.

There's the other extreme too, where couples just don't speak anything. Each person keeps everything bottled up, which is not healthy and not love, either. In the book of Revelation, Jesus is actually quite descriptive about what He wanted those churches to do differently, but it was all in love. Everything Jesus said was in love.

If something is happening in the relationship that affects you, rather than becoming hateful and hitting back or clamming up, tell the truth in love. At the appropriate time, ask, "Is this a good time to tell you something very important to me?" Then go on to explain kindly and with love, "When you say things like that, it makes me feel this way. It makes me feel so sad. It makes me feel so diminished. It makes me feel ugly. It tells me you don't respect me."

Don't reprimand your spouse, but giving your spouse the truth in the right way helps. Learn to speak the truth motivated by love instead of speaking the truth to get back at them or hit back.

> **Husbands, love your wives, just as Christ also loved the church and gave Himself for her, that He might sanctify and cleanse her with the washing of water by the word, that He might present her to Himself a glorious church, not having spot or wrinkle or any such thing, but that she should be holy and without blemish.**
>
> **Ephesians 5:25-27**

Remember, after loving and giving, then there's room for corrective, instructive words. When it's given in that order, it's so much easier for children and wives to receive instruction. They must receive it anyway, but you make it easier for them to receive it and submit if it's given in the divine order of giving of yourself and loving. This instruction is specifically to husbands, but all the roles benefit from this divine order.

Remember also that 1 Peter 3:7 says for the husbands to live with their wives "...according to knowledge..." (KJV). How are they going to get that knowledge? Probably not all on their own. You'll have to give them that knowledge of how things make you feel or the effect of their actions on you. You'll have to be honest in your communication but always in love.

I have grown in this area of knowing how to speak the truth in love. When I asked the Lord for wisdom and help in this area, He led me to books[3] that gave me tools and understanding. Oh, what a difference they made!

> And the Lord God said, "It is not good that man should be alone. I will make him a helper comparable to him."
>
> Genesis 2:18

God has intended the wife to be a *helpmeet*—somebody who reflects him as a mirror. When you receive truth about your husband from God after spending time with God every day, also speak that. Don't wait until you see the truth in his actions before you speak it. See it in Christ by faith.

If you got it from God, you know it's the truth. And what does the truth make people when they come to know it? It makes people free. Work with God by declaring the truth over one another—husbands about wives and wives about husbands. And always, speak the truth in love!

3. Faithfulness and Fidelity

> Drink water from your own cistern and running water from your own well. Should your fountains be dispersed abroad, streams of water in the streets? Let them be only your own and not for strangers with you. Let your fountain be blessed and rejoice with the wife of your youth. As a loving deer and graceful doe let her breasts satisfy you at all times and always be enraptured with her love. For why should you, my son, be enraptured by an immoral woman and be embraced in the arms of a seductress?
>
> Proverbs 5:15-20

Faithfulness is the third and very obvious way to guard our marriages, and it begins with guarding the faithfulness of our eyes. We're not even talking about guarding the bed—yet. We also need to monitor and be aware of our emotions because emotions can go to someone else even before the body does.

Unfaithfulness starts off in a sneaky way. An indicator of it is that you begin desiring to be with somebody who is not your own spouse.

If a husband begins wanting to spend time around another woman, it's often because that woman has found the key of respect that we talked about in Chapter 25.

Wife, if somebody else found your keys, and that person is telling your husband how wonderful he is, how funny he is. "You're so funny. Ha ha ha. I just can't get over that. I love your humor. You're so cute."

And then he comes home, and the wife says, "Did you remember the milk? No? What's wrong with you? I only told you one thing to get. Do you not care about us?"

Then he goes back to work the next day, and the woman says, "I saw this and thought of you. I knew you'd really like this." She's been exercising, and she's all dressed up just for him. Then she says, "I really admire the way you do what you do. You're amazing!"

Evening comes, and the man goes home. His wife looks like she crawled out from under the couch or is rolling her eyes, saying, "That idea of yours was so stupid, and why is it that you always get to watch what you want to watch on television?" Do you see what happens? The wife lost her keys, and somebody else found them. Somebody else is opening her husband's heart. You better grab those keys back!

"I don't know what to do," you might say. Well, you get yourself in the presence of God, and you'll find some keys. God will show them to you. He'll show you beautiful things about your husband, so you can use them to unlock his heart.

On the other hand, husbands, if some girl with fresh perfume acts like she really cares about you and tells you that you're just so amazing, physically take yourself someplace else. Somebody's messing with your heart! That woman doesn't belong to you, and you don't belong to her.

Before I got married, I counseled a lot of marriages, and I thought, *I don't know if I want to get married or not, ever. This is horrible. Why do single girls cry to have this? It's like hell on earth. It's awful.* It wasn't surprising for me to think that way because usually when people are coming for counseling, their marriage is in a mess.

Yet the Lord challenged me with this instruction when Tony and I were engaged, "If you don't want infidelity in your marriage, don't put it in your home as entertainment." In other words, don't be entertained with movies or magazines or any kind of entertainment that has a spouse in somebody else's arms smacking on their face. That's not entertaining! It tears people up, and it tears marriages apart. Then it tears the kids up. It isn't funny. I fast forward, turn it off, or leave the room if somebody gets to smacking on somebody else's spouse. Why? Because I don't want it in my home. It's not entertainment. It's just plain sick.

IF YOU DON'T WANT INFIDELITY IN YOUR MARRIAGE, DON'T PUT IT IN YOUR HOME AS ENTERTAINMENT.

I'm a little bit strong on that, but I hate infidelity. Why? Because it takes this particularly beautiful characteristic of the faithfulness to be seen between Christ and the Church and spits on it. It bashes it. God is faithful, and we are to image that faithfulness to one another in marriage. We're to be faithful in our minds and our emotions.

If you ever discover your emotions have drifted from your spouse, run to God, and feed on His faithfulness. Drink of the faithfulness of Jesus, and it will begin coming out in your life as faithfulness. Then the stuff that entices and pulls on your flesh will become gross and sickening to you. You will leave it alone.

Finally, the faithfulness of your sexual union must be guarded.

And they were both naked, the man and his wife, and were not ashamed.

Genesis 2:25

Originally, man and woman, as husband and wife were both naked and unashamed. Yet in chapter 13 we likened Adam's fall to an elevator ride that took all of humanity from the top to the basement. Here is yet another example. In the fall, the sexual union of a man and a woman also hit the floor. God intended for it to be without shame—no crude jokes. In the beginning God intended sex to be something beautiful.

Why? Sexual intercourse was the means by which man and woman could come together and be one. That's how the human began. Listen to this. It is by sexual intercourse that man and woman bring into existence another eternal being that will live forever. They cannot do this through having a meal together, not through working together, and not through watching a movie together. No, sex is the means through which another human begins.

So then, sex is something extremely valuable to God. Of course, anything that is valuable to God will be hated by the devil. He cannot create another human being. All he can do is fabricate and counterfeit, but he cannot create.

Has anything ever been dragged so low in our culture as the topic of sex? The sex[4] industry has been a part of human history everywhere in the world and makes enormous amounts of money. However, sex didn't need an industry to be abused. Everywhere people are, sex has been hideously abused.

Get a clue! Anything that has a curse over it so much as sex does must have an astonishing blessing. Do you reckon that redemption also targeted the sexual union? Yes—totally and absolutely. Sex is absolutely holy to God.

Not only is sex holy to God, but it's holy to an inChrist husband and wife as well. Sex is not dirty to us, we don't have shame about it. Shame is what happened in the fall. Shame came on the sexual aspect of marriage, and wherever there's shame or condemnation, it begins to spiral downward.

Yet in Christ the shame is eradicated; it's completely taken away.

Investing in the health of your body is another way to invest into the physical part of your marriage.

It would be incorrect for a believer to think, *I love God, read my Bible, pray, and go to church, but I can do whatever I want with my body. It's mine. God doesn't have a say.* Actually, He does have a say as we can see here:

19 Don't you realize that your body is the temple of the Holy Spirit, who lives in you and was given to you by God? You do not

belong to yourself, 20 for God bought you with a high price. So you must honor God with your body.

1 Corinthians 6:19-20 (NLT)

By the same token, it's pretty selfish to think like this: *I love my spouse with all my heart, but this is my body. I can do what I want to with it, and if my spouse really loves me, my spouse will accept me the way I am.* That's not correct or a loving attitude at all. It may be loving for your spouse to be accepting of you, but it's not loving or respectful of you to demand it. Look what Paul wrote to the Corinthians about this:

For the wife does not have [exclusive] authority and control over her own body, but the husband [has his rights]; likewise also the husband does not have [exclusive] authority and control over his body, but the wife [has her rights].

1 Corinthians 7:4 (AMPC

Because your spouse has rights to your body, it's important you give your spouse the best version of your body you can. Of course, age has an effect on the body, but one way to show love and respect to your spouse at any age is by taking care of your body with hygiene, exercise, and healthy food choices and portions that help you be *your* best (not someone else's best).

Remember, marriage is to mirror Christ and the Church. Therefore, after the same manner that we offer our bodies to the Lord as a part of worship, we also want to give our best "offering" in marriage. To love is to give. You cannot give to your spouse someone else's dream body. Ask God to help you give *your* best. By the same token, it would be terribly wrong for you to expect your spouse to have a dream body and compare his or her body to someone else.

GIVE YOUR SPOUSE THE BEST VERSION OF YOUR BODY YOU CAN.

Marriage, as God intended from the beginning, has incalculable value. Your marriage has the potential to be glorious and valuable to God!

Notes

1 The Hebrew word for *love* is *ahava* (הבהא), which is made up of three basic Hebrew letters: aleph (א), hey (ה), and vet (ב). From these three root letters of a-hav-a, we can discover two root words. The first is hav from the two letters hey (ה) and vet (ב), which means to give. The letter aleph (א) modifies this word making it בהא, which means I give, but *ahav* is also the Hebrew word for *loved* (Jewishmag). This Hebrew word, therefore, contains this tremendous truth: giving is fundamental to loving. http://free.messianicbible.com/feature/love-and-the-hebrew-language/

2 *Divorce Rates in Jewish Community* states: "...in American society as a whole, the best empirical research still shows American Jews are less likely to divorce than other Americans.
One difficulty with studies that compare Jews with other Americans is that they tend to treat American Jews as a monolithic group. In this analysis we wish to differentiate among Jews on a critical factor: their commitment to Judaism and the Jewish community. It is expected that those Jews who have the strongest connection to the Jewish community will have a lower probability of divorce." *Divorce in the Jewish Community: the Impact of Jewish Commitment,* Jay Brodbar-Nemzer, Ph.D., Center for Modern Jewish Studies, Brandeis University, Waltham, MA.
research.policyarchive.org/16239.pdf

3 *Keep Your Love On*, Danny Silk , Publisher Loving on Purpose 2015, redarrowmedia. com
Five Love Languages, Danny Silk, Northfield Publishing Chicago 1992, 5lovelanguages. com

4 Sex Trade – http://www.economywatch.com/world-industries/sex-industry.html
Footnote Sex and GDP https://247wallst.com/economy/2014/05/31/sex-drugs-could-add-800-billion-to-u-s-gdp/

CHAPTER 28

Sex

G od placed sex in the safest place when He set it in marriage. That is why this chapter on sex intentionally follows the one on marriage, because that is where it was placed in the beginning. After all, the sexual relationship is most holy to the Lord. But by what has often been conveyed by the church and by people of God, it would seem that sex is the naughtiest and most shameful act of human participation possible. Let's see what God actually has to say about it.

Procreation

The first recorded words God said to man are, "Be fruitful and multiply" (Genesis 1:28). To obey this first commission from the Creator, man and woman would have to have sexual intercourse. If sex is sin, then God would have commanded them to sin. Because God told them not only to be fruitful but also to multiply means God would have told them to sin a lot. And that's impossible!

Not only did God commission man and woman to be fruitful, which requires sexual intercourse, but He actually designed their bodies to accommodate this purpose.

Being fruitful, or procreation, is both the privilege and the power to bring another eternal being into existence. The person that is conceived through intercourse will live forever. There is nothing a man and woman can do that is more humanly significant. God ordained that the safest, most peaceful wholesome place for a child that results from sexual intercourse to be brought up in is in the home of a father and mother, an inChrist father and inChrist mother who surround the child with the visible characteristics of God.

Enjoying and Acknowledging Oneness

2 But because there is so much sexual immorality, each man should have his own wife, and each woman should have her own husband. 3 The husband should fulfill his wife's sexual needs, and the wife should fulfill her husband's needs. 4 The wife gives authority over her body to her husband, and the husband gives authority over his body to his wife. 5 Do not deprive each other of sexual relations, unless you both agree to refrain from sexual intimacy for a limited time so you can give yourselves more completely to prayer. Afterward, you should come together again so that Satan won't be able to tempt you because of your lack of self-control.

1 Corinthians 7:2-5 (NLT)

Sexual desire is one of the strongest appetites or cravings that God made the human man and woman to have. This verse instructs married couples to have sex regularly, which indicates procreation is not the only purpose for sex. God could have made sex to have no feeling at all or to affect us no more than brushing our teeth. But no, He designed sex to be physically pleasurable. Clearly, the sexual desire is not a curse but a part of God's perfect design.

Paul is warning in this verse that within marriage, sex is not to be abstained from except for a certain time, and only then, it's for the purpose of a mutual fasting. Paul goes on to say that this couple should come back together again sexually. Why? It's an important way to block adultery.

> **Marriage is honorable among all, and the bed undefiled; but fornicators and adulterers God will judge.**
>
> Hebrews 13:4

Notice the first phrase shows there is nothing unholy about the marriage bed. This comes in stark contrast to our culture filled with off-colored jokes on the topic and even among some people marital sex is thought of as shameful. This sort of thinking puts sex in an unholy frame of reference.

Oddly enough, the Church, which should have shown the purest and most brilliant light on the topic of sex often has been the one that turned the light off and shamed sex more than any other source. Shame is the common repercussion when someone sins, but the Church has often turned up the volume of shame on sexual sin, which generally makes things worse. We just didn't know what else to do, and our reactions of fear and condemnation were the greatest indicators of that.

However, this verse in Hebrews is very clear. Marriage is holy, and the marriage bed or sexual intimacy is undefiled and pure. In other words, when a husband and wife are intimate, God does not go out of the room and say, "Let Me know when to come back." No. God blesses sex within marriage. That's different, isn't it? Isn't it nice to see what the Word has to say? It takes the dirty out of sex.

> **1 In like manner, you married women, be submissive to your own husbands [subordinate yourselves as being secondary to and dependent on them, and adapt yourselves to them], so that even if any do not obey the Word [of God], they may be won over not by discussion but by the [godly] lives of their wives, 2 When they observe the pure and modest way in which you conduct yourselves, together with your *reverence [for your husband....***
>
> 1 Peter 3:1-2 (AMP)

Reverence toward God is only one part of the expression of reverence a wife is to show. God is limited by the wife who reverences Him but disrespects her husband. God can be God, but God is not the wife. Respecting

SEX IS A PART OF WINNING A HUSBAND OVER TO OBEYING THE WORD.

the husband is the wife's duty—not God's. God designed that reverence for the husband will open his heart, and part of the reverence the wife is to show is expressed sexually. It's not all of it but definitely an important part. Instead of despising or ignoring a husband's sexual needs, a respectful wife will "minister" to him. Put plainly, sex is a part of winning a husband over to obeying the Word.

Sex also can produce a strength that others can benefit from. It's intimate, it's private, and it's between husband and wife. If a couple has intentionally exercised and celebrated sex purposefully and intentionally, the awareness of oneness is increased, which God can use. Oneness is a benefit. Where two of you agree on earth as touching anything that you ask, it will be done. Of course, that promise is not exclusive to husband and wife, but it certainly was the intention of God that a husband and wife walk together in uncommon agreement.

Being united or kindred spiritually with someone, for instance, a prayer partner or those who share the same beliefs or values, is wonderful. But oneness in your body comes through sexual intimacy. A husband and wife have the potential to experience a very uncommon unity in the sight of God; spirit, soul, and body as well.

Children will benefit from parents who have healthy, wholesome, sexual intimacy. Your home benefits. It just puts things together.

It has been a common religious thought that we should never ever talk about sexual things. Why not? God does. It's holy. Why should it not be talked about along with other holy things in God? The Church misrepresents God if we don't speak openly about sex, because the Bible speaks openly about sex. The lack of truth on this subject makes children vulnerable to misinformation from friends, school, and what they see and hear from other influences.

Judaism teaches that sex is a holy act and even encourages that the "holy act should always be performed on the holy day[1]." For Jews, that is the Sabbath, which is our Saturday. For those of us who believe Jesus was raised on the first day of the week, we celebrate resurrection, so Sunday is our holy day. So, it would be equivalent to every Christian married couple celebrating God in this fashion on Sundays. Jewish teaching is also that the sexual drive is so strong because it is so holy. That's kind of different, isn't it?

What Went Wrong?

If sex is such a God-idea, what went wrong? We saw, first of all, that God made man and woman with the ability to procreate eternal beings. Through sexual intercourse, the image of God would be multiplied and fill the earth. Satan's plan, as we've already seen, was to fracture and distort God's image. In order to accomplish that after the fall, he utilized the very act that was originally intended to multiply God's image to now multiply and fill the earth with the fractured image.

In the fall, he defiled the sacredness of sex, wrapping it with shame and selfishness, and claiming it for his purposes. What is it that has brought noble men and women down and made them crawl like animals? I'm talking about even people of God. Sex has been that tool in the hand of the devil. He gets particular satisfaction and glee out of the defilement of things dear to the heart of God and to people. Down through the centuries, sex has been a ploy, a strategy that has caused people to stumble, fall, and even crawl.

Outside God's design for covenant relationship, sex can be brought down to animal instinct. I hope that sounds as awful as it is. There are some animals that mate for life, but the majority of animals mate by instinct and by the different seasons in that particular animal. What the devil accomplished when man fell is that he brought this holy thing—sex—down to animal instinct.

Let's picture it this way. When God created man in His image, He meant for humans not to crawl on all fours but to walk upright with Him, work with Him, and relate with Him. As a result of the fall brought on by sin, man and woman identify with something other than the Creator.

He'll let you identify with your family, your past, other people, and your culture. He'll even encourage that. But he doesn't want you to identify with God because he knows that whomever you identify with is who you will start acting like.

Until a person is born again, he or she does not have right standing, and the person's spirit man cannot stand erect before God. Though man and woman walk erect externally, being spiritually dead and oppressed, their spirits are bowed down. But that's not enough for the devil. Oppression keeps pressing man and woman further and further down until the devil has them on their knees bowing to things other than God. Because to whatever they respond is to whatever they bow (Romans 6:16).

Even that isn't enough for the devil. He continues to bring man and woman down until the way they live is like an animal on all fours. The devil's sick delight brings man and woman from walking erect through life, exercising authority over everything that crawls, to crawling through life themselves, so to speak, on their hands and knees like an animal.

Can it get worse? Sadly, yes. The devil continues to oppress further until man is spiritually brought down, down, down flat on the ground. And what animal in creation moves flat on the ground? The serpent. He will keep his foot on a man until he makes him crawl and eat dirt, finally identifying with the serpent that has to crawl on his belly. The destroyer achieves his most insidious goal when God's most glorious creation, who was modeled after God to reflect Him, chooses to identify with something lesser, lower.

Thank God, redemption gets man to stand up again. We are not animals. We are human. We are made in the image of God—not just after the first Adam's race, but we are after the last Adam's race. We are sons of God.

That's why identification in Christ and with Christ is imperative. Why? Again, you begin to look like who you identify with. Say this: "I am in Christ. God is my Father. I have His nature. I've been made His righteousness, and so I stand. *I stand.*"

Shalom vs. Taking

According to God's intention, sexual intimacy is only whole within marriage. Whole? What does that mean?

The Hebrew word *shalom*[2] means the peace that comes from being whole. This kind of peace is not just tranquility. No, if *shalom* had a shape, it would be pictured as a circle or sphere with nothing broken, nothing damaged, and nothing missing. That's shalom—that's peace.

God's idea of sex is whole—unbroken, undamaged. Do you remember what we saw about the Hebrew word for love, which is *ahava?* The definition of that word is *to give.* Granted, the sexual need or appetite is an instinct that we share with animals, yet what makes us different from animals is the potential of this giving-kind of love.

SEXUAL INTIMACY IS AN EXPRESSION OR AN ACT OF GIVING—NOT TAKING.

Sexual intimacy is an expression or an act of giving—not taking. So, within inChrist intimacy, a husband is giving in sex and a wife is giving in sex. In this way, it's unbroken. Sex is not meant to be an act of taking; it is meant to be an act of giving. Even a part of the giving is to freely receive and respond to what is freely given by the other as well. It's simultaneous giving and receiving.

Sexual intimacy practiced outside of marriage loses shalom. The individuals lose something. They lose wholeness because there's no covenant, and their sexual intimacy also lacks the blessing of the One who made it. In this experience, one person may be giving, but the other person is taking. Or maybe both people take, and when they're taken from, they're left without and in some way diminished. That diminishing then gives a sense of the need to fill in what's been taken, so they take again. In this vicious cycle, they become sexual takers instead of givers.

People who are sexually active outside of God's design are basically people taking from each other. The taking may be mutual as in, "You take from me. I'll take from you. This is what I want. That is what you want. I'm okay for you to take, but you have to be okay if I take." It's mutual taking at its best. However, only in true love can there be mutual giving. Imagine what that could be like!

And don't you realize that if a man joins himself to a prostitute, he becomes one body with her? For the Scriptures say, "The two are united into one."

1 Corinthians 6:16-17(NLT)

This verse is interesting, isn't it? You're not one flesh with somebody just because you're married. It's sex that unites you with the other person's flesh. In that way, the more people an individual is one with, the more unwhole sex becomes, as it chops up the person's wholeness.

This cycle just keeps taking. It keeps biting into people's wholeness, which will give a sense of, "I need. I need. I want." This cycle of taking makes people—even good people—takers because "I have sexual needs. I have sexual desires." But the overall and underlying motive that compels that kind of sex isn't love—it's need. Do you see that?

There are some whose innocence or virginity was taken away from them early in life or maybe by force, and this has made them feel violated, unwhole. In other words, the person became one with someone not by choice. The person didn't give sexually, but it was taken from the person. Some of these people continue the ugly later on in life by being forcible, even violent takers themselves.

Redemption is such a beautiful thing for people who have suffered from molestation or rape and lost their wholeness to takers—takers trying to fill a craving or a need due to not being whole themselves. Aren't you thankful that as a result of redemption we can become whole again as though it never happened?

Notes

1 Intimacy is encouraged on Shabbat not so much as a means to procreate as it is to create a bond between husband and wife…. There are two separate mitzvot in the Torah that involve sexual relations. One is to be fruitful and multiply (Genesis1:28). The lesser-known mitzvah is for the husband to ensure he sexually satisfies his wife (Exodus 21:10). This second mitzvah is totally independent from the first, and so the obligation to make love to one's wife applies to couples regardless as to whether they wish to or are capable of conceiving. The very notion that sexual pleasure can itself — provided it is experienced in the right context — be a mitzvah, underscores the unique Jewish attitude to life…. Nowhere is this more evident than on Shabbat where the sacred is celebrated through the physical. This holy day is observed not just through prayer and song but also through eating, socializing, relaxing and — for married couples — sexual intimacy. Shabbat illustrates the harmony that can be achieved between the spiritual and the physical. https://www.thejc.com/judaism/rabbi-i-have-a-problem/why-is-sex-allowed-on-shabbat-1.33812

2 *Shalom* – Strong's Concordance 7965 – *shalom: completeness, soundness, welfare, peace*
Original Word: שׁוֹלָם
Phonetic Spelling: (shaw-lome') – Word Origin from *shalem* – Definition: *completeness, soundness, welfare, peace*
http://biblehub.com/hebrew/7965.htm
Binary Definition – http://rabbidavidzaslow.com/the-deeper-meaning-of-shalom/

ENGENDERED

CHAPTER 29

Fractured Sex

Marriage was made to be a picture of our loving Christ and His devoted Church. Sex between a faithful husband and wife pictures a beautiful expression of mutual giving and responding. Here are some other things we see about sex *before* sin brought the fall that fractured everything—including sex.

1. The sexual organs of the male and female bodies were designed for procreation. This means that sex, according to the Creator, was designed for male and female.

2. The first male and female were husband and wife, including sex within a covenant of marriage. God meant for marriage to be the basis of a home that provides His image through a father and mother, making that home the most ideal or wholesome place to raise a child that comes as a result of sex.

3. Sex was not just to satisfy the sexual appetite, but it's also a means of expressing pure love and connecting two people wholly.

Since the fall, there are many opinions and preferences regarding sex. While God gave man the right to choose and protects that right, the characteristics and destination of the path chosen may not be what He lovingly intended. The purpose of this book is not to argue or express my opinion of what's right or wrong but to present what the Bible says on the subject. The Bible identifies expressions of sex that are alternatives to what the Creator intended. If these different paths or roads, if you will, are chosen, they will be a choice against yourself—against life. Let's look at them.

Adultery – Why is adultery different from what God intended? Because God is faithful, and unfaithfulness misrepresents Him. Becoming one sexually with someone who is not a spouse breaks the wholeness of marriage. It breaks the wholeness of family (Genesis 39:7; Deuteronomy 28:30; Leviticus 18:20).

Fornication – A person committing fornication is not married and has sexual relations with somebody(s) also not in a marriage covenant. There are various motivations for fornication. Basically, it's pleasing yourself or taking care of your own sexual appetite. Another reason is to use sex as glue to a relationship when you are afraid there may not be enough attachment to keep it together otherwise. Any of these motivations misrepresent and are alternative to God's intention (Exodus 22:16).

Rape – This also is a fractured version of sex. It's hateful, and it violently takes from women or men, which is the very opposite of God, who is loving and giving. Rape is so "un-God" and not His nature at all (Deuteronomy 22:23; Genesis 34:7).

Prostitution – Prostitution fractures everyone involved. If it is a case of a man buying sex with a woman, the man can have sexual intimacy with her and have absolutely no love or sense of responsibility. None. It's simply taking (Leviticus 19:29; 21:19). The woman, on the other hand, has no respect and honor for the man, but she takes the money or payment. Yes, that's surely nothing like what God intended (Leviticus 19:29).

Prostitution has many ugly forms depending on who wants to buy and the age and sex of the body they want. This would include pedophiliac sex. The person whose body is for sale may be forced to participate against their will to make money for someone else.

Jesus demonstrated a fury on those that bought and sold in His Father's temple. The body is far more precious than the temple Jesus drove the merchants out of and is not meant to be bought and sold (1 Cor 6:17; John 2:14-17).

Homosexuality – Sometimes people elevate homosexuality as the worst sin. But, actually, any sexual expression that is not what God intended misses the mark, which is the definition of sin. Remember what the original sin was? Murder? Robbery? No, it was simply choosing to eat fruit from a tree that God said not to eat. Again, as we have already seen, sin is essentially missing God's purpose and will either by an inch or by a mile.

This sexual expression pairs two males, while God's intention from the beginning was not so. It's not what God designed (Leviticus 18:22; 20:13; Romans 1:27). God does, however, bless loving, non-sexual relationships between men (1 Samuel 18:1).

Lesbianism – The same applies to the female gender (Romans 1:26). Love in friendship relationships between the same sex can be expressed in so many ways. Sex will not be one of those ways when there is true love. True love is God. There's no way to participate in true love outside of God's intention and design.

Incest – The reason why this is described in the Bible as confusion and wickedness is that a child should be able to look at his father, mother, uncle, aunt, brother, sister or any family member as a representation of God in modeling love. They will not experience this in incest. What misrepresentation to God's image! Incest degrades the very act that brought that child into existence (Leviticus 20:12, 20; 18:6-20; Genesis 19:32).

Bestiality – Feeding the sexual appetite outside of covenant marriage will keep bringing man and woman down, down, down until that craving is so fractured it cannot be met by another human and satisfaction is sought with animals. In the same way that sex with someone makes you one flesh with them, sex with animals makes a person one with that animal. This is fractured sex obviously at its worst (Leviticus 18:23; 20:15-16).

Pornography – Visually and purposefully stimulating natural sexual drives to the point of coveting something and someone who is not yours is an exercise in the opposite of love and a form of cannibalism. Visually it's feasting on someone's flesh. It is taking from someone with no way or plans to give to them (Psalm 101:3; Matthew 5:27-28).

Masturbation[1] – When associated with pornography (porn stars or audience), orgies or fantasizing illicit sex with another person, masturbation is another expression of sex that "takes" and mentally "becomes one" with someone who is not yours. That breaks wholeness.

Masturbation with absolutely no sexual thought is not uncommon with children and is purely a natural physical release. This type of masturbation that has nothing to do with illicit sex or sexual thoughts can be experienced by older ages as well.

Orgies[2] – Orgies are characterized by wild parties with drugs, alcohol, sex toys, and unrestrained group sex of three or more people. The red-sided garter snake provides an example of orgies in the animal kingdom (1 Peter 4:1-5 ESV; Galatians 5:19-21; Numbers 25:1-3*)*.

Let's look at 1 Corinthians 6:

There is a sense in which sexual sins are different from all others. In sexual sin we violate the sacredness of our own bodies, these bodies that were made for God-given and God-modeled love, for 'becoming one' with another.

1 Corinthians 6:18 (MSG)

SEXUAL SIN IS ACTUALLY SINNING AGAINST YOUR OWN BODY.

Sin is sin. But this verse says sexual sins are different from others. The reason that Paul gave here by the Holy Spirit's inspiration is that sexual sin is actually sinning against your own body.

What does that mean? Your body was created and meant to function in a certain way. When it doesn't, it will break down. I hope and imagine cures for sexually transmitted diseases will be found, but after they are, there will be another disease that arises. Why? Is God punishing people? No, the choice for sex outside of the Creator's design is punishing. The body breaks down, and God doesn't have anything to do with it except that He designed the body.

E. Stanley Jones[3], a great missionary to the intellectuals of India years ago, wrote:

"The laws of our being are not a novelty; they are the laws of God. Just as the engineer builds into an engine the way it is to work, so God has stamped His kingdom within the structure of our being. The Old Testament calls this stamp "creating man in his own image" (Gen. 1:27). If we live according to it, we live. If we don't, we don't.

A railway engine is made to run on tracks, and if it remains on tracks, it finds its freedom, pulls it's loads, and gets to its destination. But if in order to gain its freedom, it jumps the tracks, the result is not freedom but ruin to itself and everybody concerned.

There is a track to freedom, to efficiency, to full living, built into your being and mine."

Sexually transmitted diseases are only one repercussion of going against the God-made design. There is also the breakdown in the wholeness of the mind and soul and the breaking of precious relationships that choosing against God's plan brings to mankind. There will always be something that breaks down when man goes against creative design.

Why? Because in a personal version of sexuality apart from God, a person fights himself or herself. Each is breaking his or her own wholeness and breaking somebody else's wholeness as well.

> **Run from sexual sin! No other sin so clearly affects the body as this one does. For sexual immorality is a sin against your own body.**
>
> 1 Corinthians 6:18 (NLT)

> **Honor marriage, and guard the sacredness of sexual intimacy between wife and husband. God draws a firm line against casual and illicit sex.**
>
> Hebrews 13:4 (MSG)

Although sex may be exciting and address the sexual drive humans have, God's blessing is not upon any other sexual relationship than marriage between a man and woman. When sex is experienced the way God meant for it to be, it can be glorious.

Notes

1 masturbation – https://www.todayschristianwoman.com/articles/2014/may/masturbation-is-it-always-sin.html?start=1
https://www.summitmedicalgroup.com/library/pediatric_health/pa-hhgbeh_masturbation/

2 *Orgy* – definition – http://www.dictionary.com/browse/orgy

3 Stanley Jones, pp 134 & 135 *Abundant Living*, E. Stanely Jones, Whitmore & Stone, 1942 Edited version by Dean Merrill Summerside Press, Minneapolis, MN, 2010.

CHAPTER 30

InChrist Family

Paul begins his second prayer in Ephesians with this beautiful picture of Father and His family:

> 14 For this reason [¹seeing the greatness of this plan by which you are built together in Christ], I bow my knees before the Father of our Lord Jesus Christ, 15 For Whom every family in heaven and on earth is named [that Father from Whom all fatherhood takes its title and derives its name].
>
> Ephesians 3:14-15 (AMP)

The family, without fracture or dysfunction, has the potential to visibly represent and image the relationship of Father and His family. The world can't see God the Father. They may not even know that God is the Father "from whom all fatherhood takes its title and derives its name." Or, their idea of fathers and God as well, maybe so confused they think He's mean and condemning to His children. They may think a person never knows what God will do or if He even exists? This is not an uncommon perception due to how the fall affected fatherhood.

The family was tragically broken in the fall. It didn't take long to see the extent of the damage when in the first generation we had one brother killing the other brother. Sadly, family dysfunction has become the norm. Sitcoms have gone a long way to make people feel completely fine and find humor about being a world away from what God intended for the family.

The first promise of redemption to restore everything broken in the fall was actually the very first promise in the entire Bible. It was given by God to the head of the human race: Adam and Eve (Genesis 3:15). After that, according to the genealogy in Luke's gospel, there were 20 generations that passed, and finally, a man by the name of Abram came on the scene (Luke 3:23-38). This was God's promise to Abram:

> **And I will bless them that bless you and curse them that curses you and *in you shall families of the earth be blessed*.**
>
> **Genesis 12:3**

God gave the same promise to Abram's grandson, Jacob, when he was en route to the land of his mother's people. At night he laid down on the ground to sleep, using a rock as a pillow. In his sleep, he had a vision and saw a ladder from heaven to earth with angels going up and down. During this wonderful engagement directly with heaven, God spoke. What was it He said? It would be profoundly important because it would be a message literally from heaven. The message was this promise having to do with families.

> **Also your descendants shall be as the dust of the earth. You shall spread abroad to the left and the east, to the north and the south and in you and in your seed *all the families of the earth shall be blessed*.**
>
> **Genesis 28:14**

While there may be no earthly hope for your family to be whole, there is a heavenly promise from God concerning family.

The word here for *families* is the Hebrew word *mishpâchâh*, and speaks of a circle of relatives or tribe. This verse is saying the families of the earth will be blessed through the seed or line of Abraham, Isaac, and Jacob. We know that blessing came through Jesus Christ.

My youngest brother, Scott, has had the privilege to work with a missions organization that targets unreached ethnic and people groups. So many are yet to hear! Yet, because God uses the word *all* with families, I have a right to claim my family will be blessed through Jesus, and so do you.

The First Family

God didn't just create four random and different individuals on the earth. He made a man and a woman—husband and wife—and gave them a command to have children. They did so, making them the first family.

Remember, God commanded them to be fruitful and replenish the earth, which they did but not until after they fractured. When they reproduced, they filled the earth with fracture. But it was nonetheless, still a family (Genesis 4).

Noah's Family

When God chose people to be on the ark because the whole world was to be destroyed and He needed to save a remnant of the human race, He didn't just pick eight random people. "Hmm, I think I'll pick you and perhaps you and your friend." No. He chose a family: Noah and his wife, his sons, and their wives. He saved a family (Genesis 7:1-7).

Abraham

The promise that came from God concerning the Redeemer and His redemption of all humankind came to a man who started a family. Don't you find it interesting that the promises of God come to people with impossible situations? (Genesis 12:1-3). God's promise to Abraham could only be fulfilled by faith in God.

He gave the promise that the families of the earth were going to be blessed through a man and a woman who couldn't have children (Genesis 17:15-17). It wouldn't be unusual for God to tell you to do something you can't do without His grace and faith in His Word.

Siblings

God gave Moses a call that required him to go talk to Pharaoh, the ruler of Egypt, the superpower of that day. Moses said, "I stutter, and I can't talk very well." God gave him a helper, but not just anybody. He told him to take *Aaron*. Who is Aaron? His *brother* (Exodus 4:14).

When Pharaoh's daughter found the ark among the reeds of the Nile and found baby Moses inside, there was a young girl close by who had followed the basket as it floated down the river. She said, "Do you want somebody to nurse the baby?" The young girl was Moses's sister *Miriam*. When Pharaoh's daughter asked for a nurse for the child, Miriam took Moses back to Moses' mother. How cool is that? (Exodus 2:1-8).

Later on, after they crossed the Red Sea, Miriam led the dance and the choir as they sang this song, "I will sing unto the Lord for He has triumphed gloriously. The horse and the rider has He thrown into the sea." *Moses, Aaron, and Miriam* worked together as a family (Exodus 15:20-21).

There were two sets of brothers among the twelve disciples. *Peter and Andrew* were brothers, and so were *James and John* (John 1:40,41; Mark 3:17). Jesus' step-brothers wrote two books of the Bible, *James and Jude*.

Nephew

The King of Mesopotamia was Caleb's nephew, Othniel, which means *deliverer*. Othniel's Uncle Caleb had a similar spirit about him when he took possession of a mountain even at 80 years of age (Judges 3:9).

Cousins

When Gabriel told *Mary* she would become pregnant with the Lord Jesus, there was absolutely no one she could turn to—no one except *Elizabeth*, a cousin (Luke 1:36-56).

When Mary ran into the home of her older cousin, she didn't have to explain her situation. Instead, Elizabeth, who was very old and also miraculously expecting a child, immediately prophesied loudly about the divine baby her young cousin was carrying. The greatest encouragement to the mother of Jesus Christ was her cousin.

What person could forerun and prepare the way of the Lord Jesus Christ, the Messiah? Who could do that? Did God pick a random person who had a great ministry and preaching gift? No. He purposely chose

John. *John* is the son of Elizabeth, Mary's cousin, making him perhaps a third *cousin* to Jesus (Luke 1:41; 3:1-21).

Grandmother

Paul saw in Timothy the same gift that was in his mother, Eunice, and the *grandmother*, Lois (2 Tim 1:5).

Family Lines

We can see in the Bible that awareness of the things of God passed down in families. The call of God does not come on a person just because he or she is in a ministry family. Every call is personal and directly connected to God. Nevertheless, what God does do in family is to develop awareness and a way of responding to the Holy Spirit; children are exposed to and raised up in the things of God. You may not personally have been raised up in a home sensitive to the things of God, but as soon as you start walking in the ways of God, you're starting something new for your children or those who come through your life and influence. Isn't that neat?

YOU'RE STARTING SOMETHING NEW FOR YOUR CHILDREN.

The *priesthood* is an example of family working together in the things of God. The helps ministry within the priesthood was a family line, the tribe of Levi. The priests themselves were the men of Aaron's family line. Zacharias and Elizabeth, who were the parents of John the Baptist, were both in the family of Aaron.

Be not overcome with evil but overcome evil with good.

Romans (12:21).

This is an encouraging thought for families. If bad things can be passed down through family lines, then good things can too. Listen to this, good things cannot only be passed down but passed up as well. Maybe what your parents gave you wasn't so good, but in return, you can give good to them. That is the power of redemption!

There may have been harshness for generations in your home. But today is a new day, and life and love can come up right through that very area. God gets particular delight in you overcoming evil with good.

Don't be afraid to identify those Lists B and C traits (page 279) in your family and apply 2 Corinthians 5:17 to them. Replace all the old things that passed away and replace them with List A traits (page 278).

Tony's family illustrates this. Both his grandfathers moved to America from Italy and were tough, hard-working men. Tony's dad grew up in Ohio, and back in those days, there was a lot of prejudice against Italians in America. There was a mean Irishman who would lose his German Shepherd on my father-in-law when he walked past the Irishman's house. One day, Dad found that guy without his dog and beat the tar out of him. He said, "You're not so tough without your dog, are you?" Okay, so that was Tony's dad, and he tended to be physical in raising his seven boys as well.

After one of Tony's brothers drowned, his dad, who was a drinker, drank even more and developed cirrhosis of the liver. His sons, especially the first five who were young men at the time, were heathen!

But boy, I'm telling you what, after Tony's brother Joe got saved, salvation spread in that family like a holy contagion! I mean they got it. They *all* got it.

YOU CAN REVERSE THE CURSE IN YOUR FAMILY.

Today, two of Tony's brothers have mighty churches, and their kids are in ministry. And even the brothers who aren't pastors, serve and help in ministry as do their families. Do you see the difference of how there's a new line now?

My dad was a ranch hand and rodeo cowboy. When God got a hold of him, God saved and filled him with the Holy Spirit, and my dad became a Pentecostal preacher. All five of his kids are in ministry and many of the grandkids serve God in some capacity as well.

Daddy was the first one in his family to get saved. He never knew of any other people in the Behrman's side that were Christian—not one. Yet, through my dad, my grandparents got saved. His mom was the first one he ever baptized, and he baptized her in the bathtub because it was winter in Colorado. Salvation spreads up the line—not just down to the next generation.

You can reverse the curse in your family, too. The blessing is stronger than the curse. You're not left with the curse. You can claim the blessing, praise God!

You might want to put up a picture of your family members and begin saying, "My family is blessed." Well, part of the way they're going to be blessed is the blessing that comes up through *you*. You don't force blessing on them, but it will issue from your prayers and your life and your contact with them. They see firsthand that the love of God is stronger than hate and strife.

The devil has desired to throw families into the rubbish, but we're not going to do that. It's worth it to fight for our families. The devil wants to confuse us as to who the enemy is, so we end up fighting our family instead of him. No! We want to fight *for* our families instead of fighting members of our family. We don't wrestle against flesh and blood. We wrestle against the devil, who hates our family. One way we triumph over him is to overcome evil with good.

You can't attack hate with hate. One of the best ways to attack hate is to love. And God's way to invade a family line that has been controlled by depression is with weapons of joy and with peace.

Remember, family is part of God's redemption plan. Not only did God use family strategically within the plan itself, but family was also targeted for redemption as well. He redeemed what was broken and what it cost Him to do so shows the value that God puts on the family.

The genealogy in Matthew 1 beginning with Abraham and bringing us up to Jesus Christ has in it a variety of people. Some are known for good reasons, but there were others who were quite the opposite. If you ever had a reason to think that your relatives were hopeless, you might be encouraged to look at Jesus' earthly family line with everything from adultery and murder to sacrificing babies in fire.

Of the forty-eight individuals named in this genealogy, five mothers are included. One of the five is Mary, Jesus' mother. Because women were not included in genealogies, we should ask why the Holy Spirit inspired the inclusion of the other four women in the record of Jesus' Christ's earthly lineage. Who are they?

Tamar pretended to be a harlot and got pregnant by her father-in-law, Judah (Genesis 38; Matthew 1:3).

Rahab was David's great, great grandmother who was a prostitute in Jericho. Her lies saved the lives of Israel's two spies. In exchange, her whole family was saved. Hebrews 11:31 blatantly names Rahab "the harlot" in this chapter's list of faith heroes. Couldn't it just read Rahab? (Matthew 1:5; Joshua 2:1-18).

Ruth, an exceptional woman, was David's great-grandmother. Her own family, however, were Moabites. Who were they? The Moabites were a tribe that descended from Moab, the son of Lot. Lot's son was the product of an incestuous relationship between Lot and his oldest daughter (Genesis 19:37; Matthew 1:5).

Bathsheba was the woman with whom David committed adultery and whose husband David had killed after his cover-up plan failed for her inconvenient pregnancy. In Matthew 1:6, Bathsheba's name wasn't mentioned, but she is referred to as "her" *who had been the wife of Uriah* (2 Samuel 11).

Why would God, on purpose, put these ladies in a holy genealogy? I believe He wanted us to look straight at fractures and confusion to His image, and say, "You're not too hard for the blood of Jesus. You're not beyond redemption." Don't you love that? Nothing that's happened in your family is beyond the blood of Jesus that has power to not only forgive and cleanse, but also to completely reconcile back to God's original intention. This includes a future and a place in God's plan.

YOU'RE NOT TOO HARD FOR THE BLOOD OF JESUS. YOU'RE NOT BEYOND REDEMPTION.

Jesus, whose human body carried the divine blood of His Father God, was not born into a perfect family—one free from issues, heartache, and shame. Instead, Jesus identified with this dysfunctional family and what they did, all the while never polluting His precious blood by sinning Himself.

But listen! Jesus' fractured family line stopped with Him. A new family line began—an inChrist family line where *all* the families of the earth can find restoration, salvation, redemption, and be blessed, indeed!

Do you know what activates the blessing? *Faith* in the blessing. Believe it, and your faith will activate it. It's like throwing a match on gasoline. Jesus already did a work that provides blessing for all the families of the earth, but if you want *your* family to partake of that blessing, use your faith and believe what God said is true. Believe God's promise of blessing instead of gasping and rolling your eyes at the curse: "Oh, my family is a bunch of no goods." No! Say, "My family is blessed. Every day I call them blessed." Praise God! What can God do in your family? He can do amazing things, and He will if you believe Him.

You can believe the dysfunction, heartache, and fracture that is and has been in your family, or you can believe the promises of God for your family. Here are promises for you to take to heart. Believe and speak these promises from God's Word as you fight for your family: Deuteronomy 28:32, 41; Galatians 3:13-14; Isaiah 49:24-25; John 4:53; Acts 16:15, 31.

ENGENDERED

CHAPTER 31

Thinking Right about Generational Curses

Fractures that run in families are sometimes referred to as generational curses. The impact of sin upon a person or a family is like a fracture in your windshield that can start at one point and end up running across the entire windshield. When you do try to fix it, it may break out again or in a different place. In the same way, it's not uncommon that these fractures come down the line in families breaking out in the body and the soul as well as other areas of life.

In fact, have you ever had to fill out a registration form[1] at a doctor's office that asks you about your family's health history? If so, you know that the doctor will want to know if anyone in your close family had diseases like cancer, sugar diabetes, heart disease, or psychiatric challenges because conditions like these tend to run in families. Some diseases are carried on in the chromosomes and are even called "inherited diseases."

There have also been studies about the tendency toward negative characteristics like depression, abuse, and addictive behaviors being passed down in families[2]. You might have heard somebody say that a grandfather's temper is showing up in a child. Or, some say if a mother is an alcoholic, her child runs the risk of that problem as well. Or, some say children will likely experience divorce if their parents did.

While *generational curses* is terminology heard primarily in church or religious circles, genetic profiling and mapping is carried out by professionals who dedicate their lives to this particular research. Let's look to see what the Bible says about it.

> **But I do not excuse the guilty. I lay the sins of the parents upon their children and grandchildren;** *the entire family is affected— even children in the third and fourth generations.*
>
> Exodus 34:7b (NLT)

Research from a variety of fields is discovering what the Bible has always revealed, and it's out of this scripture verse that the term *generational curses* came. Here's the question. When a challenge like what I've mentioned arises, is it a generational curse? Whether the challenges have been passed down through your family or from another avenue, God has provided a solution.

Must these curses or genetic tendencies be broken? Absolutely! But here's the amazing truth. Jesus *has already* broken and redeemed us from the curses listed in Deuteronomy 28:16-68. These curses include physical and mental disorders.

Galatians plainly tells us:

> **13 Christ redeemed us from the curse of the law by becoming a curse for us—for it is written, "Cursed is everyone who is hanged on a tree." 14 so that in Christ Jesus the blessing of Abraham might come to the Gentiles, so that we might receive the promised Spirit through faith.**
>
> Galatians 3:13-14 (ESV)

Jesus became cursed *for* us. Knowing and believing truth about this releases God's power into your own life and situation to stop the fracture not only in your own life but also from being passed on through you (Deuteronomy 30:19; 28:32).

When it comes to generational curses, what we *don't* want to do is elevate the fracture above redemption. Regrettably, when a person has experienced or is currently experiencing a hand-me-down fracture, focusing on it is a common reaction. You can hear it in his or her conversation, even in prayers, and how the person addresses the problem. The person may even elevate it above the name of Jesus.

But when the elevation of the fracture takes pre-eminence over the redemption of the fracture, that's a problem. That's why we purposefully diminish the curse and magnify redemption instead. Practically speaking, whenever any of those kinds of things get elevated, they hijack relationships, and they hijack your words. Your consciousness fixates on the fracture or the curse, making it impossible to break out of it.

Some people can describe in detail and talk for hours about what the curse or fractures are and the damage they've caused. But what about the verses of scripture that talk about the blessing? What about their redemption in Christ from the curse? Do they think or even know about that? The blessing is so much stronger than the curse, and redemption completely restores even the worst fractures. Even though this is absolutely the truth, you won't experience and walk in the blessing of redemption unless it becomes your focus instead of the fracture.

THE BLESSING IS SO MUCH STRONGER THAN THE CURSE.

Tony and I spoke with a man who dealt with profound and debilitating depression due to abuse in his family as a child. He eventually got so he could manage to cope and carry on with some sort of life. But the Holy Spirit—the Teacher, Comforter, Shepherd, the One who guides and is his best friend—led him to truth in the Word, and he identified with the truth about himself. It broke him out of that pit, and He was free.

His wife said, "He's a different man!" But the freedom he got didn't come from examining, "Where did I get this? What wicked relative gave this to me?" and following the fracture back up the generational line. He didn't get free from studying the curse and neither will you. It might give you a sense of "Ahha." The aha-kind-of-a-feeling happens when you identify specific fractures as well as where or through whom they've come, but that is different from freedom.

Don't try to outrun what runs in your family. Ignoring or covering it won't help. Fearing it and fighting it won't stop it. Go ahead and identify the fracture or problem, and then move on to the solution.

Remember, "Moses endured as one who gazed on Him who is invisible" (Hebrews 11:27). The devil wants to captivate our attention, so instead of doing what Moses did, we gaze at the curse—the fracture, the distortion—of what God originally intended. Remember, the devil reads your attention to his destructive work as applause. And he's looking to give you an encore!

After the devil's work of curses down through your family has been identified and diagnosed, draw the line. Determine to shut down the devil by looking away from him and all his distractions. Look at Jesus, the Redeemer of all that was broken in the fall.

Even though our bodies will eventually die, we still get to enjoy the first fruits of redemption for our bodies, which is healing (Romans 8:23). God is for our bodies and our bodies are for the Lord (1 Corinthians 6:13b). The Lord loves our bodies and proved their value by taking our sickness on Himself (Matthew 8:17). Not only is there healing for our bodies, but there is also restoration and deliverance for our souls.

THE CURSE CAN BE NEUTRALIZED THROUGH FORGIVENESS.

How can this practically affect genetic disorders and generational curses? If Christ redeemed you from the curse of the law that was passed down your family line, you can use your faith to stop the fracture in your life. You can also stop it from spreading to the next generation (Deuteronomy 28:59; Galatians 3:15).

Another way the curse can be neutralized is through forgiveness. Actually, the curse is neutralized as we return blessing in place of the curse and by honoring our parents. Honoring parents opens the door for a blessing.

It's terrible to receive negative conditions from parents or other relatives, whether it's in the body or soul. Depending on what it is, it isn't uncommon for children to be bitter and despise their parents or grand-parents if those conditions have made life miserable. As much as these reactions are normal, unforgiveness and hate pave a road for those very conditions or others to break out in the child's life.

Ephesians 6 gives this instruction to believers:

> **"2 Honor your father and mother." This is the first commandment with a promise: 3 If you honor your father and mother, "things will go well for you, and you will have a long life on the earth."**
> **Ephesians 6:2-3 (NLT)**

This is one of the Ten Commandments. But notice the scripture reference of this verse. Ephesians was written to the Church, and this promise of things going well and of long life is attached to honoring parents. I believe it's because honor and blessing stop and reverse the curse from coming any further down the family line. Not only that, but it also allows the blessing to go back up the line where the curse came from in the first place.

Notes

1 Form
Sanford Health Genetic History – A family *history* is one of the most powerful "*genetic* tests" to identify if families are at increased risk for chronic diseases and certain cancers. Discovering this early can often improve, delay or prevent negative health outcomes. http://www.sanfordhealth.org/medical-services/genetic-counseling

2 Inherited behavioral traits: Today... most scientists agree that both genes and environmental factors are important in forming behavior. There is still debate as to how much nature (genes) and how much nurture (environment) affect behavior. It is generally accepted that for each trait, nature and nurture work together in different proportions. For example, scientists estimate that in deciding how tall a person will be, inherited genes have nine times more influence than the environment a person grows up in (which may influence such factors as a person's nutrition). However, researchers have estimated that in determining whether or not a person will become depressed, genes and the environment are about equally important. Read more: http://www.humanillnesses.com/Behavioral-Health-Fe-Mu/Genetics-and-Behavior.html#ixzz54gYetYvB
   Some scientists have begun trying to link certain antisocial types of behavior to specif-

ic genes. This is also very difficult, but for different reasons. It's estimated there are more than 50,000 gene pairs in the human genome. Very few have been linked specifically to any particular trait. It's especially hard to link genes to most types of behavior, because most are complex and determined by more than one gene.

Some disorders influenced by genetics are schizophrenia, alcoholism, obesity, and depression.

Read more: http://www.humanillnesses.com/Behavioral-Health-Fe-Mu/Genetics-and-Behavior.html#ixzz54gZ05TG5

CHAPTER 32

InChrist Parent

The word *parent* is both a noun and a verb. Being a parent is not only who you are, but it's also what you do. Representing, reflecting and imaging List A characteristics of God to your child in all the occasions of life is your divine purpose.

Remember, the manner in which we parent now that we are in Christ, may be different than what we experienced before. Parents have the responsibility and privilege of representing and imaging God to their children. In order to do that, we look at our inChrist model. We can only use our natural family example when it supports the characteristics that we see in the Father, Son, and Holy Spirit.

A parent is not the Holy Spirit, but the parent is responsible and anointed to work with the Holy Spirit. The female part of the human race uniquely reflects the Holy Spirit, but not exclusively because the male can also express the characteristics of the Holy Spirit. Of course, the Holy Spirit lives on the inside of both male and female.

In the same way, a dad uniquely reflects God the Father, and the husband images Christ, the head of the Church. Then again, a woman can also have the Father's characteristics and those of Jesus. She's born of God, so, of course, she should have His List A characteristics.

From what we draw from our interaction with God, here are five specific areas where parents are to represent Him:

1. Words

14 He *(the Holy Spirit)* will honor and glorify Me, because He will take of (receive, draw upon) what is Mine and will reveal (declare, disclose, transmit) it to you. 15 Everything that the Father has is Mine. That is what I meant when I said that He [the Spirit] will take the things that are Mine and will reveal (declare, disclose, transmit) it to you.

John 16:14-15 (AMPC)

A DAD AND A MOM'S VOICE IS MOST EFFECTIVE WHEN THEY SAY THE SAME THING.

In the same way that the Father, Son, and Holy Spirit agree, a dad and a mom's voice is most effective when they say the same thing. In order for the parents' voice to be one, like the Word and the Spirit, there needs to be communication within the parenting relationship that enables parents to agree and consolidate their words. For a single parent, his or her word needs to be resolute, so the parent's word, like the Lord's, is stable and doesn't cave in under pressure (2 Corinthians 1:20).

The inChrist parent is designed to amplify the voice of the Holy Spirit. You add volume—external audio volume—to the voice of God talking in your child's heart. So, your words obviously need to be one and the same with God's. Accomplishing this takes communication with God to make sure you're saying what He says.

God speaks to little children, not just adults, and when He does, He most commonly speaks these three ways: through the voice of the parents, the Word through other people, and internally in the child's heart. Parents work together with God the best when their voices don't say anything different than God's voice. Of course, it's important that children pay attention to what their parents say. Ultimately, the parents' goal is to help their children identify the voice of the Holy Spirit, and parents help them do that by talking like God.

Jesus told His disciples there was much He wanted to say to them, but He couldn't because He was returning to heaven. That's when He told them about the Holy Spirit and explained that the Holy Spirit would lead them into all truth. So even Jesus' goal was to acquaint the disciples with the One whose voice on the inside would always be there, even when Jesus, physically, was not (John 16:12-13).

When my girls were growing up, I would commonly talk with them right before they went to sleep. I remember when Annalisa was about eight years old, and I tucked her in one night. She told me something she wanted to do when she grew up. I was aghast, and I let her know so. I really let her have it. I felt like I did a superb job of straightening her out as she looked at me with so much sadness. I thought, *Good, I'm getting through to her!* I put the spiritual squeeze on it and left her room. I felt like, *Yeah, I told my daughter what to do and straightened that out.*

I was getting ready for bed, washing my face, when the Holy Spirit said, "I don't agree with what you just told your daughter." Well, if He's right, and I say something different, then what does that make me? Wrong.

A little bit defensive, because I really thought I had done a good job, I said, "What was wrong with it?"

"You didn't represent My thought or Word in that," He said. "You didn't represent Me."

"Okay," I said, "Tomorrow I'll sort it out."

"No!" He said. "I don't want her going to sleep with those words. Get in there and fix it." He was really stern with me. So, I had to go in and make it right.

Do you know what I had to say to my daughter? "I'm sorry. I said something to you, and it's not the way that Jesus talks to you." I felt so bad. I asked the Lord what to say, and He gave me something to say. The whole issue became a non-issue.

Some parents tell their children that God will be mad at them if they do a particular thing that's wrong. First of all, that's a lie. Secondly, motivating them with fear and shame will set them up for more difficulty. You don't want to put space between a child and God by misrepresenting Him. You actually need to connect them, especially when they do something wrong. You need to make the invisible—visible. You need to make the intangible—tangible. You need to make the inaudible—audible.

YOU DON'T WANT TO PUT SPACE BETWEEN A CHILD AND GOD BY MISREPRESENTING HIM.

That wasn't the only time Tony or I misrepresented God's ways or thoughts to our girls. But if and when we came to know that we misrepresented God, it was our responsibility to apologize and make sure they knew what God, indeed, was saying.

My parents did the same thing. If they misrepresented God to any of us kids, they fixed it. God is perfect, but a parent isn't. You'll drive yourself up the wall if you think, *I've got to be perfect for my kid.* No. You must be honest with your kid. No matter the age of your child, there will be times when you completely represent the Lord and His image. And there will also be sometimes when you don't.

When you blow it, humble yourself. Go to your child, and make it clear what you said or did that didn't represent God. They won't disrespect you for that. No, the opposite will happen. They will respect you. More importantly, there will be a real clarity between what you've done and God. It's important!

Have faith in God's voice to your child. When Anna was about seven years old, she woke up one night, and as she lay in bed in the dark, she decided to talk to God. The next morning when I got up, Anna said, "God talked to me." You know, there's a sweet essence, a fragrance that comes with His presence and from hearing His words and Anna had that.

I asked, "What did He say?"

"I told him I loved Him, and He said, 'I know,'" she said. That was it. I was waiting for something really huge, but actually, those two little words were huge because He said those words to her and she heard it. It was personal, and she's never forgotten it. It was holy. She knows He loves her.

He knows she loves Him and that personal relationship has kept her and grown all these years.

The day Anna identified His voice in her was a happy day for me as a mom. Why? Because I can't be with her every moment to lead and comfort, correct, and strengthen her. But He can! When she lived in China for two years, and her father and I were nowhere close, He was.

We as parents can claim supernatural help, an anointing, if you will, to parent. Not just when our children are tiny, but their whole entire life. Claim it! Your faith activates the anointing—it's a match on petrol. A parent is not the Holy Spirit, but the parent is responsible to work *with* the Holy Spirit to prepare and nurture the child—spirit, soul, and body—for what God has for him or her.

I can't count the times, lying on Lili or Anna's beds in the dark while we talked in those last moments before they went to sleep, that the spirit of prophecy would come on me. I would just be talking out of my heart. I didn't change my voice and say, "Thus says the Lord." I didn't lay hands on them and shake them to pieces. I didn't do anything like that. I would just lie beside them in the dark. Yet I knew there was a point when it wasn't just me talking, but the Lord talking through me. And while I was talking, tears were rolling out of my eyes because I was thinking, *This is so holy, and it's not in a pulpit. It's right here with my daughters before they go to sleep.*

I've watched the effect that Tony's words have had as well. When his words have communicated the heart of God, they have such impact—clarity, safety, truth, and the love God has for them too. Both Liliana and Annalisa have come to count on their father's amplification of God's Word to them.

Mercy and Grace

So let us come boldly to the throne of our gracious God. There we will receive his mercy, and we will find grace to help us when we need it most.

Hebrews 4:16 (NLT)

Children grow up knowing that if they ever need anybody to be on their side—even in the midst of trouble—an inChrist parent will be there to help. The inChrist parent doesn't lie and say their children are always right, when in fact, they are wrong. Yet, no matter the situation, inChrist parents will be on the child's side to work through whatever the situation may be.

A child should grow up knowing he or she can always go home. They don't have to go to a peer; they don't have to go to the Internet. They can go home because your home should represent the Father's throne of grace and mercy. Ultimately, you want your children running to the Father, so teach them they can run home.

ULTIMATELY, YOU WANT YOUR CHILDREN RUNNING TO THE FATHER, SO TEACH THEM THEY CAN RUN HOME.

One thing you never get from the Father when you go boldly before His throne and ask for mercy is for the Father to gasp. No matter what you tell Him, Father doesn't do that. Jesus doesn't do that. He doesn't say, "You did *what?*"

So, if you want to develop a home that is attractive to kids when they need it, it can't just be attractive on the good days. When they need a home is when they get themselves into a pickle, and they don't know what to do. You want them to beat a trail home saying, "If I can just get home, my parents will help. I've got to tell my parents." You don't want, "Home is the last place I can go. I've got to keep this a secret from my parents." No. You want to teach them that they can bear their heart to God, so they can begin now by bearing their heart to you.

I can't count the times that my children have told me stuff, and I was glad it was dark because I was lying there with the thought, *Oh my!* One time Lili told her father something that was a problem she was in, and he went in the other room until he calmed down. Then he came back out and said, "Okay, let's talk about this." But you don't want your kids running in the other direction. You want them coming home and coming home to Father in the throne room, where the first thing they receive is mercy.

Training and Preparation

Train up a child in the way he should go, And when he is old he will not depart from it.

Proverbs 22:6

All of these List A characteristics make for the best and healthiest home environment. Picture a home with all these beautiful characteristics on display on the good days but also during danger, conflict, and challenge. What your child sees, hears, and experiences not just in school or in church, but in life will be a part of their training. Don't just expect them to see through your eyes at first. Get down and see what they're seeing, hear what they're hearing, and help them to interpret correctly through the Word at every opportunity.

Life provides a wonderful opportunity and spontaneous moments for teaching and training your children. God is everywhere so you represent His thoughts and ways everywhere very naturally.

Let me give a simple example of a spontaneous moment. Annalisa was four or five, and we happened to be visiting in the States from Italy in January at the time of her birthday. We were at McDonald's for her birthday party with her cousins that she got to be with rarely. At this age, Anna had primarily been around Italians but had not yet seen the beautiful variety, features and looks characteristic of people from different places of the world. Suddenly, she looked across the restaurant and saw a little girl from Asia. Annalisa was pretty much one of those little ones where whatever went through her mind came out her mouth. She never had a lot of control over her voice, and everything was always kind of loud.

I was across the room and saw that Anna caught sight of the little girl, and her eyes got big with curiosity. Before she could say something, I ran to get to her and got down on my knees and put her face right by my face. I said, "Do you see that little girl?" I knew she did. She shook her head yes, and I could see that she was in awe.

"Yeah," she said.

"Do you see her eyes?" I asked.

"Yes," she said.

I said, "Isn't she beautiful?" I defined the diversity she saw as beautiful. She grew up thinking Asian women are the most exquisite women in the world, and she still does.

Kids need help to be prejudiced racially and in other ways. It's sad when that "help" is a parent. To be racially prejudiced is a gross misrepresentation of God. God intended for parents to image His heart of love for everyone to their children. It's important for you to be close enough to your child to bring the nature of the Father to *their* perspective. Make a point not to talk at or to them but come around beside them. See what they're seeing, hear what they're hearing, and don't make lessons an hour long. That will get tedious.

How does the Holy Spirit talk? Doesn't He often make quick statements to us? He doesn't always make you sit down or pull off the highway and take notes. Sometimes there are those pull-off-the-highway-and-take-note moments. But often He makes a statement as you're going—just an impression. Amplify that. Your child will identify His voice, and it will make it so easy to hear.

A parent also gets to expose their child to things that will inspire them—spirit, soul, and body. The Lord will help you to recognize giftings and talents that He put in your child. The parent didn't put them there—God did. But a parent is responsible for their part in nurturing these gifts and giving opportunities for these gifts to be expressed. A child is not given to a parent for the child to live out the parent's dreams. A child is given to a parent to accomplish the purpose of the Creator. As you pray about your child's giftings, God will help you to see what He sees about them.

Don't force them to be what they're not or to be like another sibling. God's Word says we are unwise if we compare ourselves with and among ourselves. It misrepresents God as a parent to compare your child to other siblings or others. Notice how God motivates you and reflect that. Through urging and inspiration, God moves us toward His will.

You don't personally have to do all the training either. God's raises up other teachers, mentors, and influencers to help your child at the right time. But you are anointed to know for your child the right schools, right seasons, right playmates, right coaches, and more. As your child grows up and starts choosing for himself or herself, absolutely use your faith and put trust in God that your child will be around people who will help him or her for good.

We all recognize there are wicked people in this world as well. Yet, in what is called The Lord's Prayer, it says, "Do not lead us into temptation, but deliver us from the evil one" (Matthew 6:13). In other words, "lead us away from things that are going to hurt us." Pray those prayers, and God will help them to not get a coach that will take advantage of them in a horrible way where they can't defend themselves.

Of course, you don't know everything about their future to prepare them, but one thing you can do is expose them to different things—like sports, the arts, various subjects in education and vocations.

One example of this is how my parents had music in our house all the time and played instruments. This inspired all the kids in my family toward music. My parents also urged us to develop and use the love and talent for music, which meant we had to practice. Momma prioritized practice. We couldn't stand it at the time, but now we're so thankful she dug her heels in and insisted. Parents who don't allow their children to be educated and developed are considered negligent. There can be legal ramifications for this in many countries in the world.

We would never deprive our child of shelter or food. That would be physical neglect and abuse. In addition to providing for a child's body and soul, what about a child's spirit? That's the part of a person that lives forever. A parent that puts everything else above providing opportunity for their child to know God is being negligent of what is most important. There is no career or achievement that is more important than a personal relationship with God. So, in addition to these natural things, also expose your children to spiritual things and to people with different giftings. It will stir up and inspire your children to know who they are on the inside and recognize their giftings when they see them in operation.

It was when I saw and heard a missionary from Alaska that I discovered something about myself. I was only six years old, but I knew that I was called to serve God in a foreign country.

Home was the place where I learned healing. It became more than a doctrine set on the shelf but something I used like a medicine cabinet. If I was sick my mother would say, "I'll get your dad to come pray." Tony and I have raised our kids the same way. Practice healing in the home, so it's a natural response and your children know what verses to use. If you have a medicine cabinet where you keep various medicines, also have healing resources ready as well.

When the girls were growing up, we had a playlist of healing songs. They called them their "sick songs." If they needed healing, we would just crank the music up and listen to the Word on healing. They would sing their colds away. They didn't know there was another way to do it.

Jochebed

Here is an example of a mother in the Old Testament who made preparations that saved the life of her son, Moses, and ultimately the lives of many a nation as well.

> **But when she could no longer hide him, she took an ark of bulrushes for him, daubed it with asphalt and pitch, put the child in it, and laid it in the reeds by the river's bank.**
>
> Exodus 2:3

There was a dark time during the Israelites' enslavement in Egypt when people were throwing their baby boys into the Nile River because of the edict of Pharaoh. Outrageous! Horrible! It's hard to even imagine. What is easier to imagine and closer to home is that throughout the Bible, Egypt is often seen as a type of the world. In this case, Pharaoh would be a picture to us of the god of this world, the devil, and the Nile River pictures to us the current of this world's system.

What the god of this world has "ordered" is that parents throw their kids into the spirit of this world. As parents, we are not under obligation to throw our kids into actual water with crocodiles and hippopotamuses, but there's definitely pressure to throw our kids into the current of, "Everybody's doing it. Everybody thinks this way."

But Moses' parents said, "No, we're not doing it. I don't care what everyone else is doing. We are just not doing it." Why did they refuse?

Because they saw something valuable about their child. Yet, the truth of the matter is that in God, every child is valuable. Don't you think every child is valuable? Which child would you pick to be thrown into the river? None. We need moms and dads like Moses' parents who say, "No, not our child. We're not throwing him in."

Instead, Moses' parents initially hid him for a while. A mother can think, "If I could just keep my child close always, I'll hide and protect him. I'll not let any harm come to him." However, you'll set your child up for harm if you see yourself as the child's ultimate protection. You cannot be that. You've got to commit them to something bigger than you like Jochebed did when she saw she couldn't hide Moses any longer. What she did then was very important.

Jochebed carefully wove a basket and knew exactly what she was going to do with it. As she finished the basket, she lined it with asphalt or pitch inside and out to make it watertight. Her plan was to put her son, Moses, in it and then put the basket in the same river that she saved him from. Initially, that would have destroyed him.

The basket is what made all the difference. What do you think the basket gives a picture of? Salvation! What does the act of weaving that basket picture for us? Teaching the Word. The unique help of the Holy Spirit to help us pray is demonstrated in the asphalt and pitch that was daubed over the woven basket, making it watertight.

I'm telling you that you can put your priceless child in that. It's the safest place. Did Jochebed throw Moses into the current of the water to drown? No. But there did come a time when she did have to let that baby go or he would never have fulfilled his destiny. She sent him into life protected by that little basket.

Noah

Hebrews 11:11 gives a similar picture of a father protecting his family much the same way. Plank by plank, with asphalt to make it watertight, this ark was a safe place during a flood that was so catastrophic that it destroyed the whole world. And yet, Noah's family remained safe from all that was happening outside the ark. Fathers and mothers in themselves are not the ultimate protection of their family. Of course, there's some natural protection that parents provide, but your child is still unprotected from the spirit of this world unless you are strategically wrapping the Word around them through instruction. Wrap the Word, wrap prayer, Word, prayer, Word, prayer, Word, prayer, Word, prayer, Word.

It can be a scary thing when a child starts school because other kids and other influencers come into the picture. Dating takes it to another level yet again when it seems that this person that your child's heart connects to has the potential to make them do something crazy and forget what you've said.

Instead of intervening much when my siblings and I came into that season, I sure remember hearing my dad and mom praying for us and our dating relationships as well as other choices we were making. Looking back now, I am so glad they prayed for me. Their prayers wrapped me. So, yes, I was in the river, but the water didn't touch me. I was in the protection of prayer and the Word. When you trust the protection of the Word and the Holy Spirit, you can release your children. You release them into their destiny.

Where did the River Nile take Moses? It took him smack dab to Pharaoh's palace where he was brought up and groomed for destiny. Could his mother or father have taken him there? No. The river was the very thing that could have killed him, but with the right protection, it took him to his destiny.

InChrist moms and dads put their children in the basket or ark they make for their children and release them to fulfill the purpose they were born for—going where they're supposed to go and doing what they're supposed to do.

The spirit of every child comes from God as does the call that connects that child to an eternal purpose. As parents, you get to participate and facilitate that God-given purpose by giving the child a body and doing all that's involved in raising that child. Your son or daughter's purpose may only take them across the street from you, but you have to trust God that if they end up going around the world, that it does not diminish you. And I can tell you, it doesn't.

I am one of five children in a very close family, and we lived in a little farming town of 2500 people. God told my momma to raise all five of her kids to go where the Lord would send us, so she prayed almost every day that Jesus would come before we grew up. But she was faithful to God, and she raised us and released us all, knowing that all of us kids, grandkids, and great grandkids would live far away from her.

Of course, this isn't the case of most moms and dads, but each inChrist parent should be willing to really and truly dedicate their baby to God's purposes wherever that may take them. Only fear and lack of trust in God would keep a parent from doing so. And that very fear is what exposes the child to what can really hurt them.

Discipline

5 And have you forgotten the exhortation that addresses you as sons? "My son, do not regard lightly the discipline of the Lord, nor be weary when reproved by him. 6 For the Lord disciplines the one he loves, and chastises every son whom he receives."

Hebrews 12:5-6 (ESV)

He who spares his rod hates his son, but he who loves him disciplines him promptly.

Proverbs 13:24

God disciplines. People often shy away from these verses of scripture. Yet, the reason why people cringe at the thought of God disciplining us is because discipline was so horrific to them. That also means it was administered the wrong way.

When discipline is given to reflect the way God disciplines His children, it will not be done in an outburst of anger but as an expression of love. God's discipline of His children is not His wrath on sin but to help them be their best. Did God ever demonstrate His wrath on sin? Yes. When? Jesus' torture on the cross pictures how much God hates sin and His punishment of it. For every one of us who receives Jesus, and what He did for us in receiving God's wrath and punishment for our sin, we don't experience God's wrath.

God's main method for discipline is His Word. An inChrist parent's main method should be the same. Notice what God's Word says about discipline:

> Every *Scripture* is God-breathed (given by His inspiration) and profitable for instruction, for *reproof* and conviction of sin, for *correction* of error and *discipline* in obedience, [and] for training in righteousness (in holy living, in conformity to God's will in thought, purpose, and action),
>
> 2 Timothy 3:16 (AMPC)

Notice in 2 Timothy that God's words to us include instruction, but it also corrects, disciplines, and reproves. After all, if the child hasn't had instruction regarding a particular issue and is clueless about what the right way is, how can he or she be disciplined for disobedience? If the child is thinking, *What do I do now?* you will frustrate the child if you punish him or her.

A child disciplined without instruction will begin to think, *I never can please my parent.* Or, *next time I'll lie or sneak better.* The child will build a wall in his or her mind between you and them. Even worse, the child will "learn" to run from God too.

If your child has done something wrong, it's important that as an InChrist parent you say, "Do you know what you did wrong?"

"No."

"Okay, then let me explain it to you."

If the child does know what he or she did is wrong, right discipline isn't bad. It hurts, but if it's done correctly, the pain is associated with the act of disobedience instead of being associated with a parent's anger. Sin hurts. Disobedience is painful. Remember this bottom line truth. The wages or consequence of sin is death. God doesn't kill or destroy, but sin does. God warns. Parents warn. Why? Because God and parents don't want their children to suffer the pain and destruction that comes with disobedience.

I don't remember all my spankings, but there were three doozies that stand out to illustrate this.

When I was a little girl, my siblings and I loved to visit our grandparents in the mountains and play in the creek at the end of the summer when the water was flowing gently. However, in the spring when the mountain snow was melting, the little creek became a raging river. My grandmother instructed us to not even go near it. Why? Because there would be no saving us if we got in. We would be killed. She was clear about this, and we all understood.

Then again, I thought that surely it wouldn't be so bad to just put my feet in right by the bank, and I did. Suddenly, my grandmother picked me up and, at the same time, spanked me. I got it! I didn't have to be dashed on the rocks and drown to get it! The pain she administered helped me associate disobedience with a consequence.

The last spanking I got was when I was 16 years old. Oh my! My friend, Cindy, and I were doing an independent study in music with some guys in our school. They were studying Led Zeppelin and ZZ Top and all other kinds of music of the '70s while my friend and I were working with music from the Jesus People movement.

Anyway, these guys were partiers, but they were also so much fun. We all got to be friends. During this time, I was developing a bit of a rebellious attitude with my dad. It wasn't over the top, but it was there. One afternoon these guys drove to my house and honked the horn, and I just ran out of the house and jumped in the car. Off we went to go "drag main." That's what we called it even though in that little bitty town, we only had one stop light. We would go down the main street, which was probably four blocks, and then we'd "flip another u" in the grocery store parking lot at the other end of the main street. We would do this again and again, waving at other people that were doing the same thing. It was a big deal, and there was not much else to do.

While these guys, who were just friends, and I were going down the main street, we passed my sister going the other way. She hollered out to me, "You need to get home!" I was embarrassed but had a scratchy feeling that I was about to have a reckoning over my attitude, so I had the guys take me home immediately.

When I got home, I could see my dad was standing on the front porch waiting for me. As I went in the house, he said, "We need to have a talk." I knew it was going to be more than talk.

I went downstairs, and I put on as much underwear as I could find. I tell you what, I was stacked up like the Michelin Man because I knew this attitude was going to be dealt with that day. Oh boy!

My dad sat down on the bed, and with his word, he first began the discipline by asking, "Do you know what you've done?" He wasn't talking about my ride up and down the main street. It was the rebellious attitude popping out everywhere.

"Yeah, I do," I said.

"Well, here's the problem," he said. "You're a Behrman, and Behrmans don't act like this. We're just not having it. Secondly, people know you're a minister." Not only were we pastor's kids, but my siblings and I sang for all kinds of community and school events. Everybody knew us from singing in the town.

"Finally," he continued, "You're a Christian, a child of God, and the attitudes you have right now aren't like Him. You're misrepresenting God, and we're not having that. This is not what I ever expected to see in you, and I'm going to have to spank you."

He wept while he was talking to me and said, "This hurts me." I could see that it really did. It was grieving his heart.

By that time even though the spanking hadn't begun, the discipline had. I was thinking, *Just spank me. This is horrible. This hurts so bad!* I could see the pain and disappointment that I had caused his heart. I saw the expectation he had for me was the best, but I hadn't done my best.

Then the spanking came. Whew! That attitude got sorted then and there. That was the hardest spanking I ever got in my life.

I looked at him while he was spanking me, and his face wasn't mad. He was crying, and he wanted me to know that the way of rebellion would end up hurting me a whole lot worse than the spanking. It wouldn't just hurt me; it would hurt other people. Instead of that spanking creating a barrier between me and my dad, it actually demonstrated that he loved me and that made me love him more.

The point is that the discipline should start with corrective words—not the outburst. Hold back the outburst! Let your words start the discipline and then attach the consequence to it. By the time the consequence comes, it's like exactly what Proverbs says it is: cleansing.

> **Blows that hurt cleanse away evil, as do stripes the inner depths of the heart.**
>
> Proverbs 20:30

If correction is done right, it actually relieves the children because they think, *What I did was wrong.* It's a type of correction where they think, *Yeah, that's just and fair. And it's better that I learn the pain of disobedience through discipline than the pain in life later on.*

Life can really belt you, but a parent who spanks in love sets up a child to not get hurt later in life. My mom was real handy with the brush.

One common element of discipline chosen by some parents after a spanking is to leave the child alone in his or her room to think over things. Ask the Lord about that, but it may be good before you leave them alone to show love and affection. Does your heavenly Father leave you alone with the feeling of failure and guilt when He's disciplined you?

I've not experienced that, but Jesus did when he cried out, "My God, my God, why did You forsake me?" He experienced that so that I don't have to. I've never felt that God left me when I sinned. No, actually, God leans in. To accurately represent God as a parent after giving out the discipline—whether it's spanking, taking away privileges, giving assignments or whatever it is—hold them close so they know the discipline you just gave doesn't separate them from you—ever.

To represent God well to your children requires that you draw constantly on your union with Him. It's good to look into the Word about discipline. Let the Word instruct you, encourage you, and give you courage to discipline and do it for the reasons and in the manner God wants. The pure and non-abusive way of discipline strengthens your relationship with your child as well as introducing your child to the ways of the Father.

Teaching the Fear of the Lord

What is the fear of the Lord? It is a reverence for God and the things of God that leads to obedience. It includes a love for pleasing God and a hate for acting against Him or His will.

> Especially how on the day that you stood before the Lord your God in Horeb the Lord said to me, "Gather the people together to Me and I will make them hear My words that they *may learn [reverently] to fear Me* all the days they live upon the earth and that they may teach their children."
>
> Deuteronomy 4:10 (AMPC)

> Call them all together—men, women, children, and the foreigners living in your towns—so they may hear this Book of Instruction and learn to fear the LORD your God and carefully obey all the terms of these instructions. Do this so that your children who have not known these instructions will hear them and will learn to fear the LORD your God. Do this as long as you live in the land you are crossing the Jordan to occupy.
>
> Deuteronomy 31:12 (NLT)

All these verses and more (Joshua 4:6; Exodus 12:13-14; Exodus 12:26-27) from the Old Testament instruct parents to teach their children the fear of the Lord and implies they may not know the fear of the Lord unless they are taught it.

The fear of the Lord is not just something you casually come by, but it literally can be taught. The best way it's taught is when it is demonstrated and strongly impressed on a child through parents who also fear the Lord. It affects your words and actions. I remember one of those "strongly impressed" occasions with my own father. I remember it as one of the three great spankings of my life!

One Sunday night we took communion at the altar. By *at the altar,* I mean there were literal altars where we kneeled in prayer at the front of the sanctuary, and in this service, we were served communion as we knelt. My friend, Sharon, and I were on opposite sides of the altar with our young heads together giggling and laughing. I don't remember what we were talking about, probably all kinds of stuff, but all the while, communion was going on.

My dad and the elders would typically walk around the altars and pray for people. When my dad came to me, he tapped me on my shoulder and said, "I'll need to talk to you at home after church." I knew exactly what that meant.

When we all got home from church that night, he said, "Come in the bedroom." He talked to me about the Lord's supper, what it meant, and its sacredness. He was so sad as he said, "You were laughing and talking when we were remembering the Lord's body and blood." He said, "You'll never do that again." He proceeded to spank the fire out of me. And I never did that again.

What I learned from that experience that I still remember wasn't just that I had better make sure my dad doesn't see me when I'm laughing at the altar over communion. No, that's not what I got. I also didn't learn to sneak. I learned the fear of the Lord, and he did not teach me only with the spanking but with his own respect for communion. I saw his grief when he said, "Don't ever do that again." I was thinking, *Please spank me. It will make me feel better.*

Like the other roles that both genders carry out, the model for parenting is actually our Creator, God. Aiming and lining up at any other model other than God will cause us to fall way short of what God intended parenting to look like and image about Himself. The more we use what we learn from our heavenly Father—His methods and motives—our parenting will more and more represent Him and assist in connecting our children to Him.

ENGENDERED

CHAPTER 33

Drop the Rocks

Our study has been focused on God's creative intention to make Him visible and tangible through the human He fashioned, both male and female. Yet, let's also consider a few practical questions in this chapter that arise when what God designed doesn't seem to match what a person is experiencing. What do you do when what you see about yourself or someone else doesn't look like an inChrist person?

To answer that question, let's first consider an important fact: We look like what we look at. What we choose to talk about, meditate on, and respond to regarding others and ourselves is the road we are choosing to take. Make sure you are on the right road for your destination to be List A.

The devil wants you to obsess on Lists B and C and identify yourself and others there, because, in this way, he keeps the realities of List A (page 278) to be exclusively how Jesus lived—certainly not you. He will press you to believe old things did *not* pass away and *nothing* became new. Of course, that's a lie, but because Lists B and C characteristics are so ugly and glaring, they do tend to captivate your attention. God demonstrated to

WE LOOK
LIKE WHAT
WE LOOK AT.

Abraham a way that faith works to change things that appear to be a way God did not intend.

> **17 as the scripture says, "I have made you father of many nations."** So the promise is good in the sight of God, in whom Abraham believed—*the God who brings the dead to life and whose command brings into being what did not exist.* **18 Abraham believed and hoped, even when there was no reason for hoping, and so became "the father of many nations." Just as the scripture says, "Your descendants will be as many as the stars."**
>
> Romans 4:17-18 (GNT)

We can do this too. If God calls things that do not exist as though they do, you can too. Call inChrist characteristics that seem to be not, as though they already are.

Why? Because in the spirit, they already are! You're not making something up. Instead, you're drawing something out that's in the spirit of a person. Your faith is drawing it out. It's important that your thinking is in agreement with God according to the realities of who that person is or who you are in Christ. But don't stop with only thinking right. Jesus taught that faith, even small faith, speaks. Say it in praise, prayer, and declaration, and reflect it in all your conversation. In this way, you can help someone take the wrong stuff off and put the right stuff on. This works for you as well.

Notice that Abraham continued to believe and hope even when there was no reason to. As a result, he became what God said about him.

Here are some practical things to do if the inChrist man or woman—including you—isn't the one you currently see:

1. Identify the List B or C characteristic that is not in Christ. Don't pretend it's not there.

2. Don't waste time scolding, condemning, nagging, getting depressed or discouraged about it. Drop the rocks!

3. Instead, remember that God laid on Jesus all of Lists B and C characteristics and judged it in Him.

4. Ask God to show you what in-Christ List A characteristic replaces the one you see and also how He wants you to think about that person.

5. Take God's thought and picture that inChrist characteristic as the real person.

6. Ask God to help you see what it really looks like to love or respect that person according to who they really are in Christ.

7. What God says about that person in Christ is then how you picture that person, what you say, and what you praise. It is what you meditate on. That's faith! And faith draws out and makes real the realities of who we are recreated to be in Christ.

Once you are in this place of faith in God, you can share with that person how the Lists B or C characteristics (the characteristics, not the person) have affected you. It comes across differently from this place and can build the relationship.

FAQs

Q: What is the right way for inChrist people to respond to those whose sexual expression isn't what God designed from the beginning?

A: Basically, as believers, we represent Jesus. We don't represent Moses. If our response is to look at people with shame and disgust, we'll not be acting like Jesus. Perhaps, we'll even be misrepresenting Him. No. Instead, we can be just like Jesus when He talked to that woman at the well who was so fractured. In all Jesus said, He never berated her. He identified what she was doing but didn't speak condemning words about it. The woman already knew what she was doing wasn't good.

BASICALLY, AS BELIEVERS, WE REPRESENT JESUS. WE DON'T REPRESENT MOSES.

Jesus didn't say, "If you'll turn, you won't burn!" "If you get rid of that man, I'll talk to you" No, He didn't do that. Instead, Jesus shared with her the greatest teaching on the subject of worship you could find in any book or download off the Internet. And this woman got it for free at the well from the Redeemer Himself. How cool is that?

While Jesus didn't condemn her, He didn't condone what she was doing either. In fact, the truth He gave her, set her free. The truth changed her from a woman known in Samaria for all the wrong reasons to an evangelist who ended up bringing the men of the city to the well where they, too, met Jesus.

Q: What do I do if my young child thinks he or she is a different gender than his or her sex?

A: As a parent, your response is extremely important. Anything said or done that's motivated by fear will not help them. It's also important to stay far away from shaming the child. We give the devil something to work with if we are disgusted or fearful that a girl wants to play with a truck or a boy wants to sew. That kind of reaction surrounds children with shame and fear and makes them think something is "off" about them. It can set them up to be vulnerable to thoughts or eventually develop conclusions about sexual preference that they may not have otherwise. Take time with God and get from Him love and wisdom to deal with your child.

A number of parents I know made this challenge a non-issue and found it was just a phase that came and went. Don't "throw your child in the Nile," meaning, don't cave to social trends to encourage them toward identifying themselves other than their sex. Kids often despise their bodies for one reason or another. Investing the truth in them of how beautiful, valuable, and purposeful their bodies are is something important for parents to do.

Q: Is it possible for someone's real self to be a different gender than their assigned sex at birth?

A: It is possible for a person to feel different than their physical sex? Yes. However, to get a Bible answer on the question, it's important to first of all understand that a person's real self is the spirit—*not* the soul *or* the body. The part of the person that will live forever is the spirit, and the spirit, like the Spirit of God, is neither male or female. Our spirit is also without race or any other natural demarcation, for that matter. Paul was explaining to the Galatian church who they were in their new identity in Christ when he said

There is no longer Jew or Gentile, slave or free, male and female. For you are all one in Christ Jesus.

Galatians 3:28 (NLT)

So, a person's spirit, who is neither male or female, lives in a body of a particular sex and that sex is meant to uniquely express that person's spirit.

What other part of a human is there besides the spirit and body? Every human also has a soul which consists of mind, will, feelings, and emotions and is also affected by other people, environment, hormones, and experiences. Challenges happen when these different components dictate feelings and thoughts that are different than the sex of the body and the chromosomes coded in each cell. The soul is *not* the "real you" but can certainly dominate the body and even the spirit, which is the "real you."

A person who is experiencing true shalom or wholeness is one whose spirit is under the Lordship of Jesus, whose soul is in agreement with and expressive of that Lordship, and whose body expresses the image of God as a male or female as the person is physically born.

God meant for the "real you," a person's spirit, to not be subservient to their soul and body, but to dominate, under His Lordship, the whole person in all aspects of life, not just gender or sexual related things.

Shame on Shame

Not compromising the truth of the Word of God no matter the sway of the world is important. Jesus is the perfect example of one who never one time in His life faltered. Not even in His words did he err. He loved righteousness and hated evil.

However, in our zeal to hate evil and uphold the truth, if we disdain people and stone them with the rocks of the law, even if only in our thoughts of them, we say goodbye to ministry as Jesus demonstrated it. Trying to shame someone (including yourself) into changing his or her thoughts and feelings about gender never works and actually contributes to the problem. So, don't do it! More to the point, using shame and disgust misrepresents Jesus.

Shame has power. It drives people down and away from God. The Gospel is the power of God bringing them to the Savior. He knows how to save. Be patient and let Him work. As inChrist people, we don't have to default to the devil's devices of shame.

Let's drop our rocks!

Truth is powerful. Truth given in love doesn't condemn or condone, but it does confront. It turns the light on so God's will and intention is not obscure and includes the empowerment to transform.

CHAPTER 34

What Was God Thinking?

In the beginning, God created the heaven and the earth.

Genesis 1:1

God created human beings *in his own image.*
In the image of God he created them; male and female he created them.

Genesis 1:27 (NLT)

Of all that was engendered, the human male and female were most amazing in their purpose. They were expressly designed to represent and image God. Yet, our ability to do what we were created to do was broken in Adam and restored in Jesus, our last Adam. God's purpose and intention in His creation of male and female can now be experienced because Jesus fulfilled *His* purpose and God's intention to save us. He saved us from everything that broke.

Everything.

That truth gives both hope and empowerment to be who we were created to be and do what we were created to do—to represent and image

God. InChrist men, women, husbands, wives, fathers, and mothers show aspects of our glorious God, making Him real. And now finally in Him, marriages and families are restored with the ability to represent the very reason they were engendered.

> Those whom God had already chosen he also set apart to become like his Son, so that the Son would be the first among many believers.
>
> Romans 8:29 (GNT)

God's Son would be the eldest brother in a large family.

Notes

Recommended Reading:
I Suffer Not a Woman: Rethinking First Timothy 2:11-15 In the Light of Ancient Evidence, Richard Clark Kroeger, Catherine Clark Kroeger 1992, Baker Books, Grand Rapids, MI

Five Love Languages: The Secret to Love That Lasts, Gary Chapman, Strand Publishing, USA, 2015

Keep Your Love On, Danny Silk, Loving on Purpose Publisher, USA, 2015

About the Author

Patsy Cameneti is a wife to Tony, mother to Lilianna and Annalisa, Bible teacher, pastor, and author. Before moving to Brisbane, Australia, where she and her husband, Tony, are senior pastors of Rhema Family Church and Bible school directors, they lived in the USA, Italy, and Singapore. These diverse settings and those where she has traveled extensively to minister have given Patsy the opportunity to strip down Christian teaching and reveal the bare and unedited truth of the Gospel of Jesus Christ, which is soluble in any culture and social setting. Patsy continues to travel internationally with a message that inspires others to live life out of an authentic relationship with God.

cameneti
ministries

For more information about Tony and Patsy Cameneti's ministry, Rhema Family Church, or Rhema Bible Training Center Australia, visit **www.cameneti.net** or **www.rhema.org.au.**

Rhema Family Church

P.O. Box 1648, Springwood, QLD 4127
19 Tolmer Place, Springwood, Qld 4127
Australia

PRAYER OF SALVATION

God loves you—no matter who you are, no matter what your past. God loves you so much that He gave His one and only begotten Son for you. The Bible tells us that "…whoever believes in him shall not perish but have eternal life" (John 3:16 NIV). Jesus laid down His life and rose again so that we could spend eternity with Him and experience His absolute best on earth. If you would like to receive Jesus into your life, say the following prayer out loud and mean it in your heart.

Heavenly Father, I come to you admitting that I am a sinner. Right now, I choose to turn away from sin, and I ask you to cleanse me of all unrighteousness. I believe that Your son, Jesus, died on the cross to take away my sins. I also believe that He rose again from the dead so that I might be forgiven of my sins and made righteous through faith in Him. I call upon the name of Jesus Christ to be the Savior and Lord of my life. Jesus, I choose to follow You and ask that You fill me with the power of the Holy Spirit. I declare that right now I am a child of God. I am free from sin and full of the righteousness of God. I am saved in Jesus' name. Amen.

If you prayed this prayer to receive Jesus Christ as your Savior for the first time, please write to us to receive a free book!

www.harrisonhouse.com
Harrison House Publishers
P.O. Box 35035
Tulsa, Oklahoma 74153

The Harrison House Vision

Proclaiming the truth and the power
of the Gospel of Jesus Christ with excellence.
Challenging Christians
to live victoriously,
grow spiritually,
know God intimately.

Connect with us on

 Facebook @ HarrisonHousePublishers

and Instagram @ HarrisonHousePublishing

so you can stay up to date with news

about our books and our authors.

Visit us at **www.harrisonhouse.com**

for a complete product listing as well as

monthly specials for wholesale distribution.

LIST A:
Characteristics of God

Characteristics of the God the Father

accepting	forgiving	kind	strong
accessible	good	long-suffering	smart
affectionate	gracious	loving	trustworthy
consistent	generous	merciful	welcoming
creative	giving	patient	wise
disciplines	honest	provider	
enduring	impartial	protector	
ever-present	just and fair	restoring	

Characteristics of Jesus the Son

assertive	consistent	humble	sacrificial
available	decisive	joyful	selfless,
caring	faithful	loving	serving
committed	forgiving	mature	submissive
communicates	friendly	meek	true
compassionate	gentle	obedient,	
conquering	good listener	peaceful	

Characteristics of the Holy Spirit

able	counselor	helper	revealer
activator	defending	honest	supportive
advocate	dependable	instructor	teacher
attentive	edifier	loving	trusted friend
bold	encourager	loyal	truthful
comforting	ever-present help	nurturing	wise
convincing	forewarner	peaceful	
corrects	guide	personal	
communicator		powerful	

LIST B:
Negative Male Characteristics

abusive
absent
angry
arrogant
cold
controlling
cruel
detached
dictatorial
disrespectful
domineering
egotistic

hard heart
harsh
inconsiderate
indecisive
insensitive
irresponsible
insecure
intimidating
jealous
judgmental
lazy
lover of themselves

manipulative
non- communicative
possessive
selfish
stubborn
temperamental
unaffectionate
unaware
unfaithful
unteachable
violent

LIST C:
Negative Female Characteristics

annoying
bossy
catty
clingy
competitive
cold
conniving
condemning
controlling
demanding
depressed

domineering
emotional
fault-finding
fragile
gossipy
gullible
hysterical
indecisive
insecure
irrational
jealous

judgmental
nagging
manipulative
materialistic
mean
needy
passive
prideful
scheming
self-absorbed
self-conscious

spiteful
stingy
stubborn
talkative
unstable
vain
vindictive
weak